FOUR WEEKS ONE SUMMER
WHEN IT ALL WENT WRONG

FOUR WEEKS ONE SUMMER
WHEN IT ALL WENT WRONG

NICHOLAS WHITLAM

Australian Scholarly

For Alice, Edward and Peter.

© Nicholas Whitlam 2016
First published 2016 by Australian Scholarly Publishing Ltd
7 Lt Lothian St Nth, North Melbourne, Vic 3051
Tel: 03 9329 6963 / Fax: 03 9329 5452
enquiry@scholarly.info / www.scholarly.info
ISBN 978-1-925333-92-3
ALL RIGHTS RESERVED
Cover design by Wayne Saunders

CONTENTS

Maps .... *vii*
Introduction .... *ix*
18 July, Saturday 1
19 July, Sunday 12
20 July, Monday 24
21 July, Tuesday 32
22 July, Wednesday 42
23 July, Thursday 48
24 July, Friday 55
25 July, Saturday 65
26 July, Sunday 70
27 July, Monday 76
28 July, Tuesday 84
29 July, Wednesday 95
30 July, Thursday 100
31 July, Friday 106
1 August, Saturday 110
2 August, Sunday 122
3 August, Monday 127
4 August, Tuesday 135
5 August, Wednesday 141
6 August, Thursday 147
7 August, Friday 153
8 August, Saturday 159
9 August, Sunday 166
10 August, Monday 174
11 August, Tuesday 182
12 August, Wednesday 188
13 August, Thursday 195
14 August, Friday 204
15 August, Saturday 212
16 August, Sunday 221

Epilogue *230*
Notes *261*
Key to Sources *279*
Index *281*
About the Author *284*

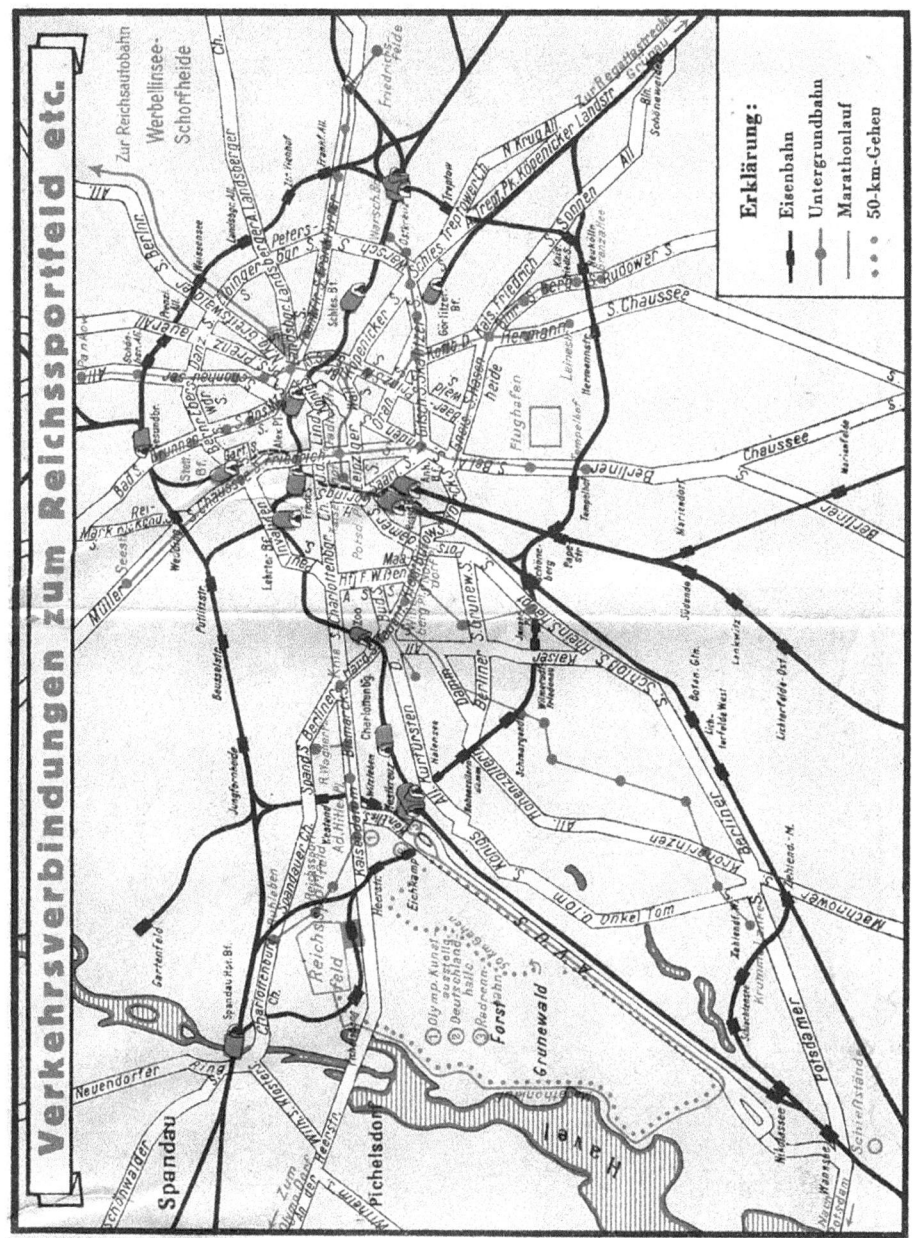

Transport links to the Olympic venues in Berlin were outstanding. Both the underground subway ("untergrundbahn") and railway ("eisenbahn") led to the Reichssportsfeld - where track and field took place in the Olympic Stadium and where swimming, hockey, fencing and the polo were also centred. The Grünewald forest could be reached by subway and railway for the marathon ("marathonlauf") and the 50 km walk ("gehen"). Deutschland Hall (② in the map) which housed the boxing, weightlifting and wrestling and the velodrome ("radrennbahn", ③) were both on a railway line. The Olympic Stadium was only 11 km from the Brandenburg Gate in the centre of the city.

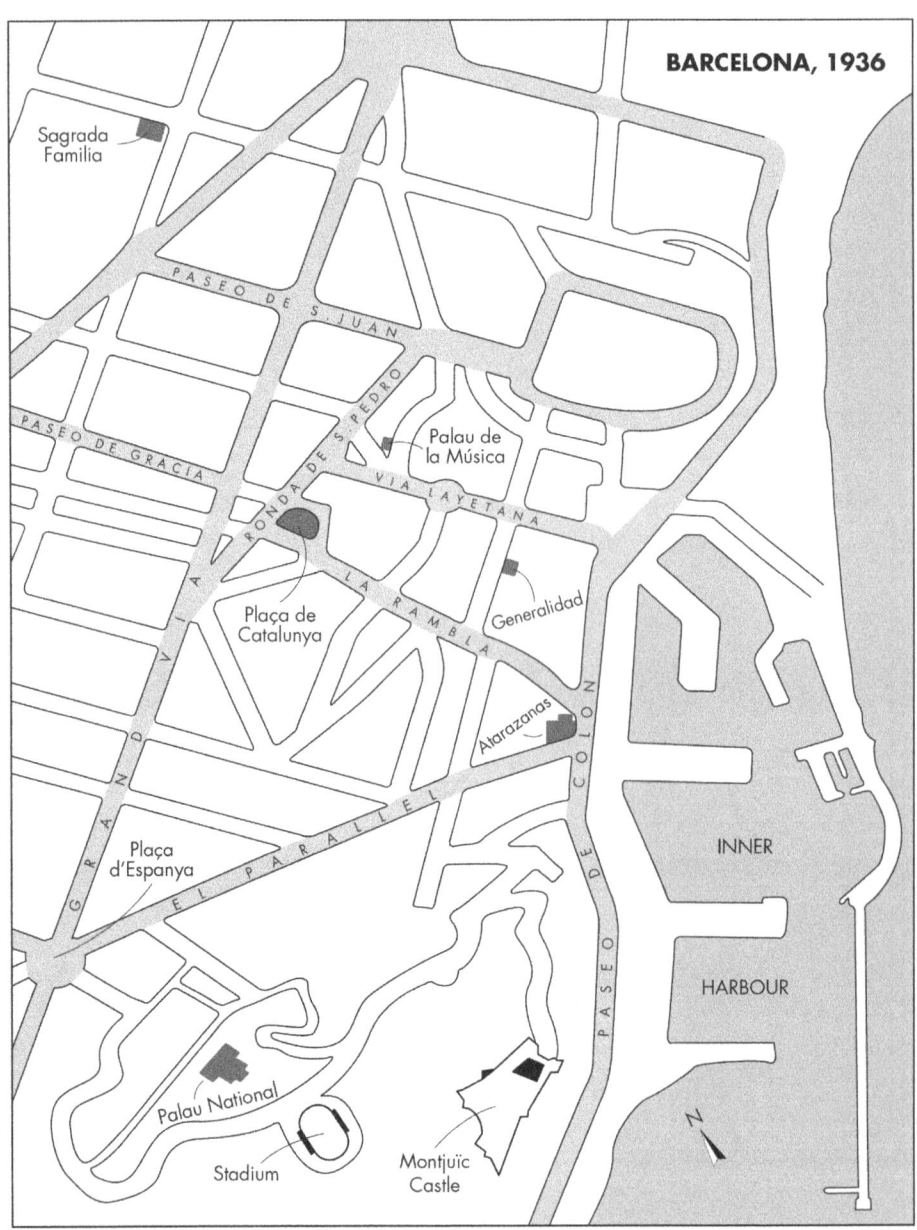

Barcelona is a relatively compact city sitting beneath a semi-circle of mountains to the north, west and south. The main thoroughfare, La Rambla, stretches about 1.5 km from the Plaça de la Catalunya to the harbour. Plaça de la Catalunya is about 4 km from the Olympic Stadium.

INTRODUCTION

In December 1972 the newly-appointed Prime Minister of Australia was presented with a list of people who should receive his Christmas card *ex officio*. He took pleasure in striking out a few names and then came to the recently-widowed Duchess of Windsor. She stayed on the list, although he corrected her style and title to "HRH The Duchess of Windsor". The PM, my father, took great delight in explaining to me that Wallis, the Duchess of Windsor had been improperly denied the designation Her Royal Highness back in the 1930s and, so far as his Christmas card list was concerned, he was going to correct it. From that point she became a subject of interest to me.

For two weeks in late 1956, the city of Melbourne hosted the 1956 Olympic Games. Members of Parliament were given two free tickets for every day of the track and field events, which were held at the Melbourne Cricket Ground. My father was an MP and a Sydney-based colleague, who could not make the trip south, gave his two tickets to my parents; as a result, my elder brother and I got to use those two extra tickets. We stayed with Aunty Ida in East Kew, and every day we took the tram to the MCG and settled into prime seats on the finishing line, well before the first event; we kept two seats for our parents who would turn up later. For an eleven-year-old boy—I celebrated my birthday during the Games—it was the most exciting time of my life. To this day I can recite the results of most heats and certainly every final.

My mother was an Australian swimming champion. She was a contender to compete in the aborted 1940 Tokyo Games. Somewhere on the bookshelves at home was a book on the 1936 Berlin Games. It must have been my mother's. I remember lapping it up, and over the years I came to understand that the

Berlin Games had been something very special.

I studied history at Harvard College—ancient, medieval and modern. Politics between the two world wars, and the thirties in particular, attracted my interest. Léon Blum and his Popular Front appealed to my left-wing prejudices; the Spanish Civil War, being the last great cause, was infinitely fascinating and the squat fascist Franco—still oppressing Spain when I was a student—was the consummate hate figure. (Funny how first impressions can be correct.)

In the early seventies, when I was working in New York and London, a fellow fledgling investment banker was a German, Michael Handrick. I learnt that his father was Gotthard Handrick, the pentathlon gold medallist in 1936. Michael and his wife became great friends of ours, and we have kept in sporadic touch from different ends of the earth. Of course I contacted Michael when I started researching this book to see if he had any diaries, a memoir or the like on which I could draw. He had plenty of press clippings but nothing personal except a replica gold medal, the original having been lost during the war. As to Gotthard's time in the Luftwaffe, Michael was "not sure we want to open that box". (I did, and there is nothing untoward.)

My wife and I visited Barcelona for the first time in 2010. I wanted to learn more about the Spanish Civil War and we both wanted to explore and discover the city. (With its climate, culture, food—and a recorded history of more than 2000 years—it is the city Sydney thinks it is or at least wishes it were.) While there I became aware of the 1936 Peoples' Olympiad that had been scheduled as a Barcelona rival to the Berlin Games—and these alternative Olympics became a matter of interest to me.

There is a consensus that World War Two had its origins in the settlement of the Great War and that the breakdown of established order, inflation, the Great Depression and appeasement all added to that original problem. And since men

Introduction

and women of goodwill can solve their disputes, there is much that has been said about how WWII could have been avoided. I don't try to traverse that well-trodden path. But *when* did it go wrong?

The year nineteen thirty-six is critical. As I delved into the developments of that year my focus became narrower. I found that many key events fell into just one month—between Saturday 18 July, when elements of the Spanish Army started the uprising that became the Spanish Civil War, and Sunday 16 August, when, among other things, the Berlin Olympics came to a close. I dug up material, some previously unpublished, on the little-known Peoples' Olympiad, the critical early days of the Spanish Civil War, the spontaneous workers' uprising in Barcelona, the drama and brilliance of the Berlin Games, Edward VIII's scandalous holiday cruise with Mrs Simpson and much more. Along the way I got to familiarise myself with Léon Blum, who remains a hero, Göbbels and Göring (whom I found, with regret, to have had considerable charm), the various British society figures who hung around Edward VIII (who gets worse and weaker with every examination) and Wallis Simpson (who gets better), Anthony Eden and British PM Baldwin, the devious, calculating and comprehensively cruel Francisco Franco, one of the truly evil men in modern history, Franco's strange colleagues and the disparate Spanish politicians of the day, Jesse Owens and his marvellous fellow athletes of the 1936 Olympics, Leni Riefenstahl and many others who make up the story of those extraordinary four weeks.

And, as best I can determine, it all went wrong in those four weeks one summer. The summer of 1936.

How to tell the story? I have adopted a diary technique, logging what took place on each of those thirty days, sometimes hour by hour. This has enabled me to record contemporaneous events episodically, moving from scene to scene, from one plot to a sub-plot, from one country to another, and so on. By setting out what actually took place at specific times, I can illustrate two truisms: first, the fact that no matter how critical to the story a protagonist may be, rarely does he or she know everything that is going on, and secondly, events are taking place elsewhere that are important, interesting and often relevant.

I hope I have come up with something more than a voyeuristic movie-type narrative which records a slice or slices of life at a particular time, with no identifiable outcome or result—although, at one level, it is that. What I found, and I hope I have conveyed to the reader, was a dramatically different world, long gone and—by and large, fortunately—impossible to reprise. At one end of the spectrum there was bravery of the first order, and decency, plus the honesty and purity of sporting endeavour that reflected the very best in humanity. At the other extreme there was bastardry and incredible violence, cowardice, two-faced diplomacy and its bedfellow, hypocrisy; there was institutionalised brutality and, given the frailty of human nature, the dominance of short-term interests—all of which helped bring on the 1939–45 War. Somewhere in between were silly self-indulgence and frivolity. Bad decisions were made.

Bad behaviour prevailed. Bad people won; not forever, but for a time. There is some fun in those four weeks, much in fact, and some things to celebrate too—four weeks, however, when it all went wrong.

Nicholas Whitlam
Scarborough, NSW
November 2016

18 JULY
SATURDAY

We do not know what was going through Pablo Casals' mind this hot summer afternoon as he rehearsed Beethoven's Ninth Symphony in Barcelona's Palau de la Música Catalana. Approaching sixty, the great cellist—the world's most famous cellist—was a much-loved national hero. Nor do we know the thoughts and plans for the weekend of high school student Juan Antonio Samaranch. He had been holidaying with his mother and siblings in Palma, Mallorca until yesterday when, in the light of the political assassinations that were traumatising the country, they had rushed back to the safety of their substantial Barcelona villa—in time to celebrate Samaranch's sixteenth birthday.[1]

What we do know is that for Casals, the Catalan maestro, and young Samaranch, a cadet fascist, today's events would forever change their lives.

Barcelona represented the extremes of the developing Spanish horror story. It was the richest city in the country. The bourgeoisie had created a city of culture and class. The arts were widely celebrated. It was the home of Picasso, Gaudí, Miró and Dalí. Talent was promoted. Yet the workers were kept down. They did not share in the city's economic success and of Catalonia more widely. As a result, the trade unions had an avid following. None more so than the CNT, the Confederación Nacional de Trabajo, which enjoyed the support of perhaps 400,000 members.

Little more than five years ago, on 15 April 1931, after Alphonso XIII had fled the country and a republican government had been installed (and Catalonia had gained a degree of autonomy), Casals had led his orchestra in an emotional performance of the Ninth Symphony. A grand crowd had gathered at Barcelona's splendid Palau Nacional. The "palace" had been built for the 1929 International Exposition or World's Fair, on the edge of the Montjuïc, the broad flat hill that forms the south western border of the established city; this new building dominated the Plaça d'Espanya below, down to which a grand set of steps flowed.[2]

Perhaps as many as 7000 people had assembled there on that day for an event that had become a famous part of recent Catalan history.

In a strange congruence, less than two weeks later, the International Olympic Committee met in Barcelona from 24–26 April 1931. The meeting's main purpose was to decide the venue for the 1936 Olympics, the choice being between Barcelona and Berlin. Presumably because of the political turmoil associated with the fall of the monarchy, the meeting did not attract a quorum—only 19 members turned up—so it was not until the following month that Berlin prevailed as the IOC's preference. Berlin won the postal ballot 43-16. Everyone accepted the result.

Less than two years later, however, in January 1933, Hitler gained power in Germany—and everything changed. The Nazis' new race laws and rampant anti-Semitism inevitably led to calls for a boycott of the Berlin Games. Although that campaign ultimately failed, one result was the establishment of a competing event—Barcelona's 1936 Olimpiada Popular, the Peoples' Olympiad.

So now, on the hottest day of the hot summer of 1936, Casals was rehearsing the Ninth Symphony. The Catalonian president, Lluís Companys, wanted Casals to reprise his 1931 performance as a symbolic opening to the 1936 Peoples' Olympiad.

The city was bursting with people. Twenty thousand visitors and thousands of athletes had arrived for the Olympiad—which was scheduled to open tomorrow, Sunday.

The invitation from the Organizing Committee, chaired by Companys himself, stated that the object of the Games was "to promote the true spirit of the Olympiad—the fraternity of peoples and races—which cannot exist in the atmosphere of Berlin."[3]

The official Berlin Games were scheduled to run from 1–16 August. The Peoples' Olympiad would precede them and would run from 19–26 July. Some athletes planned to compete in both. Others, like the great American boxer Charley Burley, not yet 19, refused the opportunity to compete in Berlin and went to Barcelona instead;[4] Canadian boxers Sammy Luftspring and Norman Yack and high jump bronze medallist for the 1932 LA Games, Eva Dawes, a fellow Canadian, did the same.[5]

The Catalonian and Spanish governments gave their "moral and financial" support to the Peoples Olympiad. Teams were sent from France[6] (with a contingent of at least 1000) and more than twenty other countries or entities—including Alsace, Euskadi, Galicia, Catalonia, Palestine and "Emigrant Jews".[7]

Most of the teams had been put together quickly. Some invitations had only been posted as late as May. That to the Committee for Fair Play in Sports in New York, the body that had organised US opposition to the Berlin Games, specifically asked that they include "Negro sportsmen for, as you will see from our manifesto, we are defending the real Olympic spirit, which stands for brotherhood between races and peoples."[8] Late in June, the Committee announced that a team of "outstanding American athletes" was sailing to Barcelona, and that it was the Committee's "final gesture of protest against the Hitler Nazi Games in Berlin."[9] They were only twelve in number. Three were indeed black, although only Charley Burley could truly be classified as outstanding.

These were not a replication of the official games. Of course there were to be events for elite sportsmen and women—and here the organizers were keen to adopt a gender balance, giving special importance to the participation of women—but there were two other categories as well: for representative athletes not quite up to international standard, and for basic athletic clubs. Moreover, the now traditional cultural events that accompanied an Olympic Games were democratised for Barcelona; the high culture of classical music was supplemented with painting, sculpture, photography and literary prizes, poster design contests, chess, folk dancing and theatre. This explains why there were so many participants in the city—perhaps as many as 6000.

Out on the high seas, mid-Atlantic, the SS *Manhattan*, a large luxury liner that worked the New York/Hamburg route, was steaming towards Germany. On board was the US team for the Berlin Olympics—with the nearly 350 athletes accommodated in third class, and the officials in first.[10]

Passengers included all the famous athletes. First among them was Jesse Owens, soon to turn twenty-three, who was expected to win the 100 metres and perhaps more. He had first come to the attention of the athletic world the previous year on 25 May 1935 at the Big Ten Championship meet at Ann Arbor, Michigan when he broke or equalled four world records—100 yards, 220 yards, 220 yards hurdles and the long jump. What's more, all this was achieved in less than one hour!

Jesse was the youngest of nine children. His father had been a sharecropper in rural Alabama, where the family lived in extreme poverty. His grandparents had been slaves. Like many poor blacks the family moved north for the better job prospects, and they settled in Cleveland, Ohio soon after the First World War. It was here that James Cleveland ("JC") Owens became "Jesse" when people misinterpreted his lingering southern accent.

Jesse Owens was an attractive character. He had been taught to please and not get "above" himself. He had a winning smile, a lithe body, a competitive spirit and a most pleasant engaging manner. And he ran like the wind.

On board the SS *Manhattan* Jesse and his teammates, black and white and brindle, were all being treated equally—which was a surprise to him because, to be fair, it was much better than the blacks were treated back at Ohio State. There, he and his great friend and Olympic teammate the high jumper Dave Albritton were heroes of the track team—but they had to live off campus, barred from the all-white men's dormitory and away from the fraternities.

Mid Atlantic weather is famously difficult, and this trip provided no exception. It was cold and wet and some of the athletes, young and spirited, were getting up to the inevitable high jinks. Notable among the merrymakers was Eleanor Holm, a swimming gold medallist from the 1932 LA Games. Holm had married bandleader Art Jarrett in 1933 and together they developed a slightly risqué vaudeville act in which she appeared in a white bathing suit white hat and high heels—thereby testing the anachronistic amateur rules of the day and incurring the wrath of US Olympic chief, Avery Brundage.

Now aged 22, Holm was a good time girl from Brooklyn and was enjoying a good time. It was now three days into the voyage. Holm had spent the previous evening in first class with American supporters bound for the Olympics. The "badgers", as the US Olympic officials were known in derogatory reference to their official badges, were up there of course. So too were many prominent people including William Randolph Hearst Jr, playwright Charles MacArthur (without his wife Helen Hayes), sportswriter and soon-to-be novelist Paul Gallico, and the famed sports journalist and hard-drinker Joe Williams.

And this morning, at 6:00 am, Eleanor Holm was seen being carried to bed—well under the weather.[11]

The five years from 1931 had been chaotic and traumatic in Spain. Middle class republicans led the new government of (what was technically) Spain's Second Republic. The Republic adopted a modern constitution. Conservative forces of the Right—led by the Church[12], the Army, landholders and an aristocracy still pining for the monarchy—simply would not accept the new government and its reforms. The Right resisted the government's popular initiatives—notably the disestablishment of the Church, female suffrage, divorce and agrarian reform—by every means available, including violence.

In 1933 a coalition of parties of the Right regained power in national elections. In response, disappointed with the loss of legitimate power, some of the Left took to the streets with strikes and riots, violence and insurrection.

A major strike in late 1934 in the northwest, in Asturias, led to an insurrection by the heavily unionised miners. Francisco Franco, a 41-year-old Army general was the local commander and he enhanced his name with the Right by suppressing the insurrection in the most savage and brutal fashion. Franco, using troops from Morocco where he had once led the Spanish Foreign Legion, "razed [Asturias] as if it were a rebellious Moroccan village."[13] Perhaps as many as 3000 were killed, mostly unionists; the union leaders who survived were executed or incarcerated.

By the end of 1935 fully 30,000 oppositionists were in prison, including many of the republican Left leadership. Then, in the national election of February 1936 the Left was restored to power in a coalition of progressive parties—the *Frente Popular*, or Popular Front.

With the advent of the Popular Front government, it took the anti-democratic Army leadership less than a month to start planning a coup. Several of them met in Madrid on 8 March 1936 when it was decided that General Emilio Mola—who was being "exiled" to Pamplona—should serve as the coordinator of a future coup.[14]

It was hot and uncomfortably sticky inside the wonderful Palau de la Música that Saturday afternoon. The orchestra had rehearsed the first three movements of Beethoven's masterpiece when Casals was handed an urgent message from Ventura Gassol, the Catalan minister of culture.[15] The minister informed him that he had cancelled the Opening Ceremony for the Peoples' Olympiad because a military uprising was expected imminently; Gassol suggested that the artists make for home without delay.

Casals read the note to the orchestra. The maestro offered his colleagues the opportunity to leave or stay and perform the final movement as a kind of farewell: "as an adieu and an au revoir for all of us".[16] They all chose to remain. Like almost everyone in Spain they knew that a military coup was a possibility and that a successful coup would mean the unravelling of the reforms of the Republic.

Casals later told of how, as the orchestra played Beethoven's final movement and the choir sang the words to Schiller's *Ode to Joy*, he shed tears of grief and frustration such that he was unable to read the score. "What a moving moment", he was to recall, "We were singing the immortal hymn to fraternity, while in the streets of Barcelona—and in so many other cities—a fratricidal struggle was being readied that would leave hundreds of Spanish families in mourning."

"When our city and country are once more at peace, we shall play the Ninth Symphony again", Casals promised his colleagues.[17] It was not to be.

On his way to rehearsal this day, Casals recalled "soldiers, Civil Guards, factory workers in overalls and crowds of agitated men and women …" as word of a possible coup started to filter through the city. When he and his fellow musicians returned to the streets—still suffocatingly hot after the rehearsal's completion—they found the city buzzing with further rumour, unease and foreboding. Loudspeakers had been set up on streets and broadcast messages such as this one: "Do not turn your radios off! Stay calm! Traitors are spreading wild rumours to sow fear and panic! Keep tuned in! The Republic is in control of the situation!"[18]

Soon after the elections and the change of government in February 1936, Franco and other anti-democratic Army generals had been dispersed to new and inferior roles throughout the country. The idea was that this would keep them out of trouble. In fact it gave them national coverage from which they could mount coordinated local insurrections.

Francisco Franco had been exiled to the Canary Islands.

The news from the Canary Islands today was that Franco, now a pudgy 43-year-old, had joined with fellow conspirators in a military uprising. He had been a late starter to the insurrection, albeit that his co-conspirators very much wanted him on board and he had been present at the initial 8 March meeting. As recently as last month, on 23 June, in his duplicitous way, he had reached out to the Republican leadership—writing a letter to PM Casares Quiroga which in its "labyrinthine ambiguity" could be interpreted as an offer to quell unrest in the Army.[19]

Five days ago, on 13 July, Franco had bought two tickets on the German ship *Waldi* which was due to leave Las Palmas tomorrow for Le Havre and Hamburg. They were for his wife and only child, a 10-year-old daughter.[20] That morning of 13 July he had heard the news in Madrid of the assassination of a prominent Right-wing politician, Calvo Sotelo. To this point, notwithstanding his being in the loop, he had yet to commit to the planned uprising. Franco now sent a message to Mola that he was in.

A plane had been procured by Luis Bolín, a Spanish civilian co-conspirator, to fly Franco to Spanish Morocco where the crack Army of Africa troops were located. The plane had arrived at an airport near Las Palmas in Gran Canaria on the afternoon of 14 July. The problem was that Franco was located in Tenerife, a separate island more than 100 miles away. And then a strange thing happened. Franco's colleague in Las Palmas, General Amado Balmes, who was an experienced marksman, shot himself in the stomach and died. Franco was being watched by Spanish government security and would ordinarily have required Ministry of War permission to travel from Tenerife to Las Palmas. Balmes' "accident" and subsequent funeral provided Franco with the excuse to get over to Gran Canaria and the escape plane. He took the overnight boat, arriving in Las Palmas at 8:30 am yesterday.[21]

Mola's plan was for coordinated military uprisings in key cities throughout the country this morning. The plan leaked in Morocco, so the putschists there jumped the gun last night—shooting their commander dead and taking the acting High Commissioner into custody. This news reached Las Palmas and Franco this morning at 4:00 am.[22] At 5:00 am Franco declared martial law, and at 5:15 am Inter-Radio of Las Palmas read his somewhat confused call to arms:

> *Glory to the Army of Africa. Spain above all. Receive the enthusiastic greeting of these garrisons which join you and other comrades in the peninsula in these historic moments. Blind faith in our triumph. Long Live Spain with honour. General Franco.*

It is noticeable that this message to his colleagues on the Peninsula made no mention or commitment to either the Republic or the Monarchy. With the Amy of Africa in the bag, Franco was defending "Spain".

The roads on Los Palmas were controlled by the Popular Front. In order to avoid them Franco took a naval tugboat to the airport, arriving there at 11:00 am. By 2:05 pm he was in the air on his way to Morocco.

The plane was a Dragon Rapide, a small six-seater biplane made by de Havilland. It had been flown to the Canaries from England by British intelligence officers.[23] With their new passenger on board they now flew to Agadir and then Casablanca, where Franco spent the night. Somewhere along the way Franco shaved off his trademark moustache, presumably as some sort of disguise. His rival, General Quiepo de Llano, opined that it was the only thing that Franco ever sacrificed for Spain.

Perhaps so, but soon Franco was to emerge as the undisputed leader of the revolt. And in less than three years he would be the *Caudillo*, leader and ruler of Fascist Spain.

Back in Barcelona, twenty thousand tickets had been sold for tomorrow's Opening Ceremony of the Olympiad. A final rehearsal of the Ceremony had been held during the day at the Olympic Stadium.[24] Later, the stadium buzzed with activity. Athletes were there to train and fraternise. Hotels were full, and many athletes, possibly thousands, chose to sleep overnight in the stadium precinct.

The British contingent did not arrive until 6:30 pm this evening, their departure having been delayed by interference from British athletic officialdom. Four Scottish bagpipers proudly announced their arrival at a hotel next to the church of Santa Maria del Pi, just off La Rambla.

Some British athletes and officials went out for a stroll. What they found was "somewhat disconcerting. Policemen were stopping cars and questioning the drivers. Several Catalonians approached them and warned them in simple English. 'Plenty revolution soon,' accompanied by hand signals imitating the firing of guns."[25]

Meanwhile, news had reached Lluís Companys that both Seville and Morocco had already fallen to the conspirators. Late tonight, probably about the time Franco arrived in Casablanca, Companys met with representatives of the CNT trade union. Convinced that the Army was about to rise in Barcelona, the unionists asked Companys to issue arms to their well organised "defence committees" which were scattered throughout the barrios of the working class areas of the city. He refused.[26]

The CNT immediately put their defence committees on a war footing, and they raided the armouries of four ships in the harbour.[27] All the elements of the Left were alerted. Motor vehicles were requisitioned from their owners and branded—prominently—with the various trade

> union and political acronyms of the Left that contemporary black and white photographs so vividly record: CNT–FAI, predominantly, the exotic-sounding neo-Trotskyist POUM and so on.
>
> The Spanish Civil War was about to begin in earnest.

Out in the Atlantic the SS *Manhattan* was steaming towards tomorrow's stop at Cobh in County Cork, a port with deep resonance for many Irish Americans as so many had emigrated from it. Tonight the American competitors attended the Captain's Ball. By all accounts it was a lively occasion. To some, however, it was unseemly in that the badgers put on a spoof of a well-known radio program and of a variety show which, while intended to be amusing, offended many.[28]

At some point Brundage made a speech in which he said that he understood the need to be flexible with the rules, the competitors aged as they were between thirteen and forty: "We are making all reasonable allowances. We are not prudish nor do we have any objection to a glass of beer or smoking by athletes who know how to behave generally and not disrupt the team's morale and discipline." This was a reference to the field hockey, rowing and fencing squads.

He extended the 10:00 pm curfew for the evening. And then he slipped in the fact that the AAU[29] would be organising a post-Olympics tour for the track and field athletes—a fund-raising activity in which they would be obliged to participate.[30]

19 JULY
SUNDAY

Lluís Companys could not sleep.[1]

Early in the morning, about 2:00 am, he and minister Gassol went out into the night. They walked up and down La Rambla, Barcelona's marvellous tree-lined boulevard that links the main city square with the waterfront. La Rambla's ubiquitous pimps and performers were asleep by now. The hotels were full in town for the Peoples' Olympiad and many athletes and spectators were sleeping rough.

Companys and Gassol must have looked an incongruous and somewhat bizarre couple to those who were awake—Companys in a soft hat pulled over his eyes for some sort of anonymity, and Gassol in his customary large-brimmed one. Companys told Gassol that he thought the Army would stay loyal, was less sure of the paramilitary police forces, but on balance he believed things were under control.[2]

In Madrid, about this time, Prime Minister Casares Quiroga resigned. His replacement was Martínez Barrio. He had been PM in 1933 in an earlier Republican administration, and he immediately telephoned General Emilio Mola in Pamplona.

At 49, Mola was the deeply conservative national coordinator of the coup ("El Director") and a rival to Franco. Tall and bespectacled, introverted and with an obsessive attention to detail, he was distinctive among the conspirators in that he looked like a leader. And like many of them he was an Africanista, that group of officers who, when younger, had gained quick promotion by their efforts in the suppression of African nationalism in colonial Morocco. With the enthusiastic help of local royalists, his troops had easily gained control of Pamplona.

Offered a cabinet position by the new PM Martínez Barrio, Mola refused:

You have your people and I have mine. If you and I should reach agreement, both of us will have betrayed our followers.[3]

And who were the supporters of the rebellion? US Ambassador Claude Bowers, identified them as follows:

- The monarchists, who wanted the King back with the old regime;
- The great landowners, who wished to preserve the feudalistic system by ending agrarian reforms;
- The industrialists and financiers, who wished to put, and keep, the workers "in their place";
- The hierarchy of the Church, hostile to the separation of Church and State;
- The military clique that had in mind a military dictatorship; and
- The fascist element, which was bent on the creation of a totalitarian state.[4]

That new central government lasted but a couple of hours. Martínez Barrio resigned. The next Prime Minister, José Giral, a 56-year-old physician turned politician and a trusted ally of President Azaña, authorised the distribution of arms to the workers in Madrid.[5]

In Barcelona, hundreds of visitors to the Peoples' Olympiad were sleeping in the main square, the Plaça de Catalunya. Blessedly, it was cooler this morning when loud sirens woke them at 5:00 am.

A CNT lookout had spotted troops moving from their

barracks at 4:15 am and informed the CNT mustering point accordingly.[6] The sirens were from textile plants where CNT operatives set off this pre-arranged signal; it was a call to arms for the CNT defence committees, and a general strike. The military had lost the element of surprise.

The US team were housed at the Europa Hotel on the Plaça de Catalunya. Frank Payton, a track sprinter and basketball player, remembered a rude awakening:

The rumbling of cannon, several thousand machine guns and rifles and the sound of marching feet.[7]

Charley Burley later told the *Pittsburgh Courier*:[8]

I was awakened at 5 o'clock in the morning by the sound of a lot of shooting and yelling. I thought they were celebrating the games by shooting off firecrackers. I got up and looked out of my hotel window, and had no sooner done that than a bullet came crashing by my head, just missing me by inches. I dropped to the floor, then rushed out to where the rest of the fellows on our team were staying, and found out what it was all about.

The team saw workers digging up the cobblestones from the streets to build barricades. Occasional machine gun fire made sure the athletes kept themselves inside the hotel.[9]

Further towards the waterfront, the British team woke to gunfire near their hotel. It appeared to come from La Rambla.[10] AR Northcott, the president of the Acton Labour Party Sports Section, who was to compete in chess, thought the firing sounded distant and went back to sleep. By 7:30 am Northcott knew the firing was "close at hand … one rifle at least apparently being fired on the roof of our hotel". The British contingent were hearing machine guns and "big gun fire". They too decided to stay indoors.

Franco arrived in Morocco at about 7:30 am. He was met by General Juan Yagüe, the leader of the already successful Moroccan uprising, an Africanista and, at 44, arguably the most bloodthirsty of Franco's colleagues.

In many ways Franco was an unlikely leader. He didn't look the part, being squat and tubby; he had a squeaky, somewhat effeminate voice; and he was the youngest of the leading conspirators. He had already held top jobs, though, having been head of the military academy at Zaragoza (when it was closed by the Republic in 1931) and chief of the defence staff—before his banishment to the backwater of the Canaries. And he was an Africanista.

It can be seen that Franco was wasting no time. He gave a rousing speech to the troops along the lines of his incoherent statement from the Canaries the day before: "Spain is saved … Blind faith, no doubts, firm energy without vacillations, because the Patria demands it …" The cries of "Viva Franco!" and "Viva España!"[11] that had greeted him on his arrival in Morocco yesterday were heartily repeated when he quickly announced that the troops' wages were to be increased.

And by 9:00 am he had despatched Bolín and the Dragon Rapide with a document they could show sympathisers:

> *I authorize Don Luis Antonio Bolín to negotiate urgently in England, Germany and Italy the purchase of aircraft and supplies for the Spanish non-Marxist Army.*

On the SS *Manhattan*, the US team had been at sea for four days. Conditions were hardly ideal for training. There was a rudimentary gym and a single rowing machine (which the rowing coach discouraged his charges from using, believing such devices caused his men to lose the feel for the water); calisthenics were feasible, but the swimming pool was a bath sloshing around with the roll of the sea.

The badgers had responded quickly to complaints about the

food. The new menu was so good the athletes started putting on unwanted weight. And Glenn Cunningham, the team captain and a truly decent human being, reached out to the black athletes; he succeeded in creating genuine camaraderie among a diverse group of black and white, established athletes and youngsters, many leaving home for the first time, among urban sophisticates and rustics alike.

Jesse Owens led the athletes in runs around the decks. US diplomat George Kennan, who surely should have chosen another vessel to return to his post in Moscow, complained that "For a week we dodged the motions of gum-chewing supermen with crew cuts and a variety of hefty amazons, as they practiced their particular skills on deck."[12]

Avery Brundage had been a fine athlete, competing in both the pentathlon and decathlon in the 1912 Stockholm Olympics, and, after a successful career in the building industry, was now president of the US Olympic committee. Nearly 49, Brundage had led the successful resistance to the Berlin Games boycott and was starting to give vent to his authoritarian nature.

This morning he lectured the athletes on good behaviour. He said they were allowed to accept the hospitality of the well-wishers upstairs but reminded them of their sworn undertakings not to drink alcohol. He said the badgers, not his term, were not "deaf, dumb and blind." (Everyone knew of the beer window in tourist class that many of the men, notably the rowers, regularly patronised.[13]) He almost certainly knew that his young and fit and frisky charges had found some privacy for their amorous encounters in the lifeboats.[14]

> The situation this Sunday morning in Madrid was confused. That in Barcelona was clearer: in the Catalan capital an almighty battle was about to start.

War brings death and trauma. Civil War is no different. Men and women, usually men alone, set out to kill and maim one another. No amount of bravery can hide the savagery and horror of war and its consequences. And over the next two days about 600 people were to die in Barcelona, with 4000 seriously wounded.[15]

The Barcelona army garrison totalled about 6000. In addition, as part of Spain's peculiar police system, there were 3000 Guardia Civil ("civil guards") and 2000 Assault Guards, all armed.[16] The blue-uniformed *asaltos*, as the Assault Guards were colloquially known, were a paramilitary police corps created by the Republic in 1932 to defend "public order", and it was assumed they would be on the side of the Republic. The allegiance of the green-uniformed Guardia Civil, which had been created in the 19th century to guard large estates from their workers and had a well-earned reputation for brutality,[17] was less certain.

The unionists' strategy was to not engage troops in their barracks, where they might dig in, but to wait until they were some distance away from that refuge.

CNT militia soon sealed off La Rambla, thereby preventing the rebels from linking the seaside Atarazanas barracks with the Plaça de Catalunya. Controlling this key artery also allowed for swift movement of their people through secondary streets across the city.[18] Then they blocked El Parallel, the main road from the docks to the Plaça d'Espanya.

The army quickly gained control of the Plaça d'Espanya. Earlier, to the great benefit of the loyalists, supporters within the Atarazanas barracks had handed over some weapons to the CNT; but then, with heavy fighting, control of the barracks returned to the army rebels.

Moving through the city army troops were instructed to cry out "Long live the Republic!" thereby confusing their opponents and the Republic's supporters, and they soon appeared to have captured the Plaça de Catalunya. Machine guns were erected at strategic points around the square, the most obvious nestled in a flowerbed in the centre; yet the rebels did not control the Plaça de Catalunya. An American tourist, who watched from an hotel overlooking the square, wrote "carnage reigned supreme for the next fourteen hours", and of how "from all side streets, came armed [workers], running, nondescript, mad and wild."[19]

Throughout the city there was great confusion: deadly hand-to-hand combat took place at key points while close by, within sight of the combat, the army rebels and the loyalist workers stood off from each other behind freshly built barricades.

Meanwhile, high up on Montjuïc, Carlos Pardo arrived at the Olympic Stadium for the Opening Ceremony. He was a member of the Spanish water polo team and as such was housed—along with the Catalan, Basque and Galician teams—in the Exhibition Halls of the Palau Nacional. He found the gates of the stadium locked. Someone knew what was going on, because a sign was affixed to the gates reading: "Games cancelled because of war."[20]

In their hotel, the British team rushed from window to window, watching the action in the streets below. One sniper took their particular attention: a priest—a supporter of the rebels—was using the cover of the Del Pi church to shoot at the militias and loyal troops.

Alfred "Chick" Chakin—a CCNY official, former champion wrestler and now coach to the US team—wrote in his diary:

> *Rifle and pistol fire, stuttering machine guns, bombing and shelling. They don't do things by halves out here. We are locked in our hotel room and every time we shove our heads out of the windows, we are shot at.*[21]

He saw the local militia ferret snipers from their positions in the churches: "Each time a nest of snipers was routed, the church would be set ablaze."[22]

And yet, some people were still going about their business. One reliable journalist even reported Sunday "picnickers coming down the street with hampers hoping to get on a train for their customary trip to the countryside."[23] (He also noted popular outrage that many military rebels and their civilian sympathizers had been permitted to establish the machine-gun emplacements in church towers.)

Early on workers commandeered an armoured car that was used by the tramways system to carry wages and fare collections. It became an armoured militia vehicle and was soon plastered with CNT–FAI red and black livery.

Critically, both the Civil and Assault guards stayed loyal to the Republic. In the Plaça de Catalunya a police captain led a mad dash against the rebel machine gun stationed in the centre of the square. He was inevitably mowed down—but as he flaying about in a dramatic death dance, he fell on the machine gun and dislodged it. Those who followed him turned the gun on the rebels.[24] Control of the square was passing to the loyalists. The square itself was strewn with dead men and dead horses.[25]

Control of the Telefónica building on the corner of the square went back and forth between the antagonists.

Callow army recruits who had been cynically induced to raise the Popular Front clenched fist to confuse their opponents, were now asked the question:

Soldiers, brothers, why are you fighting us?

Some started to reply:

We don't know.[26]

By 11:00 am CNT leaders could rightly cry what soon became a mantra, "We're a match for the army!" A US athlete left his hotel, grabbed a crowbar and helped the locals dig up the cobblestones and build a barricade.[27] Frank Payton reported that "Women held barricades. Some women even led detachments of workers against the fascists."

At 12:30 pm General Manuel Goded flew in by seaplane, as arranged, from Mallorca. Like Franco and other conspirators, he had been exiled to the provinces earlier in the year. He was 53. The rebels' plan was for Goded to take command in Barcelona after he had led the uprising in Mallorca. That done, he was now in Barcelona. What he found was a city where the Republic was very much getting the upper hand. The local air force had remained loyal, the police forces too—and now he

> found the army divided.
>
> In the Plaça de Catalunya, white handkerchiefs began to appear from the rebel side. There was confusion and misinformation. Armed civilians mingled with the soldiers, thereby breaking up their formations. Asaltos hugged and fraternized with newly loyal soldiers while their leaders withdrew to the Hotel Cólon. The Guardia Civil fraternised with CNT fighters.
>
> At about 4 pm white flags appeared in the Telefónica and the Hotel Cólon, both on the Plaça de Catalunya.

The situation in Madrid was still a stand-off. General Joaquin Fanjul, the 56-year-old leader of the local conspirators, had visited the Montaña barracks late this afternoon with some Fascist supporters and addressed the troops. When he tried to lead the troops out of the barracks, however, they were surrounded by trade unionists and asaltos. Trapped in their barracks, the rebel troops fired their machine guns on the milling crowd.[28]

> Back in Barcelona, Manuel Goded came to accept the fact that the insurrection had failed there. He surrendered at 6:00 pm. By 1930 he had been persuaded to broadcast a simple radio message:
>
> *This is General Goded. I make this declaration to the Spanish people, that fate has been against me and I am a prisoner. I am saying this so that all those who are still fighting need feel no further obligation towards me.*[29]

Goded's surrender gave enormous comfort to supporters of the Republic and those who had stayed loyal to it. It was broadcast widely throughout the country. In Madrid, the crowd outside the Montaña barracks were further enthused by Delores Ibárruri's famous *No Pasaran!* ("They shall not pass!") speech:

> *Workers! Farmers! Antifascists! Patriotic Spaniards!*
>
> *Everyone rise to defend the Republic against the Fascist military uprising, to defend the people's freedoms and the democratic triumphs of the people!*
>
> *Through the statements by the government and the Popular Front the people understand the gravity of the situation ...*
>
> *Under the battle cry "Fascism shall not pass! ... workers and farmers from all Spanish provinces are joining the fight against the enemies of the Republic that have risen in armed rebellion.*
>
> *Communists, Socialists, Anarchists and Republican democrats, the soldiers and services loyal to the Republic have inflicted the first defeats on the Fascist foe, who drag through the mud the very same honourable military tradition that they have boasted to possess so many times.*
>
> *The whole country cringes in indignation at these heartless barbarians who want to hurl our democratic Spain into an abyss of terror and death.*
>
> *However, THEY SHALL NOT PASS! ...*
>
> *Long live the Popular Front! Long live the union of all anti-fascists! Long live the Republic of the people! The Fascists shall not pass!*
>
> *THEY SHALL NOT PASS!*[30]

Ibárruri, a 40-year-old communist deputy from Asturias, spoke with such power and conviction that from this day she became universally known as La Pasionara. And *No Pasaran!* became the eternal slogan of the Republic.

> In Barcelona, the terrified athletes started to slink out from their hotels. The British team continued to be alarmed that rebels had holed up in the adjacent Santa Maria del Pi church and were using it as a sniper point. The hotel's food had quickly run out and two volunteered to get some. Only after careful explanations to trigger-happy Republicans did they return safely.[31]
>
> Chuck Chakin, the US coach, reported a sorry scene:
>
> *We are finally allowed out when things are comparatively quiet. Martial law and we can't stay out late. We go around picking up bullets and taking pictures. This beautiful city is a mess. Churches are burning all over town.*

Far away in southern Germany, Adolf Hitler was officiating at the opening night of the Bayreuth Festival. He was a keen and knowledgeable admirer of Wagner and, in the fourth year of his twelve-year government, the Festspeile had become the feature of his cultural calendar.

Winifred Wagner, Wagner's English-born daughter-in-law, the widow of his son Siegfried, headed the festival throughout the thirties and, as chatelaine of the family estate, *Wahnfried*, she provided Hitler with his own small guesthouse in the grounds. She was an enthusiastic supporter of the Führer. This year, because of the forthcoming Berlin Games, the Festival had been split in two, one part 19–30 July before the Games, and 18–31 August after.

With the official opening set for 10:00 pm tonight, Hitler conformed to correct form. He arrived to open the event dressed in white tie, for once forgoing one of his chilling and silly Nazi outfits.

19 July

Mid Atlantic, on the SS *Manhattan*, Eleanor Holm was upstairs for another round of champagne with her fancy new friends. A chaperone, the unfortunately named Ada T Sackett, told her to go to bed.

"Look," Mrs Holm Jarrett unwisely replied, "it's my third Olympic team. I don't think you've been on any before. I know what I'm doing. And what are you doing up here? Why aren't you down stairs watching the athletes?"[32]

France and Spain enjoyed fraternal Popular Front administrations, Spain's *Frente Popular* having won the election of February 1936 and France's *Front Populaire* having won the French election in May. Accordingly, late at night, after the tumultuous events throughout Spain and in particular in his two biggest cities, Spanish PM Giral sent a telegram to Léon Blum, the newly elected French Prime Minister:

> SURPRISED BY A DANGEROUS MILITARY COUP. BEG OF YOU TO HELP US IMMEDIATELY WITH ARMS AND AEROPLEANES.
>
> FRATERNALLY YOURS GIRAL.[33]

20 JULY
MONDAY

The San Andrés barracks, Barcelona's main armoury, had surrendered during the night. This provided a windfall 30,000 rifles to the CNT and other militias.[1] Yet remnants of the rebel forces and their allies fought on.

The British Peoples' Olympiad team again woke to gunfire. Taking to the hotel roof, they determined that it was still coming from the adjacent Del Pi church tower.[2]

> In Madrid, fifty churches had been set on fire during the night.[3] Huge crowds gathered in their Plaza d'España. "All aid to the Republic!" and "Death to Fascism!" were the ubiquitous mantras. Loyal aircraft bombed the Montaña barracks and loudspeakers broadcast calls for the troops to overthrow their officers—but when white flags appeared and the crowd of loyal Republicans moved forward to accept the surrender of the rebels, they were greeted by machine gun fire.
>
> Just before noon the Republican loyalists' constant assaults broke down the barrack's huge main entrance door. A bloodbath ensued. Of the 2500 Rightists in the barracks—2000 troops and perhaps 500 neo-fascist supporters—several hundred were killed in a savage retribution. "One giant revolutionary conceived it his duty to fling officer after officer, disarmed and yelling, from the highest gallery upon the insensate mass of people in the courtyard beneath."[4]
>
> At the end of all this, General Fanjul was arrested—lucky to escape, albeit temporarily, with his life.[5]

Meanwhile, in the western Peloponnese, at Olympia, a new Olympic ritual was underway; it was to become a "tradition".

Precisely at twelve noon a flame was kindled in the ancient stadium. Fifteen "young Greek maidens" carried it through the arched stone doorway of the stadium to an altar in the Sacred Grove.[6] There, representatives of the Greek and German governments made the necessary speeches and read a long message—in French—from the ailing founder of the Olympic Movement, Baron Pierre de Coubertin. Part was strangely prophetic:

> *We are living in solemn hours. Everywhere around us are occurring the most extraordinary and unexpected things. Like a thick morning mist there are taking shape before us the figures of a new Europe and that of a new Asia. It seems to be that, now more than ever, the crisis that we must face and debate is, above all, a crisis in education.*[7]

The German National Anthem was played (as was the Nazi marching anthem, the frightening "Horst Wessel" song), and then a weedy Greek youth lit a torch from the altar and set off on the first leg of the first ever Torch Relay.

Originally known as the "Olympic Fire", the Torch Relay was to pass from Greece, though Bulgaria, Yugoslavia, Hungary, Czechoslovakia and Austria before arriving in Germany in time for the Opening Ceremony. It took twelve days and, as expected it was wonderful publicity for the Berlin Games, allowing many people to "participate" in them. (Within a few years each of these countries had been either invaded or annexed by the Third Reich.)

Leni Riefenstahl filmed it all. Riefenstahl was 33, indeed nearly 34, about which she was unnecessarily sensitive. A former actress, she was Hitler's favourite director. She had put together two brilliant propaganda films for the Nazis—*Sieg des Glaubens* ("Victory of Faith")[8] in 1933 and *Triumph des Willens* ("Triumph of the Will") in 1935, and the Führer had now engaged her to make a movie of the Olympics. For *Olympia*, as the film was eventually christened, she prepared a long prologue with pictorial references to ancient Greek statues and architecture which would provide a bogus historical link between ancient Greece and the new Germany. She tricked up attractive maidens dancing in a past paradise interwoven into the faux history; in the movie, this morphed into the Torch Relay, which would then lead to the opening of the Games. Unfortunately, none of the Greek youths on the first legs of the relay met her demanding standards for male beauty. Certainly not the first one. Nor the next few, some of whom appeared in native costume! All this was overcome on the fourth leg.

Anatol Dobriansky and his family were refugees from Communist Russia.[9] He barely spoke Greek, let alone German. But, at 20, slim and muscular, with black wavy hair, he was what Leni Riefenstahl wanted.

Leni soon had young Anatol stripped to a pair of shorts recreating the unsatisfactory first leg. She found they could converse in French. The early *Olympia* scenes were reshot in picturesque Delphi, with Dobriansky featured. He soon joined Riefenstahl's convoy to Berlin where, for the filming of the Games, he was a general dog's body and provided Leni with personal services.

Despite their prominence in these early days of the attempted coup, neither Mola nor Franco was the designated leader. That was José Sanjurjo. Like most of the conspirators, Sanjurjo had made his name and had gained his promotions in Morocco with the Army of Africa. Although an avowed monarchist, he had won early support from the Second Republic and, to the surprise of many, was kept in charge of the important Guardia Civil; there he maintained his reputation as a brutal traditionalist.

By 1932, however, Sanjurjo had been demoted. So, at the age of 50, he attempted a coup; the *sanjurjada*, as it became known, was a success in Seville but failed miserably in Madrid. Condemned to death, his sentence was commuted by the Republican Government. In 1934 the re-elected Right released him from goal, and he took exile in Portugal.

As soon as the uprising was underway, Mola sent a prominent adventurer and pilot to Estoril to bring Sanjurjo back to take command of the new rebellion. This was Juan Antonio Ansaldo.

Ansaldo had arrived last night, on the Sunday evening, and had flamboyantly announced to Sanjurjo and his hangers on that he—Ansaldo—was at Sanjurjo's command; he was, as he put it, "at the orders of the head of the Spanish state!"[10]

The Portuguese authorities ordered Ansaldo to move his plane from the main airport in Estoril to a more discrete one. And now, the next day—today—he was ready to go, to bring the designated leader back to Spain to take command of the insurrection.

It was a small plane, a Puss-moth, and Sanjurjo was a vain man. For his triumphal return ("I need to wear proper clothes as the new caudillo of Spain"), Sanjurjo packed a large trunk, full of uniforms and decorations and squeezed his heavy frame into the plane.

It was all too much for the Puss-moth. It clipped some trees on take off and burst into flames. Ansaldo survived but not Sanjurjo.

In Barcelona, Olympiad coach Chakin wrote in his diary:

> *... saw the wounded fall on both sides. Boys of 14 and 15 picked up guns and awkwardly raised them to their shoulders. It seemed as if all the workers were out on the streets bearing arms against the soldiers ...*
>
> *During this time the churches were burned because they provided havens for the Fascist soldiers, who used many of them as fortresses from which to snipe at the citizens. I personally saw*

no fewer than twenty-five churches burned, the flames leaping high into the ... sky ...[11]

It may be incredible to contemplate today, but in July 1936 there were more than 150 churches in Barcelona—and few escaped some sort of attack. The hatred of the Church ran deep: its historic support for the established order was resented by many, and now it was seen to be backing the attempted coup. Santa Maria del Mar was gutted. The Cathedral itself was protected by Assault Guards, however, and the never-finished Segrada Familia was left relatively unscathed.

A British athlete reported young fighters brandishing rifles from speeding cars daubed with the bold CNT and FAI identification. He and his colleagues saw parties of two or three Republicans checking out the Del Pi church; they heard its door being broken down and then saw a fire coming from its innards. This they tried to extinguish and, in so doing, found the horribly burned body of the priest who had been sniping from the belltower.[12]

These foreigners were not disinterested observers. Charley Burley was already active in the labour movement, and his coach Phil Goldstein was Jewish. Burley's entry on the Peoples' Olympiad team sheet is illustrative of the situation:[13]

*CHARLES BURLEY—57 Fullerton Street, Pittsburgh, Pa.—
BOXING. 147-pound class; Golden Gloves Championship
1936; Golden Gloves Junior Championship 1934; National
Runner-up, Cleveland, 1936; AAU tournaments. Was asked
to try-outs for Olympic Team, 1936, refused to compete on the
grounds of racial and religious discrimination in Germany.*

To a man and women the athletes in Barcelona had chosen to come to these alternative games as a protest against German racism and as a celebration of democracy. They were politically motivated members of trade unions, workers clubs and association;

many were socialists and communists.

But the violence against the Church was new and perplexing to these foreigners.

> For the best part of a century there had been a history of violence in Spain against the established Catholic Church. It flowed from the privileged position the Church was granted in education and welfare and its seeming irrelevance and indifference to the daily needs of the people. About two-thirds of the population were not practising Catholics.[14] Churches were used for funerals and weddings, even baptisms—but the people did not attend mass or confession. This was particularly so in the south and east: interestingly, "the very regions of the final expulsion of the Moors and Catholic reconquest in the 15th century seem never to have truly been conquered for the Church."[15] In Andalusia only 1% of men attended church. Apostasy was the norm. As a result, Manuel Azaña, the first Prime Minister of the Second Republic and later President, had tellingly, if unwisely, publicly concluded that Spain "had ceased to be Catholic"[16]
>
> Of the nearly 120,000 clerics and nuns of one sort or another, about 40,000 were employed by the State and paid by it as educators in the nation's schools and colleges—where the Church enjoyed a near monopoly. But they did a bad job. In nearly twenty Spanish provinces literacy was less than 50% and in only two (Barcelona being one) was illiteracy less than 25%.[17] Tens of thousands of the priests were poor and uneducated and incapable of other employment.
>
> It is worth noting that the Spanish Church was an embarrassment to the Papacy: the local Church embraced an enormous range of cults and superstitions, most unauthorised; processions to shrines and veneration of relics and statues were daily occurrences. These activities went well beyond and overwhelmed the minimal obligations of church on Sundays and confession.
>
> Most of the State's welfare system was administered through the Church. And here the priests and nuns succeeded in making religious observance a condition of welfare. The poor naturally resented this.

> In summary, reformers saw the Church as an impediment to the modernisation of Spain. Accordingly, the Constitution of 1931 put an end the Church's privileges when it was, in effect, disestablished. As a consequence the Church identified itself with the defeated Right. The aspiration of Republicans to a free, secular secondary education for all was anathema to the Church. It weighed against divorce, telling its female adherents that their husbands would abandon them as a result of the law change.
>
> In Madrid, in May 1931, more than a dozen churches were torched. Many other religious sites, notably, nunneries, were set alight through southern and eastern Spain. At this point the otherwise thoughtful and measured Azaña again had the memorable quote:
>
> > *All of the convents in Spain was not worth the life of a single Republican.*

In Madrid, although the fighting continued through the day, the socialist-led UGT was in effective control of public administration such as food and transport. That said, the victorious militia—socialists, communists, loyal police and simple workers—lost control of themselves. Newly armed militants indulged in spontaneous extra-judicial executions and reprisals. Ad hoc peoples' courts "authorised" execution orders. And the victors occupied and torched clubs, public buildings and the houses of the rich.[18]

> By this evening the rebellion was well under control in Barcelona. As a politician Lluís Companys represented the middle class owners of small businesses, minor landlords, lawyers and other professionals. He was a lawyer and had formerly represented the CNT professionally, but was clearly not one of them. In the circumstances, though, he had no choice but to embrace the CNT and the loyal supporters of the Republic. He met Buenaventura Derruti and the other leaders of the militias

in his office. His interlocutors were still dressed in their fighting gear, and he made this confession:

> *First of all, I admit to you that the CNT and the FAI have never been accorded their proper treatment. You have always been harshly prosecuted, and I, who was formerly with you,[19] afterwards found myself obliged by political exigencies to oppose you. Today you are the masters of the city.*
>
> *You have won and the power is in your hands. If you don't need me and if you don't want me, tell me now and I will only be one more soldier in the struggle.[20]*

It worked. Companys' Maoist self-criticism brought the CNT on side. What emerged was a proposal to form the so-called Central Anti-Fascist Militia Committee (CCMA) in which there would be representation from all progressive forces. Later that night, after a great debate within the CNT in which it examined the alternative of "ruling alone", the union decided to work with Companys. Overnight the CCMA became the de facto government of Barcelona with the CNT at its heart.

21 JULY

TUESDAY

News of Sanjurjo's death reached Mola in Pamplona at dawn. This changed the dynamic of the rebellion, not least because Sanjurjo would have restored the monarchy.

Also, it could not have escaped Mola's attention that he—as El Director—would now be a candidate to succeed Sanjurjo, and that his likely competitor was Franco.

In Barcelona, the CCMA took control of almost all administrative duties of the provincial government. Much more dramatic, and revolutionary, was the spontaneous social revolution that now took place. Emboldened by their success at the barricades, workers simply took over most businesses.

First up, they took over the transport system. The top management of the Transvias de Barcelona had fled the city yesterday, Monday. Today, Tuesday, a mass meeting of transit workers—and fully 6500 of the total 7000 were CNT members—voted to expropriate the assets of the company in the name of the people.[1]

The tram network had been badly damaged in the street fighting. The workers, now in control of their affairs, repaired it within days. Logistical solutions, known to the workers but not necessarily disclosed to their erstwhile superiors, soon improved service. A flat fare was introduced to help longer distance commuters. The red and black livery of the CNT adorned the system and became a feature of revolutionary Barcelona. Over the coming weeks, with wartime restrictions on private automotive travel, usage of the system increased dramatically.

And in the next days and weeks more than 3000 businesses were taken over by the workers. Just about every industry—the telephone company, electric power, textile mills, paper factories, department stores and hotels, picture theatres, live theatre and the opera, breweries, banks, gas and water companies, even haircutting—was collectivised and controlled by its workers.

None of this could have happened without the failed military coup. Ironically, it was the rebel uprising that had empowered the unions and their sympathisers.

The dominant political philosophy behind these events was anarcho-syndicalism, the philosophy of the CNT. Anarcho-syndicalists, also known as "anarchists" or "libertarian syndicalists", believe that power corrupts and that economic, social and political privilege flows from the power of the state and that the primary purpose of the state is the defence of private property. To them, this power denies most people the ability to enjoy material independence and social autonomy. Accordingly, as an alternative to the power of the state, anarcho-syndicalism advocates collective ownership by the workers of all enterprises, with that ownership deriving from the initiatives of the workers within individual enterprises. It advocates the liberation of the people from below, with autonomy and self-realisation working its way up the system, as opposed to communism ("dictatorship of the proletariat") or socialism ("claiming the commanding heights of the economy") where liberation comes from above. Further, if necessary, they believed that this liberation may be achieved through industrial action, expropriation and violence.

In Barcelona in 1936, the expropriation extended beyond industrial enterprises to other private property such as expensive large apartments. Some adherents opposed these actions, seeing them as unnecessary and part of the "politics of jealousy", but their views were ignored. The expropriations naturally caused alarm among the rich and established.

Founded in 1910, CNT membership was open to workers, students and the unemployed. Its stated aim was to develop a sense of solidarity among workers. Those who worked for "repressive organisations", such as the military and the police, were unwelcome. Its sister organisation, the Federation Anarquista Iberica (FAI), which had been founded in 1927 and whose membership was secret, came to think of itself as the conscience of the CNT—a sort of super politbureau for the union. In the late 20s and early 30s the FAI had effectively taken over the CNT when, according to its terms, it had seen the CNT becoming a mediator between capital and labour, rather than a pure representative of the workers.

A CNT–FAI leader said "If I were to sum up Anarchism in a phrase I would say it was the ideal of eliminating the beast in man."[2] And in answer to the charge of anarchist violence, he opined: "Anarchism has been violent in Spain because oppression has been violent." A sympathetic British observer offered the alternative view that anyone who is "not either a hopelessly impractical dreamer, or else a certifiable half wit, realizes that the programme that [anarcho-syndicalism] wishes to introduce is utterly impossible unless you can first eliminate one or two trifling little disadvantages, such as human nature and the basic laws of economics."[3]

A present day advocate of anarcho-syndicalism is Noam Chomsky. Critics and supporters of him alike would find comfort for their opinions on anarcho-syndicalism (and perhaps Chomsky) in the utterances recorded in the previous paragraph.

Released at last from their hotel, the athletes at Peoples' Olympiad started to check out the damage done to the city over the previous two days. They saw many armed men patrolling the streets—women too—and in nearly every side street they observed grinning Republic supporters manning barricades made of stones taken from between the tramlines.[4] The British contingent counted seventeen dead and rotting horses and mules in the Plaça de Catalunya, stinking in the heat; they saw burnt out churches too, and bullet holes and broken glass everywhere. And there were corpses piled up on the Catalunya metro station stairs.

21 July

With the CCMA in control of the city, the word went out that the Peoples' Olympiad would now go ahead in a truncated form—from the coming Friday to Sunday. In celebration and in anticipation of the re-activated Olympiad, teams from several countries marched the 4 km from downtown to the Olympic Stadium up on Montjuïc. Led by the Scottish bagpipers, they made a "very colourful procession", and were cheered all the way.[5]

At the stadium the athletes spent a few hours exercising and practising. When they came to return to their digs, however, they could only use one stadium exit. The battle for Barcelona was in fact not quite over. And to get home athletes had to run through the streets in twos and threes, dodging bullets from rebel snipers; they would take refuge in doorways, and then make a run when loyal militiamen gained them safe passage.

While the rebel uprising had failed and the CCMA was gradually imposing its control, a safe Peoples' Olympiad could clearly not be guaranteed.

Britain was once the most powerful country in the world. Although economic power had shifted to the United States post the Great War, the US had largely abstained from exercising its potential political power. As a result, largely by default, Britons of every station, rich and poor, still thought of Britain as a great power. It had a huge empire. Its navy was still supreme. And they had a new King.

Edward VIII had succeeded his father on 29 January 1936. At 41, he was handsome in a boyish way, unmarried, and enormously popular in Britain and throughout the Empire. His popularity was founded on a charming public persona, many years of successful public duty and a reputation as a man who wanted to be modern monarch.

One of the anachronisms of the Court was the presentation to it of distinguished women as well as young women of wealth or high birth who had come of age; for the young women this was their "coming out". The Season per se had proceeded pretty much as usual in 1936 except that, because of the Court mourning period for the late king, the usual four presentations to Court had been deferred and there was now a considerable backlog.

It was decided to hold two large ceremonies—outdoors for the first time—as garden parties, in Buckingham Palace. With the six month mourning period not quite up, today was the first such event.

This was an incredibly important occasion for the young women and their families. No end of preparation was involved, from choosing the right outfit and having it made, selecting the right young man to serve as an escort (and hoping he would accept the role), and so on.

Rows and rows of expensive cars rolled up the Mall to Buckingham Palace this Tuesday afternoon, bumper to bumper. On board were 300 debutantes, their families and the chosen escorts. Once inside the Palace grounds the visitors were crowded into a roped-off enclosure. Their expectations were intense.

The King and his entourage of royals and worthies sat grandly under a crimson canopy protected from the elements. And the elements were not kind. Rain threatened. The King himself looked glum and petulant.[6]

Soon enough, lines of young women were assembled in front of the King on the great lawn. One by one the Lord Chamberlain read their names; the poor named girl then walked forward with her escort along a Persian carpet stretched across the garden, and she curtseyed. The King acknowledged her with a nod, and another unfortunate repeated the ritual.

It started to sprinkle with rain. By this time barely half the girls had been presented. Edward ostentatiously summoned the Lord Chamberlain and the Prime Minister for an impromptu conference on the dais:

"Isn't this becoming ridiculous?" asked the King.

"It is indeed, Sir!" replied the Lord Chamberlain.

"Then I'll stop it."[7]

21 July

> Thereupon the Lord Chamberlain abandoned the proceedings. The girls and their families were left to huddle under the chestnut trees or in the overcrowded refreshment tents. Word only gradually reached them that the presentation was over.
>
> This was appalling public relations. Here were some of royalty's most ardent supporters, and they had been poorly treated. The hurt was hardly assuaged when those who had missed the opportunity to actually go forward and curtsey ("unable to pass the King's presence") later received an official card from the Lord Chamberlain acknowledging their presence at the presentation and informing them that they could now consider themselves "officially presented at Court".

Among the guests on the dais that afternoon was Mrs Ernest Simpson. She had become the King's favourite, and the King immediately withdrew with her to his retreat, Fort Belvedere in Windsor Great Park.

Later that evening, Mrs Simpson's husband, Ernest, checked into the Hotel de Paris, a smart inn at Bray on the river Thames.[8] The hotel was popular with Bright Young Things, usually hosted the Guards' passing-out parade party and had come to enjoy a somewhat louche reputation. The Hotel de Paris was barely ten miles away from Fort Belvedere, and today was the Simpson's eighth wedding anniversary.[9]

Simpson registered himself at the Hotel de Paris as "Ernest Arthur Simmons". There was, however, no plan for Mrs Simpson to join him. Indeed he had another companion, a woman who answered to the name "Buttercup" and registered as T.H. Kennedy, his "wife".[10] Overnight Ernest and Buttercup shared bedroom Number 4 and they took breakfast in bed together. This was a staged event: Mrs Simpson had engaged agents to record it all.[11] It formed the basis for their forthcoming divorce.

The King's romance with Mrs Simpson was the talk of British

high society. Discussions of it—and objections to it—were largely confined to the upper classes and political circles. Indeed it was correct form to keep the news from one's servants: many a dinner party guest was fined a guinea for speaking about the romance in front of the help. More importantly, there was a code of silence among the British press barons; they agreed to keep the story from widespread public knowledge.

Ernest Aldrich Simpson was 39, a year younger than his wife. Both had been married previously. He had been born in New York of British parents and had abandoned his Harvard education in 1917 in order to sign up with the Coldstream Guards.[12] The family, which was of Jewish extraction (although that was not publicly acknowledged), had a shipping business of which he was a partner. A tall handsome man, with fair curly hair and a moustache worn in the manner of a British gentleman, Simpson was a fastidious dresser. He had chosen to be British rather than American. A keen member of the Guards Club, he embraced all things British, not least the monarchy.

Simpson's sister Maude was twenty years his senior. She had married a wealthy Ulsterman who became an MP in Westminster, and she was a well-accepted member of London high society. When Earnest and Wallis married in 1928, Maude was their entrée to "society".

Edward, the Prince of Wales and heir to the British throne, had a penchant for married women. His first serious relationship was with Freda Dudley Ward, the wife of a much older man, William Dudley Ward, who was a Liberal MP and something of a womaniser; Freda was Edward's mistress for five years from 1918. By the late 1920s the Prince had taken up with Thelma (pronounced "Telma") Furness, the American-born wife of Viscount Furness of the Furness Withy shipping empire.[13] Lord Furness too was a much older man than his wife, and Lady Furness had become bored with him.

21 July

By late 1930, through Thelma, the Simpsons had made the Prince of Wales' acquaintance. They soon became part of his circle.

Wallis was a brilliant hostess. She served interesting and flavourful food, often with an American twist—and she made a great cocktail. She had an engaging banter which was "modern", direct and amusing—which Edward found enchanting. The Prince was first entertained to dinner at the Simpsons flat at 5 Bryanston Court, 133 George Street, Marylebone in early 1932. Wallis served black bean soup, grilled lobster, chicken Maryland (after all she did come from Baltimore), and cold raspberry soufflé.[14] The Prince stayed until four in the morning.

The Simpsons soon received a longed-for invitation for a weekend at Fort Belvedere. Thelma was the hostess.

The Prince began to drop in to the Bryanston Court flat, unannounced. The Simpsons became regulars to the Fort weekends. With the global economy in depression, the Simpson family shipping business suffered like so many. As a result, Ernest frequently absented himself on business in New York—but the Prince and Thelma's invitations to the Fort continued. By late 1933 Wallis wrote "The association imperceptibly but swiftly passed from an acquaintanceship to a friendship."[15]

In January 1934, Thelma returned to the US to visit and support her family in a crisis. She had a famous farewell lunch with Wallis at the Ritz Hotel in Piccadilly where, according to Wallis, Thelma jokingly said: "I'm afraid the Prince is going to be lonely. Wallis, won't you look after him?" That she did.

By May 1934 Wallis was the Prince's new hostess.

On instructions from Edward, Freda Dudley Ward's telephone calls were no longer put through to him. Also, after her return from America Thelma Furness got just one more visit to the Fort—before her calls too were stopped.[16]

Come the summer, the Prince took a house in Biarritz. Business pressures precluded Ernest Simpson accompanying his wife, so Wallis' aunt Bessie Merryman came along as chaperone. When the Guinness heir Lord Moyne invited the Prince's party to take an extended cruise into the Mediterranean on his luxury vessel the *Rosaura*, however, Aunt Bessie stayed behind. More than twenty years later Wallis confessed: "Perhaps it was during the evenings off the Spanish coast that we crossed the indefinable boundary that marks the line between friendship and love."[17]

The affair prospered and Edward and Wallis became more brazen about it. He took a skiing holiday with her (and friends) in Kitzbühel in February 1935, and again holidayed with her in the South of France that summer. Ernest Simpson did not accompany Wallis on either holiday. The King—Edward Albert Christian George Andrew Patrick David—had since birth been known to the royal family as "David". In due course, as she became the hostess at Fort Belvedere, Wallis adopted the familiar sobriquet.

The Simpsons necessarily drew apart. They continued to appear together in public, albeit less frequently.

Simpson is usually portrayed as a cuckolded chump; good subject that he was, the king wanted his wife and, in a variant of *droit du seigneur*, he ceded her to his sovereign. By late 1935, however, Simpson had taken up with Mary Raffray, an old friend of Wallis'. Mary had in fact been a bridesmaid to Wallis at Wallis' first wedding in 1916 and, ironically, ten years later had introduced Wallis and Ernest to each other at a Christmas party. By the autumn of 1935 the vivacious Mary had separated from her husband and was seeing Ernest on his business trips to New York.[18]

In early March 1936, while Wallis was in Paris on a shopping trip, Simpson confronted the new King.[19] Accompanied by Bernard Rickatson-Hatt, editor-in-chief of Reuters, they met in York House, St James's Palace. Simpson explicitly asked the King what his intentions were towards Wallis: she would need to choose between the two men.

With this, according to Rickatson-Hatt, Edward rose from his chair and answered: "Do you really think that I would be crowned without Wallis at my side?"

What followed was a changeover and a handover.

Mary Raffray came to stay with the Simpsons at Bryanston Court in late March. She stayed for two weeks. For the weekend of 27/28/29 March, the King invited the Simpsons, Mary and some others to Fort Belvedere.[20] (Weekends tended to start early for the King; the 27th was a Friday.) Soon after Edward gave Wallis a diamond and ruby bracelet with the cryptic inscription "Hold tight 27.iii.36".

By Easter, Mary was at the Carlton Hotel in Cannes. From there she posted two letters to Bryanston Court, one a thank you letter to her hostess and the other a love letter to Ernest. The letters were put in the wrong envelopes. Wallis confronted Ernest, who confessed his adultery and announced his intention to marry Mary. Ernest Simpson then discretely moved out of Bryanston Court to the Guards' Club.

It was all very civilised. In the early summer, the two couples spent a weekend at Himley Hall, the country house of Lord Dudley in the Midlands.[21] Ernest had a new partner and his wife was now explicitly with Edward.

Some time later, the Earl received a visit from Queen Mary, Edward's mother. "I understand that my son was here recently," Queen Mary said to Lord Dudley. He confirmed that this was so. "And that so was Mrs Simpson." Again Dudley confirmed her understanding. "And Mr Simpson. And Mr Simpson's lady friend." The Earl agreed that this was true too. Queen Mary then insisted on being shown the sleeping arrangements. It soon became apparent that the bedrooms of the Prince of Wales and Mrs Simpson shared a connecting bathroom, as did those of Simpson and Mary.

"I see," said the Queen stiffly. "Very convenient."

22 JULY
WEDNESDAY

In Barcelona, fighting had subsided sufficiently for the British Olympiad contingent to once again leave their hotel. Anxious to assure loved ones of their safety, some joined a 100-yard long queue outside the post office.[1] Others were heartened to see that a British cruiser HMS *London* had arrived at the docks.

Meanwhile, management of the water, gas and electrical services had been transferred seamlessly to worker control.[2] The transport system was working well with the CNT in charge. To be sure, the CNT–FAI livery was new—and the transport workers revelled in their newfound power—but otherwise things were normal.

When employees arrived at their places of work they found, with few exceptions, that the businesses had been collectivised. Many owners and managers had fled or gone underground; if not, they lost their leadership role and now formed part of a team to run the business. Francisco Samaranch, Juan Antonio's father, a self-made textile merchant, appears to have been a benevolent factory owner.[3] He had been in Vichy when the uprising started, taking the waters for his gallstones. When he returned home to join his family, the border guards at Portbou telephoned the Samaranch textile factory at Molins de Rei, west of Barcelona, to check on the owner's record; the leader of the team now running the factory gave him high marks. Accordingly, Samaranch senior was allowed to travel on home to Barcelona where, for the duration of the war, he worked in his own factory.

Many of these requisitioned enterprises were surprisingly successful. For example, as of this day—only three days into the working week post the attempted coup—useful armoured cars were coming off an assembly line.[4] This had been achieved by harnessing a set of previously unrelated factories, including the Hispano-Suiza automobile plant, into one co-ordinated production unit.

Everything had changed, though. The city was on a war footing. The barricades were becoming fixtures, and the militias controlled all movement through the city.

Under the soft guidance of the CCMA, the CNT's former defence committees transformed themselves into "revolutionary committees" in each barrio; as such, they:

- commandeered buildings for administrative centres and supply depots;
- maintained hospitals and schools;
- searched private homes for weapons, food, cash and valuables;
- arrested priests and "fifth columnists";[5]
- established recruitment centres for the militias; and
- collected a "revolutionary tax".[6]

Inevitably, some zealots took on these extensive responsibilities in an unnecessarily authoritarian and even unscrupulous manner. The rich and the bourgeoisie rightly felt threatened; they *were* threatened. Anything suggesting wealth or privilege put you in danger. No-one was safe.

Pablo Casals had retreated to his substantial villa at El Vendrell on the coast south of Barcelona. On more than one occasion his life was in danger from Anarchists who had no idea of who he was.[7] Once he had to pick up his cello and play Bach—and only this convinced his potential assassins that what they saw as simply a "rich man" was indeed Casals, a known supporter of the Republic.

Those members of the middle class who were already out of town for summer holidays simply stayed away. Francisco Samaranch had been unable to persuade his wife to have the family join him in Vichy; Senyora Samaranch felt obliged to stay and look after her ailing mother.

Any fancy car left behind was invariably requisitioned for the Republican defence cause. All three Samaranch cars were confiscated, including Francisco's beloved Hispano Suiza.[8] With handsome villas such as theirs being requisitioned daily by the CNT–FAI, Senyora Samaranch took matters into her own hands. First, the family moved to the top floor of their house; then they took in friends who had lost their house; and finally, ingeniously if ingenuously, Senyora Samaranch erected a large sign: "This house is seized by the CNT–FAI". As a result the lorries carrying gun-toting, red-kerchiefed militants passed them by; they no longer visited the house to liberate it.

Roundups of political opponents put pressure on them to conform to the new reality. Even low-level apparatchiks like the young Juan Antonio Samaranch were intimidated. He had joined the youth arm of the right-wing CEDA party. In these early days of the counter-revolution he was instructed to report to police headquarters on the Via Laietana. Always resourceful, Senyora Samaranch dressed her small and slight son in a tennis outfit and, accompanied by an ex-policeman friend, presented him to the authorities as a "lad [who] has caused them a lot of problems and was so young … that he had done this without telling them anything about it …" The authorities let him go, but they knew who he was and where he lived; they made it clear they'd be watching him and that they would be back.

Meanwhile, as part of their revolutionary zeal, the new masters of Barcelona made a major mistake: in echoes of the Bastille, they "liberated" the prisons. Common criminals were now on the streets, and some returned to their former ways—often under the guise or cover of the new regime.

Spontaneous acts of anti-clericalism continued. Of the city's 500 religious buildings perhaps only ten were left untouched. Gaudí's Segrada Familia, always a decade from being "completed", lost many of its original designs. About fifty churches were totally destroyed. Priests and nuns were terrified, and rightly so. Many of them were killed in the anti-clerical violence that was both inexcusable and inexplicable to outsiders.

Beyond the burning and burned churches, there were other physical manifestations of change. The Hotel Cólon, which dominated the Plaça de Catalunya, was commandeered by the PSUC, the communist trade union; in the manner of Mao's portraits in parts of modern China it would soon sport massive canvas portraits of Marx and Stalin. The Hotel Falcon on La Rambla was taken over by the POUM, with the obligatory banner advertising its POUM affiliation.[9]

The CNT–FAI seized the Ritz Hotel as a canteen "for those in need". A banner carrying the CNT–FAI graphics rebranded it "Hotel Gastronomic No. 1". Although the waiters continued to serve in their crisp tuxedo uniforms, their new clientele—militia men and women, factory workers—enjoyed a more utilitarian menu than the lobster thermidor and bombe Alaska that was featured less than a week ago.

Léon Blum, French Prime Minister for barely seven weeks, had not been sitting on the telegram he had received from his Spanish counterpart Giral a couple of days ago. A thoroughly decent man, the 64-year-old Blum was leading a fractious Popular Front government whose supporters expected much and who, in many cases, had gone too far or too fast. And Blum's opponents in the French Right—politicians, businessmen and journalists—seeing the Left over-reaching itself, took every opportunity to bring the new government down.

Blum received Giral's fraternal call for "arms and aeroplanes" with empathy. There was no question that the French government or indeed French private firms could supply war matériel to another properly-elected government; that was perfectly legal in French and international law. Aviation minister Pierre Cot gave his enthusiastic support to the request too. Both knew that while the immediate issue was the Spanish Government fighting an army insurrection in their own country, it was entirely possible that the French Government itself could face a similar same problem in the future—particularly if the Spanish rebels were to prevail.

The Spanish Ambassador followed up his Prime Minister's telegram with a meeting today in which specific requests for twenty bombers, various heavy field guns, machine guns, rifles, bombs and other munitions were made.[10] After consulting with two others, foreign minister Delbos and war minister Daladier, Blum agreed to the requests.[11] A Franco-Spanish commercial agreement negotiated as recently as December 1935 had specifically covered such arms sales. Accordingly, Cot prepared for their despatch—albeit in secret; a cabinet meeting which would be needed to authorise the sales as the munitions industry had recently been nationalised by the Popular Front government.

The French Government's decision did not stay a secret for long. The British Foreign Office was on to it immediately. The French Ambassador to the UK telephoned his head office in the Quai d'Orsay. His message was that the British Government was concerned about Blum's support for Giral; further, since meetings on other foreign policy matters were scheduled in London with Delbos tomorrow—Thursday—would it be feasible for Blum to accompany Delbos? Blum agreed to go.

And then the Spanish Ambassador resigned—his sympathies lay with the rebels—leaving the negotiations on the arms sales with two air force officers of dubious loyalty.

22 July

The British athletes in Barcelona were now advised by the British vice-consul to take advantage of the presence in the harbour of HMS *London,* and to board it a soon as practicable.[12]

The US team had never had the support of US officialdom. The US consul in Barcelona was panicked and threatened to wash his hands of the American team: "To make it short," wrote gymnast Bernard Danchik, "after several meetings we find that we have to leave town, because it is too dangerous to stay. We hate to go, but we must."[13]

Meanwhile, somewhere off the Dutch coast the SS *Manhattan* was passing its last night in the open sea before it would start moving up the Elbe river to Hamburg. There was a party mood and the journalists—Paul Gallico and Joe Williams and others—planned a serious drinking session. Williams loved a drink and invited Eleanor Holm to join him and his colleagues in first class. For Eleanor, it was champagne as usual. They played dice and talked baseball, the Brooklyn Dodgers being Eleanor's team.

The party went into the night.

23 JULY
THURSDAY

Early this morning Helen Stephens, the "Fulton Flash" who was expected to win the track sprint events at the Berlin Games, went for a walk on the SS *Manhattan*'s third class deck. She had retired to bed early but couldn't sleep. The vessel was now moving slowly along the Dutch coast. As Stephens was passing the lifeboats she noticed that one was moving rhythmically. Then the movement stopped. Intrigued, Stephens waited to see what was going on. After a few minutes Jesse Owens emerged and, just as Stephens went to move on, a woman whom she didn't recognise stepped from the same boat and whispered merrily: "Good morning".[1]

Meanwhile, Eleanor Holm—"the glorious Brooklyn mermaid" as Joe Williams had christened her overnight—had really turned one on. She and the journalists got plastered. According to Holm it was a "humdinger of a party—everybody got pleasantly soused."[2] This morning, as an unidentified young man was escorting Mrs Holm Jarrett to her room, they came upon the ever-zealous Mrs Ada Sackett. Eagle-eyed Mrs Sackett dutifully recorded their intimacy and insobriety.

Some hours later, well into the morning, Mrs Sackett and the ship's doctor, J. Hubert Lawson, woke up the fast asleep Eleanor in her cabin. Lawson diagnosed her as suffering from "acute alcoholism". All the female athletes were then paraded through Holm's cabin to witness her unfortunate state.

The game was up. Brundage fired Holm from the US team. He banned her from competing in the Berlin Games and therefore

23 July

defending her Olympic title. And he announced that she was to be sent home.

> The foreign policy discussions in Whitehall—which were technically among Britain, France and Belgium—started in the morning at a leisurely pace. They had been scheduled for some months, and the principal subject was Germany's unilateral takeover of the Rhineland in March 1936. This was the first international act of aggression by Hitler's Germany, and by its occupation of the territory Germany had violated and repudiated the Treaty of Locarno. In response, France and Britain did nothing. There was an overwhelming wish for appeasement in both Britain and France, and this meeting today was to look at the possibility of suggesting a new five-power treaty of collective security ("a new Locarno") with Hitler and Mussolini. No mention of Spain appears in the official record.
>
> Blum was a secular Jew. Early on in his literary career, and he was a great literary and drama critic for decades before he entered politics, he referred to "religious beliefs of which I do not retain the slightest trace."[3] He did not resile from his Jewish heritage at all, and he was traduced by the Right for it: "It is as a Jew that one must see, conceive, hear, fight and destroy this Blum," wrote the anti-Semite polemicist Charles Maurras of *Action Française*, "This man is anything but French."[4] This accusation was totally false. It deliberately misread Blum. He was in fact French through and through. Blum self-identified as French; he described himself as "… a French Jew, of a long line of French ancestors, speaking only the language of this country, nurtured predominantly on its culture."[5]
>
> In this context it was perhaps a little unnecessary that Alexis Léger, the head of the French foreign office, today engaged Blum in ostentatious conversation next to the statue of former British PM Benjamin Disraeli in Parliament Square. Disraeli was a Jew by birth, of course; he was also reliable and a gentleman—and this was something shared by Blum that Léger was asking the British to understand.
>
> In London, Blum was questioned by journalists as to whether the

> French Government would come to the aid of the Spanish Government. Blum told them he was firmly resolved to aid the Spain as best he could. When informed by his interlocutors that the British Conservatives were fearful of that approach, he replied impatiently: "Never mind all that, the Government of Spain is a legitimate Government; what's more, it is a friendly Government."[6]
>
> After luncheon, as he was preparing to depart for Paris, British Foreign Secretary Anthony Eden came to Blum's room in Claridge's Hotel to bid him farewell. In doing so, he asked:
>
> "Are you going to send arms to the Spanish republic?"
>
> "Yes," replied Blum.
>
> "It is your affair," said Eden, "but I ask you one thing. Be prudent."[7]
>
> It was a warning to which Blum attached the greatest importance. To him the Franco-British relationship was supreme and overarchingly important, and anything that would jeopardise it was a problem.

It seems likely that the British team in Barcelona had a more frugal lunch than the diplomats at Claridge's. That morning they had joined in a celebratory march down La Rambla with a large group of militiamen and women who would be setting off the next day to "liberate" Zaragoza. The US team joined in too; they wore black in honour of those who had died in the previous few days fighting the rebels.[8] The rag tag Zaragoza-bound militia themselves wore a variety of uniforms but showed "a spirit of elation…at the defeat of the rebels."[9] Everyone listened to inspiring speeches and enjoyed the Scottish bagpipes.

At 3:00 pm, this last show of support done, most of the British team of forty boarded HMS *London* on the first sad step of their way home. Perhaps as many as ten stayed behind to fight for the Republic.

The British contingent had been in the thick of things in

23 July

Barcelona these last few days. From their hotel in the Plaça del Pi they had seen a rebel priest shooting at loyal militia; they'd found his charred body in the desecrated church and seen it torched. And, now, a key political event in the battle for Spain was taking place in the Bar del Pi. This evening in that excellent bar four major Catalan left-wing parties agreed to create a new merged party: the formidable *Partit Socialista Unificat de Catalunya*, the PSUC.[10] Perhaps the British athletes were there, with Caridad Mercader, toasting the new socialist power.

Seville had fallen to the rebels in the first days of the uprising. The leader of the local putsch was General Gonzalo Quiepo de Llano y Sierra, a handsome 61-year-old cavalry officer given to delirious egotism and personal vanity.

Mola, as Director of the planned coup, had assigned Quiepo responsibility for Seville; this was confirmed in May and June. So when, on 16 July, one of Mola's Madrid agents asked Quiepo to go quickly to Seville, he had travelled overnight. He sauntered into Seville at 8:00 am on 17 July—ostensibly in his capacity as Inspector General of Borders, a role which enabled him to travel around the country unsupervised.

Quiepo had then moved swiftly on 18 July, employing 4000 men to win his takeover of Seville. He soon promoted and established the myth that he had achieved his victory with but a handful of men.[11]

There was no mythology about his tactics, however. Quiepo was savage. Having first taken control of the city's key command points, he was then overwhelmingly brutal and bloodthirsty in mopping up the workers' resistance. All opposition was viciously eliminated. Women and children were at much at risk as men. On one occasion he set a ten-minute deadline for Republican graffiti to be removed from defeated workers' houses, on pain of death; victorious rebels gloated as the surviving men, women and children frantically scrubbed their houses—leaving their dead or dying in the streets.[12]

Today, he issued a decree that made passive resistance a serious offence. A separate order required that, for every strike leader identified, he and another striker (chosen at the discretion of the military authorities) be shot. [13]

He was hideously self-indulgent, vulgar and uncompromising. This evening, in what was to become regular nightly radio broadcasts laden with vulgarities and threats, Quiepo authorised his troops to "kill like a dog anyone who dares oppose you and … if you act in this way, you will be free of all blame."[14]

He had succeeded in landing a handful of troops of the feared Army of Africa at the local airport and wanted to let this be known. In part of a speech that Quiepo's own censors did not allow to be printed, he made an explicit incitement to rape:

Our brave Legionarios and Regulares have shown the red cowards what it means to be a man. And incidentally, the wives of the reds too. These Communist and Anarchist women, after all, have made themselves fair game by their doctrine of free love. And now they have at least made the acquaintance of real men, not wimpish militiamen. Kicking their legs about and squealing won't save them.

And with this, rape and the denigration of Republican women as "whores" became key elements of the rebels' on-going campaign.

Quiepo established a personal fiefdom in Seville. With Seville and the adjacent provinces of Cadiz and Huelva soon in rebel hands, a landscape was now settled as to where the rebels had succeeded and where not. The new battlelines had been drawn.

Essentially the zones of control conformed to the voting patterns of the February 1936 national election. Where the conservatives had won in that election, the rebels now prevailed. Where the Popular Front had won, the rebels had failed.

The insurrection had succeeded in the south west around Seville. Looking at a map, from the rebels' south west redoubt and

23 July

moving up the Portuguese border, there was an ominous gap—with the province of Badajoz holding loyal to the Republic—before rebel territory became contiguous up the Portuguese border, west to the maritime provinces of the Atlantic coast, and then east, south of the northern industrial cities (of Santander and Bilbao) and the Basque country—all of which had stayed loyal—through Old Castile (Burgos, Segovia, Valladolid) to Pamplona and the French border. The uprising had failed in the two most important cities, Madrid and Barcelona, and also in Valencia. Perhaps 40% of Spain was now in rebel hands, although less of the population—and none of the industrial areas had fallen.

The key 30,000 strong Army of Africa was under Franco's command in rebel-held Spanish Morocco. And the Republic's loss of Seville was critical because, together with the port of Cadiz, it was a potential mainland staging point for Franco's Moroccan troops.

It is about 70 miles from the mouth of the Elbe to the port of Hamburg. At dusk the *Manhattan* sailed gently past fields on either side of the vast river, the athletes waving and crying out to the welcoming Germans on the riverbank. Many remember it as a highlight of their trip. The *Manhattan* was elegant enough with its red hull and gleaming white superstructure, but for this special arrival the crew lit up the red, white and blue striped funnels and, as night fell, trained floodlights on an enormous Olympic flag and an American flag. Boats passed and hooted their horns. Germans in the riverside beer gardens happily hoisted their steins in spontaneous toasts to the visitors.[15]

That evening Brundage made oblique reference to Eleanor Holm's disgrace in his valedictory lecture:

> *We are a free and easy people who scorn discipline. Other nations are taught to respect it. I hope you will not be outdone in politeness and courtesy any more than you are on the field …*

> *I won't have the opportunity again to address you. Remember we are representing the grandest country in the world and we are here to win for the honour of our country and for the glory of sport.*
>
> *Good luck to you all.*[16]

Cot and Blum's plans for the sale of aircraft and arms had been organised in secret. The decision had been made yesterday. Today rebel sympathisers in the Spanish embassy leaked the news to the French press.[17]

The French knew from the timing of British overtures that someone had instantly told Britain's Foreign Office of yesterday's decision. At least they were an ally. Now, unbeknown to the Spanish or French authorities, the news had been conveyed to the Germans. This evening the German Ambassador to France sent a message to his head office in the Wilhelmstrasse:

> *I have learned in strict confidence that the French government has declared itself prepared to supply the Spanish government with considerable amounts of war materiel during the next few days ... Franco's situation is likely to deteriorate decisively, especially as a result of supplying bombers to the government.*[18]

Barcelona promoted the Peoples' Olympiad with this iconic poster

Programa Deportivo de la Olimpiada Popular
Barcelona, 22-26 de julio 1936

I. ATLETISMO

1. *Campeonatos Internacionales*

   Hombres:
   Carreras: 100, 200, 400, 800, 1500, 5000, 10000 metros llanos
   3000 m. steeple, 110 y 400 m. vallas.
   Carrera a pie: 25 kilómetros. Marcha: 50 kilómetros.
   Saltos: Altura, longitud, triple con impulso y Pértiga.
   Lanzamientos: Peso, Disco, Javalina y Martillo.
   Relevos: 4 x 100 y 4 x 400 metros.

   Mujeres:
   Carreras 100 y 600 metros llanos y 83 metros vallas.
   Saltos: Altura, longitud con impulso.
   Lanzamientos: Peso, Disco, Jaalina.
   Relevos: 4 x 100 metros.

2. *Competiciones Internacional de la II.ª y III.ª Categorías*
   Carreras: 100, 400, 1000, 5000 metros llanos.
   Concursos: Salto de longitud y lanzamiento de peso.

3. *Competiciones Internacionales por Equipos Regionales o Provinciales*
   Relevos: 20 x 500 y 10 x 100 metros.
   Carrera 3000 metros llanos por equipos de 5 corredores con puntuación de 3.

   * * *

   En el *Campeonato Internacional* pueden participar 3 atletas por nación y prueba individual o un equipo nacional con las carreras de relevos. En la carrera de 25 kilómetros y la marcha, el número de participantes no se limita.
   En la *Competición Internacional de la II.ª y III.ª Categoría* la inscripción no es limitada. Los participantes tendrán que enviar junto con su propia inscripción las marcas habituales en las pruebas respectivas. La Comisión de Atletismo hará la distribución necesaria.
   En la *Competición Internacional por equipos nacionales o provinciales*, pueden participar un equipo por región o provincia.
   Los participantes a los Campeonatos Internacionales no podrán participar en las pruebas de la competición internacional de II.ª y III.ª categoría ni en las pruebas de la competición internacional por equipos regionales o provinciales.

II. NATACION

1. *Campeonatos Internacionales*

   Hombres: 100, 400 y 1500 metros libres.
   100 metros espalda y 200 metros braza.
   Saltos: Trampolín y Palanca.
   Relevos: 3 x 100 metros estilos (braza, espalda y libres) y 4 x 200 metros libres.
   Water Polo.

   Mujeres: 100 y 400 metros libres.
   100 metros espalda y 200 metros braza.
   Saltos: Trampolín palanca.
   Relevos: 3 x 50 metros estilos (braza, espalda y libres) y 4 x 100 metros libres.

2. *Competición Internacional de la II.ª y III.ª Categoría*
   Hombres: 100 metros libres, 100 metros espalda y 100 m. braza.
   Mujeres: 50 metros libres, 50 metros espalda y 50 metros braza.

3. *Relevos Internacionales por equipos regionales o provinciales*
   Hombres: 10 x 100 metros libres.
   Mujeres: 10 x 50 metros libres.

4. *Competición Internacional Infantil*
   Niños: hasta los 14 años. Niñas: hasta los 13 años.
   50 metros libres.

5. *Demostración de salvamento de náufragos*

   * * *

   En el Campeonato Internacional pueden participar dos nadadores por nación y prueba individual o un equipo nacional en las carreras de relevos y en el Water-Polo.
   En la Competición Internacional de II.ª y III.ª categoría, la inscripción es ilimitada. Los participantes tendrán que enviar junto con su inscripción sus marcas individuales en las pruebas respectivas. La Comisión Organizadora hará la distribución necesaria.
   En la Competición Internacional por equipos regionales o provinciales pueden participar un equipo por región o provincia.
   La participación a la Competición Internacional infantil y la demostración de salvamento de náufragos no se limita.
   Los participantes a los Campeonatos Internacionales no podrán participar en ninguna de las pruebas de la Competición Internacional de II.ª y III.ª categoría ni en las pruebas de relevos de la Competición Internacional por equipos o provincias.

III. FUTBOL

1. *Campeonatos Internacionales*
   Puede participar un equipo por cada nación.

2. *Copa Internacional por equipos regionales o provinciales*
   Puede participar un equipo por cada región o provincia.

3. *Copa Internacional por equipos de clubs de diversas categorías*
   Pueden participar todos los equipos locales, forasteros y extranjeros. La Comisión de Futbol hará la distribución de las categorías.

IV. RUGBY

1. *Campeonato Internacional*
   Puede participar un equipo por cada nación.

2. *Copa Internacional por equipos regionales o provinciales o de clubs*
   Puede participar un equipo, por cada región o provincia. La inscripción para los Clubs no se limita.

V. BASKET BALL

1. *Campeonatos Internacionales masculinos y femeninos*
   Puede participar un equipo masculino y femenino por cada nación.

2. *Copas Internacionales por equipos masculinos y femeninos Regionales, Provinciales o clubs de diversas categorías*
   Pueden participar un equipo masculino y femenino por cada región o provincia. La inscripción por los equipos masculinos y femeninos no se limita.
   La Comisión de Basket hará la distribución de las categorías.

3. *Copa Internacional por equipos masculinos y femeninos infantiles*
   Pueden participar equipos locales, forasteros y extranjeros sin limitación.

VI. TENNIS

1. *Campeonatos Internacionales*
   Simple Hombres, Simple Mujeres, Doble Hombres, Doble Mixto.

2. *Torneo Internacional de Segunda Categoría*
   Simple Hombres, Simple Mujeres, Doble Hombres, Doble Mixto.
   Las inscripciones han de cursarse señalando la categoría en que desea participar.

VII. BOXEO

1. *Campeonatos Internacionales*
   Puede participar un representante de cada nación en cada categoría de peso.

2. *Torneo Internacional de Consolación*
   Podrán participar todos los boxeadores que no hayan tomado parte en los Campeonatos Internacionales.
   La inscripción por todos los pesos no se limita.
   Los combates se efectuarán a un límite de 3 rounds de 3 minutos con descansos intermedios de un minuto.
   Las categorías de pesos serán: Mosca, hasta 50 kilos 802; Gallo, hasta 53 kilos 524; Pluma, hasta 57 kilos 152; Ligeros, hasta 61 kilos 237; Medio Mediano, hasta 66 kilos 678; Mediano, hasta 72 kilos 574; Medio Pesado, hasta 79 kilos 378; Pesados, más de 79 kilos 378.

VIII. LUCHA GRECO ROMANA

1. *Campeonatos Internacionales*
   Puede participar un representante de cada nación en cada categoría de peso.

2. *Torneo Internacional de Segunda Categoría*
   La inscripción para todos los pesos no se limita.
   Las luchas se efectuarán a un límite de 20 minutos. Las categorías de pesos serán: Mosca, hasta 52 k.; Gallo, hasta 56; Pluma, hasta 61 k.; Ligero, hasta 66 k.; Medianos, hasta 72 k.; Semipesados, hasta 79 k.; Medio fuertes, hasta 87 k.; Fuerte, desde 87 kilos.

IX. CICLISMO

Campeonato Internacional
Carrera por carretera de 100 kilómetros.
No se limita la cifra de participantes por cada nación.

X. AJEDREZ

1. *Concurso Internacional en diversas categorías*
   No se limita la cifra de participantes.

2. *Competiciones por equipos regionales o provinciales de cinco jugadores.*

XI. DEMOSTRACIONES SIN COMPETICION

1. *Gimnasia*
   Libre participación para toda clase de grupos masculinos, femeninos, mixtos e infantiles.

2. *Hand Ball*
   No se limita la cifra de participantes (equipos).

3. *Basse Ball*
   No se limita la cifra de participantes (equipos).

4. *Bailes y canciones típicas de los folklores nacionales*
   De libre participación por todos los grupos masculinos, femeninos, mixtos e infantiles.

XII. EXPOSICION ARTISTICA

Artes Plásticas, Fotografía y Arquitectura relacionadas con el deporte popular.
De libre participación de los artistas de todos los países. Las obras tendrán que ser recibidas por el Comité Organizador antes del 15 de Julio.

* * *

La inscripción para todos los concursos y demostraciones tendrán que estar en posesión del Comité Organizador de la OLIMPIADA POPULAR (Rambla Santa Mónica, 25, Barcelona, España), hasta el día 15 de Julio.

Sports program for the Peoples' Olympiad

Facilities for the Peoples' Olympiad were centred on Montjuïc: athletes were housed in the Hotel Olímpico on the Plaça d'Espanya (foreground) and in the Exhibition Halls (midground), while events were planned for the grand Palau Nacional and the stadium beyond

Main ticket booth for the Peoples' Olympiad

17 July 1936, Gare d'Austerlitz, Paris: French athletes took a special train to Barcelona

US team for the Peoples' Olympiad; Charley Burley second from right

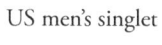
US men's singlet

Charley Burley

19 July 1936 in Barcelona

Left
Plaça de Catalunya

Lower Left
At the barricades

Below
Barricade on La Rambla

Barricade at El Molino on El Parallel

Many religious buildings were torched and gutted on 19 July and the following days

Basilica Le Merced

Santa Maria del Mar

Ecclesiastical buildings adjacent to La Sagrada Familia

Barcelona celebrated the defeat of the Army rebels

24 JULY
FRIDAY

At 6:00 am the US team assembled in their smart uniforms for disembarkation at Hamburg. The men wore boaters and were dressed in their blue blazers and white trousers. Thousands of Germans had gathered at the docks to greet them.

"Yessay Oh-vens", "Yessay Oh-vens," they cried out. A fellow athlete had to point out to Jesse Owens that the cry was for him. Whatever racism existed in the German psyche, and Hitler's government certainly encouraged whatever was there, these Germans loved a hero. "Yessay Oh-vens", "Oh-vens! Oh-vens!" was a mantra that would be heard throughout the drive to the Hamburg Town Hall and on to Berlin.

At Hamburg's grand neo-renaissance town hall there was a formal reception where, apart from the usual portentous speeches, the athletes were offered orange juice and, according to pentathlete Charles Leonard, a West Point graduate who would have known about these things, "the best sherry I have ever tasted."[1] Meanwhile, a petition was circulating amongst the athletes, calling for Eleanor Holm's reinstatement.

The team saw Hamburg at its best. There was a sprinkling of rain, but the lakes sparkled, the wonderfully named *Planten un Blomen* botanic gardens were appropriately in full bloom and buildings were decorated with flowering window boxes. All this the athletes took in on their way to the main railway station.

It was here that many of the US team first took in the military aura of Hitler's Germany. Soldiers were everywhere.

By noon they were on the train to Berlin. This was no ordinary train. The *Fliegender Hamburger* was a stunning example of German technology, efficiency and comfort. Diesel powered, its maiden run had been 1932, and it was famously promoted as being able to travel comfortably at 99 miles per hour. The trip to the capital would take just three hours, and during this time the athletes enjoyed a full silver service luncheon. This was genuine luxury. The train itself was festooned with Olympic flags and Nazi flags. As it passed through the fields on the way to Berlin the Americans could not help but notice that ordinary fieldworkers stopped their activity and gave Nazi salutes to their visitors. The flags and the salutes were something all visitors to Berlin would come to take for granted over the coming weeks.

Eleanor Holm had been allowed to take the train with the team while her appeal was heard. She was grateful for the support she was getting with the petition: "If you want to do it, I won't stop you, and I'm grateful. They said I could come on the train and they'd at least listen to me. I'll tell them I'm sorry, I'm done drinking, and ask for another chance … but if that asshole Brundage thinks I'm gonna beg—at least beg *him*—he's got another guess coming."[2] A majority of athletes, more than two hundred, signed the petition—but it was all to no avail. The ban stood.

The Berlin welcome for the US team was overwhelming.

Thousands greeted them at the palatial neo-Renaissance Lehrter Bahnhof[3] near the Tiergarten. The platform was jam packed. Brundage exchanged cheek kisses with Theodor Lewald, the head of the Berlin Games organizing committee. Lewald greeted the team in English and a band struck up "the Star Spangled Banner". Brundage reciprocated the welcome with a boring and predictable set of platitudes which were translated periodically into German; he then concluded with a truism, which the crowd lapped up:

24 July

... more than fifty nations will participate in what probably will be finest competition in the history of sport. Conditions in Berlin are the finest ever provided in modern sports competition. We in the United States who pride ourselves on being the first in so many fields cannot equal the facilities here.[4]

As the team moved through the crowd, the Germans eagerly sought their autographs. "Wo ist Yessay?", the asked. And when the saw him, "Yessay Oh-vens", "Yessay Oh-vens" was again struck up. Next came the cry *"Zehnkampf"* (decathlon) as they recognized Glenn Morris, the US decathlon champion who was featured on the cover of the Games program.

The team was loaded into open cars and open-decked buses for the trip to another Town Hall reception. Olympic flags again shared equal billing with the Nazi flag. (In fact, of course, the Nazi flag was the new German National Flag—this having become official in 1935.) The crowds did not let up. "It was like a Broadway parade," wrote one participant to his parents.[5] While they had hoped for the cheers, of course, and these continued throughout their stay in Berlin, the athletes were non-plussed by the ubiquitous Nazi salutes which punctuated the crowd's continued "Yessay" cries.

The Nazi salute and "Heil Hitler!" had become part of German life. Over the next few weeks every visitor would need to get used to it. Many of the more outgoing athletes came to parody the greeting by substituting their own leader, for example, "Heil Roosevelt! or, amusingly, if sadly, "Heil E-selasse!" after the recently deposed Ethiopian emperor.

In Barcelona, the general strike continued in name only. The CNT had called for a return to work. CNT transport workers were already back running the trams, trains and buses. The POUM flexed their revolutionary ardour by advocating continued strike action until fascism was crushed everywhere—but fascism and its agents the Army rebels had already been resisted and defeated in Barcelona.

Meanwhile, an event was underway that would become part of Civil War folklore.

Zaragoza, 200 miles to the west of Barcelona, was an anarcho-syndicalist stronghold and had unexpectedly fallen to the rebels. This was largely because the local Guardia Civil had fallen in with Mola's rebels. (In many cities the key to the success of the insurgents was the backing of the well-trained and well-armed Guardia Civil; it transpired that whomever they backed tended to win the day.)

The masters of Barcelona were enjoying their newfound power and decided it was time to take the battle back to the rebels. Local hero Buenaventura Durruti organised a militia unit and today led one of two groups through and out of the city to great fanfare. Under the black and red colours of the CNT–FAI, they were off to liberate Zaragoza. This came to be known at the Durruti Column, the most recognized and celebrated of all Republican militias and a symbol of the anarchist movement. Many of the Durruti Column volunteers were athletes from the Olympiad.[6]

More than 2,500 troops marched through the streets this famous day. It was to become a landmark in the Civil War's history. Cheered on by the thousands of citizens lining the streets, the volunteers flew Spanish and Catalan flags and proudly carried CNT–FAI banners. Bands played revolutionary songs. And the marchers showed off their new crude "tanks"—the armoured fighting vehicles manufactured under worker control at the Hispano-Suiza plant and elsewhere.

Buenaventura Durruti was basking in the success of the revolution and was starting to display shades of self-aggrandisement and hubris. He made an important speech in which he warned of the need to stay vigilant against the possibility of counter-revolution; he argued that the success of the revolution to date should be preserved until Zaragoza had been liberated, cryptically saying that only then could the new masters "go for broke."[7] In an interview with a Canadian journalist, he

> summarised the situation:
>
> *There are only two roads, victory for the working class, freedom, or victory for the fascists—which means tyranny.*
>
> *Both combatants know what's in store for the loser.*
>
> Two hours out from Barcelona the Durruti Column was embarrassed to discover that, in their enthusiasm, the participants had forgotten to take their supplies. But the enthusiasm was maintained. As towns were liberated along the way and the land collectivised, peasants joined up—such that by the time the Column reached the outskirts of Zaragoza it had grown to 6,000.
>
> In the coming days and months, perhaps as many as 20,000 followed this first group to the front. They went both by road and rail, since the railways were working well under worker control, always flamboyantly displaying their sectional affiliation—POUM, CNT–FAI, liberal republican, Catalan nationalist, communist, socialist and umpteen variants thereof.[8]

It was late afternoon by the time the US team was released from the festivities at the Berlin Town Hall. This had been a long day, starting in Hamburg with a reception, then the train ride and finally the reception in Berlin, and at last the athletes were loaded on to buses for their final destination—their Games accommodation.

There was to be no fraternisation between the sexes. Most of the women were to be accommodated in the Friesenhaus in the Olympic complex or *Reichssportsfeld*, which was about twelve kilometres west of the CBD; the men were off to the *Olympicshe Dorf* or Olympic Village, a similar distance (and about 25 minutes by road) further west in Döberitz.

The American women found the Friesenhaus somewhat Spartan, apparently, and expressed concern at the tiny rooms and inadequate bathrooms.[9] In contrast, Australian swimmer, Evelyn de Lacy found the rooms in the smaller Frauenheim, which was also in the Reichssportfeld, "gorgeous" and the Olympic swimming pool, just 200 yards away, wonderfully convenient: "What a place to live in …", she wrote in her diary, "It is surrounded by lawns and on one side a deep gully. There is a tennis court and from our window we can see the Olympic Bell and the Arena where the Games take place, and the swimming pool. Oh, it's simply heaven."[10]

Whatever the merits of the women's accommodation, the Olympic Village—exclusively for men—was a dream.

About 136 acres had been set aside in a bucolic birch forest. 142 new cream-coloured cottages were built on the ridges of a handsome meadow; each dwelling had white-washed walls, new fitments and bright red tiled roofs. The cottages housed between sixteen and twenty athletes, two to a room with specially constructed mattresses, a communal bathroom, telephone booth and a common room which opened to a terrace and a view.[11] Each was named after a German city—the Australians were housed in "Worms", which they found amusing—and each was decorated with scenes from the relevant city.

Fifty-one countries had been invited to send teams to the Games. Notwithstanding the boycott campaign, all accepted. In order to accommodate the unexpected numbers, the Village was extended into the adjacent Air Defence Barracks—which were quickly refurbished for the German, Japanese and some other teams. One of the teams assigned to the Barracks was the Spanish contingent. Four Spanish athletes arrived on 17 July. As a result of the Army uprising, however, the team officially withdrew on 20 June—and the last Spaniard left the precincts on 4 August.[12]

A special message of greeting was received by each athlete:

Welcome to the Olympic Village!

This is your home during the weeks to come. Here you will

dwell together with your friends and fellow participants, a community of comrades serving the same ideal, who are overjoyed to greet you, live with you and pass pleasant hours in your company.

Everything that has been provided here is for your comfort and convenience, and the regulations have been considered and drawn up in your interest so that you may be assured undisturbed enjoyment of your new home.
Over this Village waves the Olympic flag and the national banner of your native land. Each morning the chimes play the Olympic Hymn.

May the Olympic spirit and Olympic peace reign here from the first to the last day.
Help us to ensure and preserve this peace.
The German Army erected this Village for the Olympic guests. It performed its task gladly in the interest of sport and because it reveres the Olympic ideals. Thus the German Army as well as the German people extends to you, its guests, a hearty welcome.

[signed]

Field Marshal von Blomberg, Reich War Minister

Dr Th. Lewald, President of the Organizing Committee for the Eleventh Olympic Games

The grounds were immaculate. Every convenience was provided—from a barbershop and post office, to a cinema, extensive dining rooms, a large hall (the Hindenburg House) for evening entertainment, a medical and dental clinic, and at one end of the meadow, a bucolic swimming lake with a Finnish vapour sauna at its edge. The Japanese didn't take to the sauna, so their ever-accommodating German hosts quickly built them a special Japanese one up in the Air Defence Barracks.

Lou Zamperini, the US distance runner, wrote home: "They

had everything there. They had wild animals running over the grounds … green grass mowed like a golf course. The buildings we lived in were like motels."[13] The wild animals were rabbits, deer, squirrels, water fowl, storks and ducks—to which the Australians added their own mascot, "Aussie", a kangaroo they had brought all the way from the Antipodes and presented to the commandant of the Village[14].

Apart from the comforts of the accommodation, the Village also had a full-size 400-meter running track with facilities for each track and field event—even a water jump for the steeplechase—a fully equipped gymnasium, and an indoor swimming pool.

The dining hall was in fact multiple rooms, each catering for the appetites and cuisines of the visiting countries. This first evening the Americans settled down to meal of steak, lamb or veal, fresh green vegetables and baked potatoes, fresh fruit, stewed fruit, custards, ice cream, milk, tea, coffee and fruit juices.[15]

Many of the Americans had put on weight on the SS *Manhattan*. Glenn Morris was alarmed to find he had put on nearly four kilos according to the bathroom scales in his Village cabin.[16] With the first Olympic event a mere nine days away, everyone would need to quickly re-establish their fitness and watch what they ate.

In Barcelona, the last of the Olympiad's athletes were leaving the city. At least one French athlete had been killed in street crossfire. The provincial government had few enough responsibilities after ceding so much to the CCMA, but one was "public safety". They concluded that the situation was unsafe for their Olympiad visitors, so they ordered everyone out.

In fulfilment of the order, the Belgians hired a small Spanish vessel, the *Cuidad de Ibiza*, to transport their team members to the port of Sète just over the border in France.[17] The Hungarian team joined them. And

> when this evening a group of Spanish soldiers came to the Europa hotel, seven of the US team were happy to be escorted down La Rambla to the docks and the relative safety of the *Cuidad de Ibiza*. Five of the US team stayed behind to fight with the militias.
>
> The dream of the Peoples' Olympiad was over. It had been scheduled to run from 19 July to 26 July, had been stillborn and then briefly revived—and now, within a tumultuous week, the participants had been dispersed.

On their return from London this evening, Blum and Delbos were met at Le Bourget by minister of state Camille Chautemps. He told them that the government's decision to sell arms to Spain had already appeared in the right-wing press, with full details of the government's plans having been disclosed in *L'Écho de Paris* and *Le Jour* the previous day. *L'Écho*'s headline read: "Will the French Popular Front dare to arm the Spanish Popular Front?" *L'Action Française*, admittedly a truly rabid right wing organ, even referred to the "treason of Léon Blum and Pierre Cot"[18]

A wily and successful careerist, the 51-year-old Chautemps was a former and future Prime Minister. He was widely described as "intellectually bereft". Even so, his interlocutors were conscious that Chautemps had influence amongst their peers, notably their Radical Party partners in government. Chautemps informed Blum of a veritable "insurrection" brewing in Paris, arguing: "No one can understand why we are going to risk war on the behalf of Spain when we did not do so over the Rhineland."[19]

Blum confirmed Chautemps' report in conversations with other colleagues. Jeanneney, the President of the Senate, told him "We are certain that if there were European complications provoked by intervention in the affairs of Spain, England would not follow us."[20] Édouard Herriot begged him not to "meddle in that business". They were all afraid of war.

Later this evening, at about 10 pm, Blum called a meeting at his elegant ex officio apartment on the Ile St Louis. Blum and other ministers including Cot and Delbos (who had an apartment in the same block as the PM) met the new Spanish Ambassador, de los Rios; de los Rios had hurriedly moved to Paris this very day from Geneva. They discussed how French planes might be delivered to Spain under the 1935 Agreement. The question was who might pilot them without causing undue problems with France's allies, most importantly Britain. (Nor, it must be said, did they want to upset Germany and Italy.) Delbos was opposed to using French pilots.[21]

Later still tonight, Pierre Cot telephoned the sleeping de los Rios and asked him to come to his house. At that meeting Cot and de los Rios agreed that French pilots should fly the planes to the south of France where Spanish pilots would take over.

25 JULY
SATURDAY

It had only been a week since Franco and his colleagues had started the Spanish conflict. With Barcelona and Madrid safely in Government hands, the battlelines had now been drawn.

Decisions made in the next few days would deny an early resolution of the conflict and prove to be critical to its ultimate outcome. What was fast becoming a stalemate, with neither the rebels nor the Government in complete control, would soon turn into a protracted Civil War. The critical decisions were not made on the battlefields or cities of Spain but far away in France and Germany, Italy and Britain. What's more, the decisions soon to be made in Germany and Italy firmed up a working relationship between the two Fascist countries, making them allies—something that helped bring on the Second World War.

> The French cabinet was scheduled to meet later on today to formally consider its response to the Spanish Government's call for assistance. Conscious of this, the French Right-wing press continued to run sensational reports. The actions of the government were "abominable" and "criminal", they reported, and would naturally arouse legitimate anxiety and anger in Germany and Italy.[1] The government was involved in "arms traffic"[2], and so on.
>
> When the new Spanish representative de los Rios visited the French air ministry to finalise arrangements this morning he found that the two remaining signatories on the Spanish accounts—the chargé d'af-

fairs and the military attaché—had both resigned. These two men, supporters of the military uprising, apparently saw no irony in telling the French press that the reason they had resigned was that they were not prepared to be a party to the purchase of arms for use against their own people.

In Burgos, to which city he had moved the putschists' headquarters a few days ago, Mola was worried. In particular he was concerned about the failure of the usurpers to make ground in Madrid. The coup was at a critical point and, as Mola saw it, a stalemate was entirely likely. Mola sent a telegram today to Franco expressing his concerns and informing him that he was contemplating a retreat back to the Duero River.[3]

Franco would have nothing of it: "Stand firm, victory certain," he replied. Franco's optimism was unstinting. It had always stood him in good stead with his troops; now it sat well with his fellow rebel generals, where his optimism helped consolidated his authority.

French President Lebrun bought into the situation. A conservative, he warned Prime Minister Blum that the contemplated support for the Spanish Government was leading France to war or revolution[4]. On the other hand, the French Communists, who were part of the Popular Front but provided no ministers in the government (and therefore got no say in cabinet), were keen to support the Spanish Government. It can be seen that Blum was being subjected to great pressure from all sides.

One of Chautemps fellow ministers, a Radical, reported that Chautemps "took to one side the young ministers, and walking up and down with them on the rue de la Varenne and the Boulevard des Italiens, lectured them vigorously, pointing out that the [Spanish] military insurrection could be victorious in a few weeks and that the Republican government would crumble like a house of cards."[5] Nevertheless, immediately prior to the cabinet meeting this afternoon, an emotional Blum assured de los Rios that he would not be moved. "I am heartbroken," he said, but the original decision would stand "at all costs and despite all risks."[6]

It was not to be. Key Radicals went to water. A number of Radicals were outright careerists, and this important decision provided opportunities for people like Chautemps and Daladier to advance their ambitions while purporting to represent the will of the people. That the country was divided on this issue, as with so many other issues, is without dispute: the usual alliance of the working class, intellectuals and students were on one side and some of the middle class, both rural and in the cities, plus the Church on the other. Blum feared for his government and the British alliance. It is said that Blum let the cabinet discussion run its course until, in order to save his government, he allowed cabinet to refuse government aid to Spain. There is little doubt that Blum was playing for time and that he hoped to be able to reverse the decision and provide Spain with assistance.

That evening a French communiqué was issued announcing that the Government would refuse the Spanish Government's request for arms of any kind; it would "in no way intervene in the internal conflict in Spain." This was later "clarified" by a foreign office announcement that the decision did not apply to private sales of aircraft provided the aircraft were not armed.

The effect of the decision was to allow non-government sales of any planes except bombers. Within the cabinet Pierre Cot was the most enthusiastic backer of the Spanish Republic, and so long as he remained Air Minister he did whatever he could to support Spain. Together with his chef du cabinet, Jean Moulin, the future Resistance leader, Cot quickly arranged the sale of fifty aircraft—ostensibly to Finland and Brazil. These aircraft, sadly not the most modern, were paid for by gold from the Spanish gold reserves—and soon found their way to the Spanish Republic. Other sales followed, some mediated by

> the self-important (and financially astute) adventurer André Malraux. But the course had been set. The French Government would not help Spain, officially.
>
> The Rightist were exultant. In due course the refrain "Plutôt Hitler que Blum" [7] came to be embraced as a slogan among Blum's opponents in parliament and in wider conservative circles.

While the French were deciding their official position, PM Giral took it upon himself to telegram the Soviet Ambassador to France thus:

Gracious Sir!

The Government of the Spanish Republic needs to supply its army with a significant quantity of modern weapons to wage war on what began as and continues to be a civil war against the legal authority and constitutional government, As head of my government, and knowing the possibilities and availability of weapons at the disposal of the USSR, I decided to apply to you so that you would inform your government of our government's wish and necessity to seek and supply from your country a great quantity of weapons and all categories of military supplies.

> The Festspeile in Bayreuth had enjoyed a most successful seven days. This evening Hitler attended Wagner's Siegfried with Wilhelm Furtwängler conducting. Hitler was staying at the modest yellow house on the Wahnfried estate known at the time as the Führer annex.
>
> Very late this evening, after the performance of Siegfried, Hitler received three emissaries from Franco. They had come to seek Germany's support for the Spanish insurrection. [8]

Two were German expatriate residents of Spanish Morocco. Adolf Langenheim was the 64-year-old leader of the group. He and his 39-year-old colleague, Johannes Bernhardt were both members of the small Nazi party in Morocco. They were accompanied by a low ranking rebel, Francisco Arranz, an ex-airforce officer who had sided with Franco. When they first arrived in Berlin they had been rejected by the German foreign office; then, through Nazi Party connections, they gained access to Rudolph Hess, Hitler's deputy—and through him to the Führer. A Dr Kraneck, the head of the legal section of the Nazi Party's foreign department was with them.

While the emissaries knew their mission was of vital importance to the Spanish rebels, it can now be seen that the meeting and their mission came to have a significant influence on global affairs.

They were greeted by a Hitler suffused with excitement from the brilliant performance he had just witnessed. The emissaries then presented what Hitler called the "terse" letter of request from Franco. The rebel general asked for fighter aircraft, arms, anti-aircraft guns although not, importantly, transport aircraft. Forgetting his supper, Hitler cross-examined the men about the situation in Spain. What did Franco stand for? How would he transport the Moroccan troops across the Straits of Gibraltar? How were they to pay for any assistance?

Hitler was well informed. He would certainly have been informed of France's initial intentions and probably now knew of the French communiqué. He seemed sceptical about the rebels' plans and planning, and was hesitant to accept, as was suggested by his visitors, that the rebels might be able to pay for aircraft and armaments from the raw materials of an Andalusia that was still in contention.

"That's no way to start a war," Hitler said. And then, when Bernhardt agreed that the war could last many months and it would be catastrophic if Franco did not receive help immediately, Hitler opined: "Then he is lost."

Hitler wanted to talk on, though, and he would not be going to bed early.

26 JULY
SUNDAY

As the clock passed midnight in the Führer annex, Hitler went into full flight. Perhaps the histrionics of *Siegfried* were still with him. Perhaps it was just part of his mad persona. Whatever its genesis, Hitler now set off into a two-hour diatribe attacking Bolshevism and how, if it prevailed in Spain, that would be the end of the country as we know it; how, with the Soviet Union flanking Germany to its east and unreliable France and Spain to its west, the spread of Bolshevism was intolerable.

Eventually Hitler resolved to help Franco "to keep the Straits of Gibraltar from falling into Communist hands."[1] He announced that he would provide the requested arms and aircraft, and more: he would provide the rebels with transport aircraft to get the troops across from Morocco to Spain. There was just one condition: the German aid was to go to Franco and Franco only, thereby avoiding conflict with the competing generals. Hitler had decided to back Franco as the future Caudillo.

Both Hermann Göring, who had founded the Luftwaffe the previous year, and Field Marshall Blomberg, the War Minister, were staying in Bayreuth this very evening. So too the obsequious Joachim von Ribbentrop, who was soon to be appointed Hitler's Ambassador to the UK and was the Führer's personal guest at the festival. Hitler summoned them all to his villa.[2] By this time it was about 2 am.

Whatever caution they felt towards Hitler's decision, and both Göring and Ribbentrop did express some caution, Hitler had made his decision. The decision must now be implemented.

Apart from his ideological support for the rebels, Hitler had strategic reasons to back them. A Fascist Spain would be more likely to supply iron ore and other minerals to a Fascist Germany than a democratic one would; it would stand between France and Britain "athwart the sea of communications" between those two powers, and Spain's ports would be available to German naval vessels including submarines. Moreover, as he later explained, his intervention in Spain would "distract the attention of the western powers … and so enable German rearmament to continue unobserved."[3]

"If there had not been the danger of the Red Peril's overwhelming Europe, I'd not have intervened in the revolution in Spain," Hitler later said. On the other hand, he shared Communism's rejection of religion. Hitler was not a believer, and he would have been happy that "The Church would have been destroyed [without his intervention]"—but the Führer had more important goals than that.

Today, in the battlefields of World War I, King Edward was to show how good he could be when he took his role seriously and applied himself. He was King of the United Kingdom and Northern Ireland, all the Dominions—like Canada, Australia, New Zealand, and South Africa—His Other Realms and Territories, Emperor of India and so on. Today he was playing King of Canada.

He had sailed overnight from Portsmouth aboard the Admiralty yacht *Enchantress* to Calais. From there he would travel to Vimy Ridge, near the town of Arras close to the Belgian border. At Vimy he would oversee the dedication and unveiling of the huge and dramatic Canadian National Memorial.

On arrival in Calais he received annoying news. He had planned an August holiday in the south of France at Chateau de l'Horizon, a grand villa at Golfe-Juan owned by American actress of Maxine Elliott. He had stayed there before. It was reasonably secluded and since "Wallis's companionship had become [his] only solace in a job which otherwise would have been intolerably lonely",[4] he was planning to holiday there with her and some friends. The British Ambassador, meeting the King on his arrival in Calais, advised Edward against his planned visit—not the Mrs Simpson part, about which he may well have been ignorant, but because of the "security situation". The Côte d'Azur was "blazing with red flags,' he reported, "One indeed, had been raised in full view of l'Horizon." It should not have surprised the Ambassador that the Popular Front had support throughout the country, even in salubrious Golfe-Juan, but apparently it did.

Léon Blum and the French government were only too happy to contemplate the British king holidaying on the Côte d'Azur, whatever the British assessment of the situation. Indeed, Blum was prepared to post a battalion of infantry at the villa if such comfort was required.

It was too late to find an alternative villa, though, and taking the Ambassador's advice, Edward instructed him to thank "Monsieur Blum" and then turned to his equerry Jack Aird:

Jack, when we get back to London, your first order of business is to charter a yacht, a big, comfortable one, around two thousand tons. She must be in tiptop condition. I want nothing to spoil our cruise. Nothing.

It would prove to be a terrible mistake. Peeved, he wrote to his mother: "I am really very annoyed at the F[oreign] O[ffice] for having messed up my holiday in this stupid manner."[5]

Vimy is to Canadians what Yorktown is to Americans and Gallipoli to Australians—it represents the nation's "coming of age". The First World War battle itself, in 1917, was heroic and bloody, albeit not necessarily the most important battle in which Canadians had distinguished themselves. But it had been an all-Canadian affair and, in the manner of these things, it represented all that was brave and good about the new country.

Edward had a special affinity for Canada. In 1919, just after the War, he undertook an incredibly comprehensive and enervating royal tour right across the country as Prince of Wales. It took three months and involved countless functions and hand shakes through the major cities of Montreal and Toronto, the capital Ottawa, from the towns and villages of the maritime provinces through to British Colombia. Always impeccably dressed, whether in army or navy uniform or civvies, at 25 he was boyishly handsome—the prince charming personified. The trip was an enormous success, and all Canada took to him. The affection was returned when he acquired a small 100-acre farm in Alberta.

Prince Edward was back again for further tours in 1923 and 1924, when he visited his farm, and then again in 1927. Canada loved him.

Edward arrived early in Vimy today. It was a warm sunny day, and his early arrival gave the youthful-looking King the opportunity to mingle with some of the 6200 Canadian visitors. The "pilgrims", for that is what they were designated, had travelled from Canada in five ocean liners. Most were ex-servicemen who had served on the Western Front. The Great War had been a major influence on Edward, and he had a genuine affection for service personnel. The affection was reciprocated, with the veterans greeting "Good old Teddy!".[6]

At 2:00 pm the ceremony started with rousing performances of *God Save the King* and *O Canada*. Fresh from the political manoeuvrings over Spain, President Lebrun was received by the King—because the Memorial land had been gifted by France to Canada. The *Marseillaise* was played. There was a vast crowd of perhaps 100,000 in the large natural amphitheatre. The huge new limestone monument, gleaming white, dominated the countryside for miles. Four squadrons of RAF and French aircraft flew over the Memorial, dipping their wings in salute.

Edward started his speech in French before moving to English. He had a fine voice and something of a mid-Atlantic accent, which appealed to a wide audience and certainly to the Canadians. His speech, which Churchill had helped refine, was eloquent and moving. Sixty thousand

> Canadians had died in the Great War and 12,000 had no known grave. The Vimy Memorial celebrates them all.
>
> As the King took his leave the crowd burst spontaneously into a hearty rendition of *For He's a Jolly Good Fellow*. The day had been an enormous success, and no one could have done his job better than King Edward.

Back in Germany, Hitler's henchmen were quickly on the job. Although it was a Sunday, by early afternoon the German naval commander in Hamburg and the Secretary of State for Aviation, Erhard Milch, had been flown on Hitler's personal aircraft to Bayreuth. It took two hours for them to develop detailed plans for what was named *Operation Magic Fire*—a reference to Siegfried's passage through a ring of flames to rescue Brünnhilde.

By this evening Milch was back in his office in Berlin. He had been the first managing director of Lufthansa and, at 54, he was now enjoying a well-deserved "can do" reputation as Göring's right hand man. Milch immediately announced the appointment of his colleague Helmuth Wilberg, commander of the Luftwaffe's leadership academy, as head of the Spanish military mission:

> *You all know the Spaniards, under the leadership of General Franco, have risen to liberate Spain. The greater part of Spain is in the hands of the enemy. Franco has asked the Führer to put at his disposal a fleet of Junker52/3ms and crews to take his forces from* [Morocco] *to Seville.*
>
> *General Göring has decided to entrust General Wilberg with this task.*[7]

Secrecy was paramount. Apart from the leaders to whom Milch had made the announcement and Wilberg's own chief of staff, no one was to be informed of the ultimate destination of the personnel or war matériel that were to be assembled.

> When the rebel General Goded and his top brass had surrendered in Barcelona on Monday the 20th they were incarcerated in the oppressive Montjuïch prison. Today, after six days, they were transferred to the abandoned ocean liner *Uruguay*. It was something of a rust bucket sitting in the Barcelona harbour but the prisoners were treated well, being allowed to sit on deck and enjoy the sun. Unwisely, however, they misbehaved—notably by standing at attention and giving the fascist salute to passing Italian naval vessels. It would not augur well for their ultimate fate.
>
> And in Seville, this evening, as a sign off for his weekend, Quiepo de Llano let off yet another of his outrageous radio outbursts:
>
> *Sevillanos! I don't have to urge you on because I know your bravery.*
>
> *I tell you to kill like a dog any queer or pervert who criticises this glorious national movement.*[8]

27 JULY
MONDAY

The Spanish Army of 1936 was a disgrace.

In an establishment of about 130,000 fully 700 were generals. One in six was an officer. With the loss of Cuba and the Philippines in 1898, the essential elements of the Spanish Empire were gone. For nearly forty years the Army's main interest or purpose was the control of the barren, if strategic, strip of land at the Straits of Gibraltar that formed the Protectorate of Spanish Morocco. And the Army cost about 25% of the national budget.

In Morocco, the Army of Africa comprised the Spanish Foreign Legion, the *Legionarios*, and the regular Moorish troops—the *Regulares*. Together they numbered about 30,000.

The Regulares were both conscripts and volunteers to the Spanish Army—a regular unit of the Army, from Morocco and based in Morocco. As such they were invariably Muslims and dark skinned. To the Spanish they were "Moors", an exotic, if inferior race of infidels, useful subordinates in the shrunken greater Spain. First established in 1911, the Regulares' main task was to expand and hold land beyond the main protectorate enclaves of Ceuta and Melilla. They developed a reputation for extreme machismo and bravery, even foolhardiness.[1] With both infantry and cavalry squadrons, Spanish officers commanded the Regulares.

A slight and slim nineteen-year-old Francisco Franco first came to Morocco in 1912. He joined the Regulares as a junior officer in 1913 and was to spend nine of the next thirteen years in Africa. Decades later, in 1938, when he was on the brink of victory in the Civil War, he portentously said:

> *My years in Africa live within me with indescribable force. There was born the possibility of rescuing a great Spain. There was founded the idea which redeems us today. Without Africa, I can scarcely explain myself to myself, nor can I explain myself to my comrades in arms.*[2]

There can be little doubt that Franco's time in Morocco was crucial in developing the icy and ruthless person he was to become. As a young Regulares officer he was serious, ambitious and brave. He was cold, not yet icy, and calculating. Wounded in battle and thought unlikely to survive, his commander once cited his "incomparable bravery, gift for command and energy deployed in combat."[3] As a young man Franco gained a reputation of being blessed with good luck, a sort of divine protection; as he moved through the ranks this luck or protection was felt to be shared by those who stood with him. Franco was also a prude; he frowned on his colleagues' sexual adventures and abstained from any participation in them.

By 1917, after five years in Morocco, a newly promoted Major Franco was back in Spain.

Spain sat out the First World War: Alfonso XIII was closely related to monarchies on both sides in the conflict and prevailed in his wish that Spain should back neither side. Wise as this might be per se, it meant that the Army was inexperienced in the latest fighting techniques that were developed and experienced by the major powers.

The Spanish Foreign Legion was founded in 1920, largely modelled on its French namesake. It was to be an elite special force of shock troops who enjoyed much better pay than regular Spanish troops. And while there were some Beau Geste types to be sure, it drew upon a similar cohort to the French Foreign Legion: "a motley band of desperados, misfits and outcasts, some tough and ruthless, others simply pathetic."[4] The Foreign Legion was based in Morocco and, unlike the French model which attracted men from many countries, 90% were Spanish.

Its first commander was a wild one-armed one-eyed veteran of the Spanish-American War, José Millán Astray. Millán was 41 when he was given command of the *La Legion* in 1920 and was already given to mad harangues of his troops in which his "whole body underwent an hysterical transformation." He would tell the legionnaires that they were "bridegrooms of death." They were the scum of the earth, according to Millán, whose only retribution was death; indeed, it was he who established the Legion's catch cry: "Long Live Death!" His deputy was Francisco Franco.

When the indigenous Berbers declared an independent *Confederal Republic of the Tribes of the Rif* (the "Rif Republic") in 1920, the new legion led Spain's brutal colonial response. The ensuing Rif Wars were to last six years and involved many of the future leaders of the 1936 uprising. Sanjurjo, Mola, Quiepo, Goded, Yagüe, Millán Astray, Varela and—not least—Franco, were all Africanistas.

Here in the Rif Wars the future putschists established a lasting bond among themselves. A mystique developed around all Africanistas as they emerged as the Army's elite with a shared sense of destiny.[5] They were insufferably arrogant. And, in the Rif Wars, they came to share a tolerance for savagery and violent repression. This was an attitude and policy the future putschists fervently embraced when they became leaders of the Civil War rebels.

The Rif Wars did not go well for Spain. Vastly outnumbered, the Berbers employed guerrilla tactics and, with the support of the local Kabyle tribesmen, they were able to drive the Spanish troops back towards sea; at one point they even threated the enclave of Melilla. That said, service in the Rif Wars made the career of many an Army officer.

Francisco Franco Bahamonde was one. In 1923, at the age of thirty, he became commander of the Spanish Foreign Legion. A short man, barely 5 foot 7, pallid and still slim—with a high-pitched voice that seemed strangely out of place for a man with his newfound power—he was promoted to Lieutenant-Colonel. Before the year was out he had married his long-standing fiancée, 21-year-old Maria del Carmen Polo.

The Legion embraced iron discipline, and the troops were harshly disciplined for any infractions of the rules. Men were shot for the most minor offences. This culture formed the basis of their experience of life and their attitude towards the enemy. Brutal annihilation of the enemy was the goal; sadism was common, with severed heads a speciality.

Franco himself was all business in Morocco. He imposed capital punishment for seemingly innocuous matters.[6] An example often quoted was the legionnaire who refused to eat his food and threw it an officer and who, as a result, was put before a firing squad.

The savagery of La Legión was dehumanising to all who were part of it. When one of Franco's officers stopped his men firing on some Berber women, a fellow officer opined "but they are factories for baby Moors"; to this Franco provided the supporting comments "and we remembered that during the disaster [at Melilla], the women were the most cruel, finishing off the wounded and stripping them of their clothes, in this way paying back the welfare that civilization brought them."[7]

France held the rest of colonised Morocco, the fertile and attractive part. In 1924 it came in to assist Spain. By 1926 the Rif uprising was all over. Spain had committed 90,000 troops at one point, and the final battle was one between 125,000 Spanish and French troops versus 12,000 Berbers. This overwhelming force plus better technology (and chemical weapons) overcame the brave Moroccans nationalists. It had been a humiliating "victory" but one that forged a deep loyalty to each other among the Africanistas.

In early 1926 Franco returned to Spain, a hero of the Rif, and at just 33, thought to be the youngest general in Europe. Admirers made ambitious comparisons with the young Napoleon.

> At the outbreak of the Civil War the Spanish Army's establishment was split between 100,000 in the Peninsula and 30,000 in Morocco. This total of 130,000 was an exaggeration in that about one-third of the Peninsula troops were on leave.[8] (Conscripts were given three months training and then sent on leave.) Of the active regular Army on the Peninsula, about half (32,000) were now in the rebel zone and half (34,000) in the Republican zone. And the 30,000 Moroccan troops—the Army of Africa—were of course led by the rebels.
>
> Everyone knew that control of the Army of Africa was a crucial advantage held by the rebels. So too was the backing of the Church. The Church's support gave the uprising a legitimacy and a purpose beyond it being a simple grab for power. Franco and his cohort enthusiastically embraced the call to return Spain to Christendom; the uprising became a "Crusade" against atheist socialism. The irony, indeed hypocrisy, inherent in their relying on an overwhelmingly Muslim fighting unit to achieve that end is self-evident.
>
> In addition to the ostensible 130,000 strong Spanish Army, there were 32,000 in the Guardia Civil; they were split slightly in the Government's favour—probably 18,000 to 12,000. The Assault Guards were also split in the Government's favour—perhaps 12,000 to 5,000. (Both sets of guards or police were made up of hardened experienced men, all located in major centres; as noted, their allegiances, one way or the other, were always critical in determining whether the rebels or the Government would prevail in each particular theatre.) Then there were Carabineers, an armed paramilitary force that had largely stayed loyal—4,000 were now with the rebels but 10,000 with the Government. The Airforce, such as it was, was largely in Government hands. The

four fighter squadrons were based in Government-held Madrid and Barcelona. Of the serviceable aircraft, both airforce and navy, the Government controlled about 200 and the rebels less than 100.[9]

As for the Navy, it appeared to be very much in Government hands. In the first days of the uprising loyal seamen mutinied and overthrew the officers commanding the Republic's largest vessels. Valiant and useful as this was, it meant that the Republican-controlled navy, run by sailors' committees, had few men with the authority or experience to navigate or direct the navy's guns. So while control of the vessels denied the rebels troopships to ferry the Army of Africa across the Straits of Gibraltar, the loyal naval personnel had proved ineffective in blocking small craft crossings. What's more, the rebels had won control of El Ferrol in the northwest. This was the location of the main naval dockyard, and two new cruisers and the country's only two minelayers were nearing completion there.[10]

With the outbreak of war, the distinguished American journalist Jay Allen had sought an interview with Franco. In due course word had come through last weekend, on the Saturday evening, that if he presented himself at the Spanish Morocco border and asked for the right person Allen would be granted access. He immediately travelled from Gibraltar to the international city of Tangier and then to its darkened border with the Protectorate. Everyone in Tangier told him he would not get across. Regulares challenged and threatened him on the border, as did the blue-shirted the Falange (i.e. fascist) youths who actually manned the border post. After some hours, however, Allen was let through. A harrowing 60 km ride to the protectorate's capital, Tetuan, followed. Allen arrived there late on the Sunday to the sound of loyal naval cannon harassing the city and the news that loyal Republican aircraft had bombed it the night before.

Franco had by this time commandeered the High

Commissioner's office which stood on the main square opposite the caliph's palace; the caliph deputised for the Moroccan sultan but, in the scheme of things in the Protectorate, took his orders from the Spanish High Commissioner. The acting high commissioner, Arturo Alvarez-Buylla, had been "arrested" on 17 July by Franco's men when he opposed the rebels' insurrection. Franco had installed himself as High Commissioner when he arrived from the Canaries eight days ago.[11]

Allen got to interview Franco this evening, Monday at 8:00 pm. The venue was an ornate office in the High Commissioner's mansion, and they spoke next to a massive table on which maps were strewn out to plan the coming battles. It was the first interview Franco had granted the international press, and was held "in the temperature of a Turkish bath."

Allen was taken aback at what he saw: "Another midget who would rule," he wrote. "He is barely five feet tall.[12] His voice was a shock. It was gentle and even sad. He was very tired. He talked and I looked at the man who has plunged Spain into the ghastliest civil war in its history."[13]

Many accounts have commented upon the femininity of Franco's appearance—his large and luminous eyes, long eyelashes and soft voice.[14] Allen added to this Franco's high forehead, beak nose, "tiny feet and hands" and "nascent paunch." The moustache regrowth would have been evident too. Appearances, however, defied Franco's steely resolve.

He would have nothing of Allen's suggestion that there was a stalemate.

"No," he said quietly.

There has been a setback. There were defections at the start in the mutiny of the fleet. But no matter. We will bring ships from the northern coast to clear the Strait. We will win ...

There will be no let up. I am going through with it. I will advance on Madrid.

Franco confirmed his support for the role the sclerotic Army had adopted for itself—an obsession with "national unity", order and the defence of established privileges. A consummate politician himself, Franco told Allen he would have nothing to do with politicians:

I will pacify Spain and put a stop to hunting down one class of citizens by another. Spaniards are tired of politics and politicians.

And then, in ominous and prophetic anticipation of the oppressive dictat he would make as Caudillo, by which all laws passed in the Second Republic (1931–1939) were thrown out by his Fascist Government, he opined:

The revolution of 1931 was artificial…In the name of liberty there was frightful licence. The constitution was a unilateral affair. Half of Spain is persecuted.

"Then no truce, no compromise?" asked Allen.

No. No, decidedly, no. We are fighting for Spain. They are fighting against Spain. We will go on at whatever cost.

Allen asserted that "You will have to shoot half of Spain." Franco shook his head and smiled, and then looking straight at Allen, the committed and experienced Africanista that he was, and answered steadily:

I said whatever the cost.

28 JULY
TUESDAY

It is dawn, birds are twittering, rain drops are falling from the birch trees, and through the mist athletes run in the woods and over the fields. A squirrel nibbles on a nut and "Aussie" the kangaroo hops between the cabins as the Olympic Village awakes. It is a tranquil pastoral setting that gradually comes to a busy life. These are the opening scenes of the second part of Leni Riefenstahl's *Olympia*.

Riefenstahl, a connoisseur of the male form, next indulges herself with a segment featuring naked male athletes gambolling in the Village lake and later birching and watering their fit bodies in the vapour of the Finnish sauna. Partly clothed calisthenics and various warm-ups follow. Then we are shown track suited athletes in the uniforms of all nationalities going about their training—Indian, Japanese, Italian, even black Americans—on the athletic track, taking hurdles, conversing among themselves and eating hearty meals in the Village's canteens.

Catering for the athletes in the Village was a mammoth task. North German Lloyd Company fulfilled it with German efficiency and success. Special menus were created, almost on demand. Every food style or preference or dietary law, kosher included, was catered for. Today, 28 July, it being Peruvian Independence Day, a special menu was devised for the Peruvian team.

Here are some examples of the demands German Lloyd met on a

regular basis:[1]

Argentina: Steak à la plancha or empañada à la Creole once daily; chicken with saffron rice and risotto with fish often requested; dumplings and tallerines with extras; comparatively little veal and pork; spices, including sweet paprika and garlic; ample quantities of oil; tomatoes; few vegetables; "mate" in the afternoon.

Austria: Dishes such as fricassees, Schmorbraten, etc. prepared with flower [*sic*] preferred in general; macaroni, noodles and rice popular; steamed vegetables prepared with cream; following the usual meal, cold cuts or a sweet dessert with coffee requested; eggs and ample quantities of white bread desired for breakfast.

Brazil: Large quantities of meat, especially beef and pork; veal and lamb less popular; black beans daily (with dry rice); little butter but large quantities of olive oil; six oranges daily and one pound of bananas per person; strong coffee.

China: The Chinese were also moderate in their requests, pork and fowl being preferred as meats although beefsteaks were also demanded occasionally; no lamb; fish requested now and then; curry as a principal spice; large quantities of salad and fresh fruit, but few vegetables; 300 grams of rice daily per person; iced tea and orange juice as beverages.

Finland: Cold cuts from roast and sausages served with black bread, white bread, milk and large quantities of butter; fruit consommé, principally blueberry; oatmeal porridge and milk before training; cheese of all kinds; large quantities of smoked ham and bacon (which they brought with them); warm meals usually only in the evening with sweetened vegetables and potatoes; buttermilk popular; the consumption of fruit limited during training periods.

France: The French sportsman is also an epicure, paying less attention to practical nourishment than to tasty and varied dishes. English steaks Chateaubriand fashion with white bread and red wine preferred for the weight-lifters; all kinds of meat requested, this being prepared in the form of steaks, filets, cutlets, roasts and ragouts; delicacies such as mushrooms, anchovies, sardines, corn on the cob, green peppers, etc. popular; stewed fruit with every meal; vegetables steamed in butter but without sauces; cheese, fruit and coffee after the principal meals.

Germany: The weight-lifters received beefsteak Tatar [*sic*], chopped raw liver, cream cheese with oil and considerable quantities of eggs, often four per meal. Light refreshment before training and more substantial food afterwards. The athletes required normal meals, steaks, cutlets, pork chops, roast beef and fowl being principally requested. Large quantities of fruit; vegetables prepared with flour; potatoes but practically no rice; tomatoes and salads popular; milk with grape-sugar and fruit juices preferred as a drink; various kinds of bread with large quantities of butter.

Holland: Breakfast egg dishes also requested for second breakfast; steaks, cutlets and roast meat preferred for dinner in addition to salad with mayonnaise; green vegetables and large quantities of white bread as well as fruit, especially bananas; ground steak preferred by the cyclists.

India: No beef or pork; principally fowl or lamb prepared in curry and eaten with rice only; few vegetables and salads; four to five eggs daily; large quantities of fruit and fruit salads. Several sportsmen were vegetarians.

Italy: The Italians' diet was prescribed by their sporting physician. Principally soups, spaghetti, macaroni, tallerines and large quantities of Parmesan cheese; noodles, ravioli and strudels of all kinds; starchy foods at every meal; the weight-lifters ate considerable quantities of meat, while the boxers consumed only bouillon with egg two days before competing; daily portions of meat average in size; normal quantities of fruit; coffee and chianti wine preferred as beverages; large quantities of rolls.

Japan: For breakfast, soup with meat, vegetables, soy and rice, then eggs, fruit and bread; for lunch, meat (pork preferred), vegetables, rice, potatoes and often a sweet dessert; for dinner, steaks, ragouts, fish and other similar dishes with rice; vegetables and salads always mixed with soy; preserves which the Japanese brought with them also popular.

Luxemburg: Fowl as well as beef, veal and lamb steaks especially popular; mixed salads (lettuce, beans, asparagus); sweetened water preferred as a beverage; large quantities of white bread; two raw eggs for the cyclists before the start of each race.

Mexico: Steaks and fowl served with black beans, pimentos and rice; all meals prepared after the Spanish fashion with oil; eggs daily; baked potatoes with the principal meals; large quantities of bananas and oranges; saffron, tobasco [sic] and garlic used for seasoning purposes.

Peru: Meals similar to those prepared for the Mexicans. As many as ten eggs per day were eaten by the weight-lifters.

Philippine Islands: Meat well done and served with rice or vegetables (no spinach or cauliflower); large quantities of fruit, especially apples; tea, but little coffee; one lemon per person per day; no honey or cheese.

Sweden: As in the case of Norway and Finland, the "Smörgasbrød" was popular for lunch; roast potatoes with cold dishes; 150 grams of crisp bread and 250 grams of butter daily for the rowers; large quantities of raw tomatoes; cream was usually mixed with ordinary milk; the wrestlers ate no meat but large quantities of eggs and fish as well as oatmeal and blueberries.

Turkey: No pork, no pork fat; eggs eaten for breakfast only by certain athletes; large quantities of fruit; oil used for preparing meat and braising vegetables; the consumption of meat not especially large; grilled lamb and fowl with pommes frites very popular; small Turkish sweet dishes often requested; eggplants, green peppers and onions were the principal vegetables.

USA: Beefsteaks as well as lamb and veal daily for lunch and dinner; no form of fried meat except fowl; underdone steaks be-

> fore competition; for breakfast, eggs with ham, bacon, oatmeal or hominy and orange juice; large quantities of fresh and stewed fruit; no kippered herrings; vegetables and baked potatoes with principal meals; sweet dishes including custards and ice cream.
>
> Milk was by far the preferred beverage, usually straight but also with Ovaltine or grape-sugar. Remember this is the 1930s. The world was still in a serious depression. Fresh milk was delivered to the Village promptly every morning from the nearby Spandau Dairy.[2] Being Germany, records of all sorts were kept and it was the Indians who emerged champion milk drinkers, consuming two litres of milk per person per day.
>
> Alcohol was requested by a few European teams. The French and Italians asked for wine with their meals—the French taking it straight and the Italians typically watering it down. The Dutch and Belgians (of course) drank beer. Apart from these special requests, all based on ostensible cultural demands, alcohol was not technically available or allowed; the Australians and others ignored this and, in any event, there was an excellent beer garden just outside the Village's main entrance.
>
> Fruit demand exceeded expectations, vegetables were less popular than anticipated. Among all the teams only the Indians expressed (polite) disappointment with the enormous effort that had been made. It had to do with creating genuine Indian dishes.

Catering to the needs of the athletes did not stop with their appetite for food. In discussing the Village layout, the *Official Report* of the Games coyly refers to how "the primaeval forest to the north-west, known as the 'Enchanted Forest' (*Märchenwald*), was left undisturbed"; it had, we are told, "special bird houses, baths and feeding troughs ... distributed throughout the woods..."[3] Several reports inform us, however, of a racier role for the sylvan setting.[4]

28 July

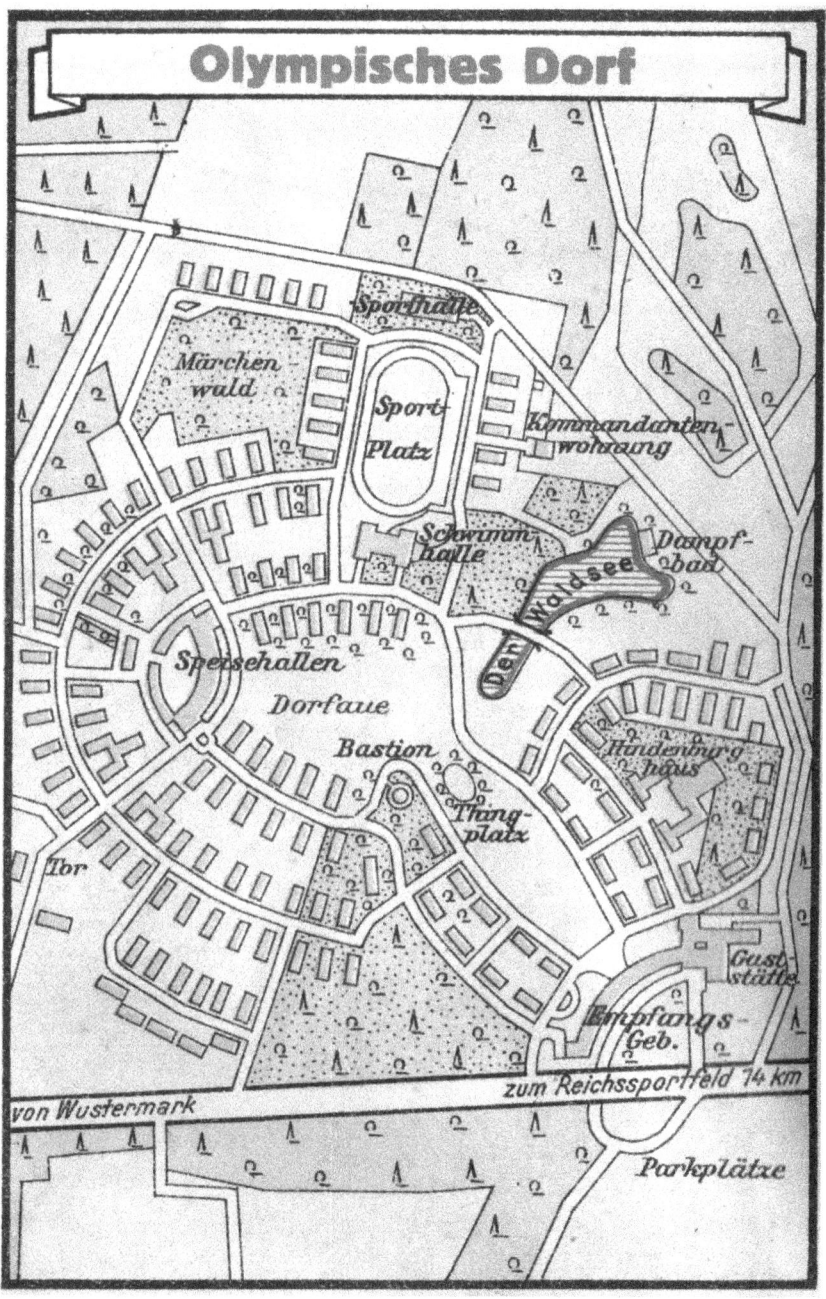

Paul Martin, a five time Swiss Olympian, was thirty-five in Berlin. He had won a silver medal in 1924 in the 800 meters, and this was his last Olympics as a competitor:

The Olympic athlete in Berlin was elevated to a godlike creature ... The Germans had even reserved a sort of heavenly forest for those gods. And there the prettiest hand-picked maidens would offer themselves to the athletes—the good Aryan types ... The maidens were usually sports teachers or members of Hitler's Bund Deutscher Mädchen ["German Girls"] *and they had special passes to enter the Village woods and mingle with the athletes. It was a lovely birch forest which had a pretty little lake, and the place was ringed with* [Berlin city police] *so no one could disturb the sportive couples. It was interesting that before submitting to the Olympic god of her choice, the girl would request her partner's Olympic badge.*[5]

The Australians had been in the Village since 23 June and the New Zealanders since 28 June. They knew the ropes. When they crashed one of the American dinners—it was their goal to sample as many of the available cuisines as possible—the conversation came around to sex.

"It's kind of creepy, actually," admitted one of the Aussies:

Policemen are guarding the area. Couple of Gestapo types had to wave me past. Then the girl had to approve me, too. Had to hand her my Olympic badge and she wrote down every goddamned word of it. It was like filling out a form at the doctor's office. She said no way could I use a wrap.[6]

Who knows? Perhaps it was all part of a Nazi eugenics breeding plan for the 1956 Olympics and beyond. Whatever, the set up had been dismantled by the time the Americans checked it out, apparently—and the enchanted forest had been returned to the birds.

> The Olympic athletes may not have known it, but the Village was on the edge of a major military base straddling the Berlin–Hamburg highway.
>
> The area had been used for military manoeuvres since the 1700s. In 1894 Kaiser Wilhelm II's Imperial German Army had acquired 4400 hectares at Dömeritz, 25 kilometres west of Berlin on the Berlin–Hamburg road; the plan was to establish a permanent military base—the Truppenübungsplatz Döberitz. The hapless inhabitants of the village of Dömeritz were moved and three-quarters of the site was quickly deforested.
>
> In 1910 an aviation school and an airport were constructed within the site. This was the original home of the Luftwaffe; the Red Baron, Manfred von Richtofen, learnt his craft here. And then, in during the First World war, the base was partly used a prisoner of war camp for 30,000 French and British soldiers.
>
> The Olympic Village was north of the highway. For the 1936 Olympics, some of the base's vast rolling hills and woods to the south of the highway were developed for equestrian use—specifically for the riding event of the pentathlon competition and the cross-country parts of the 3-day equestrian event.

Today was wet and rainy. Ninety military and civilian volunteers assembled at the Döberitz base.[7] Others would soon follow from various parts of Germany. They were responding to a request from General Milch for men prepared to volunteer for service as part of an expeditionary force to an unnamed foreign country. In fact the destination was probably not too secret.

One fighter pilot explained: "On 28 July 1936, whilst serving … at Köln [as part of the occupation of the Rhineland], I received a telephone call from my [commander] … His first question was 'Are you engaged to be married?' I stated I was not. He then swore me to secrecy and began to explain the situation in Spain and the need for well trained pilots in that country. Before he even had the chance to ask me if I would be prepared to go there, I said to him 'I volunteer'." Five other pilots were targeted. They were the foundation members of what ultimately became the Condor Legion, the German air-arm that backed Franco and infamously destroyed the Basque city of Guernica on 26 April 1937.

Such was the degree of secrecy that the volunteers' commander, who knew the code name *Magic Fire*, of course, was unaware of the exact nature of their mission; he still believed it to be simply a large-scale training and transport mission.

Each of the volunteers were officially discharged from the armed forces. They were required to hand in their uniforms and were given "cheap" civilian clothing in exchange, and were issued with new identification papers that showed them to be engineers, salesmen and so on—all tourist members of the Union Travel Association. They were given 200 marks in Spanish currency, which must have been some give-away, and a mail box address to which relatives could write.

Meanwhile, in Rome, Franco had received further support, this time from Fascist Italy.

It will be recalled that on 19 July, on his arrival in Morocco, Franco had authorised Luis Antonio Bolín to seek arms from "England, Germany and Italy", and that Bolín had flown off in the famous Dragon Rapide to do so. Bolín got to Rome on 21 July and the following day was received by Count Galeazzo Ciano, Mussolini's foreign minister (and son-in-law). Ciano was told that twelve transport aircraft were all Franco would need to win the war and he could do so, with the planes, over a few days. Whether he believed this or not, Ciano was keen to help. Mussolini, however, resisted two written approaches from his foreign minister.

At the same time as Franco's representatives were engaging with Cia-

28 July

no, General Mola sent a separate delegation to Rome. The delegation was led by a distinguished and well-known Spaniard, but Mola's requests were more modest than Franco's—rifle cartridges rather than aeroplanes—and, perhaps as a result, were hardly taken seriously. More importantly, Mussolini had come to understand that, with the death of Sanjurjo, Franco was likely to emerge as the leader of the putsch.

While these two sets of emissaries were in Rome, Franco himself sought "twelve bombers or civilian aircraft" from the Italian government representative in Morocco, a proposal the Italian representative happily supported.[8]

As a result of these approaches, Mussolini—through Ciano—decided to back Franco. Italy would send Franco twelve bombers immediately.

Where, one might ask, was US President Franklin Delano Roosevelt through all this?

On 27 June he had been renominated—by acclamation—as the Democratic Party candidate for President at their convention in Philadelphia. He accepted the nomination with his famous "A Rendez-vous with Destiny" speech—albeit that he never uttered those words; that memorable invocation was simply the title of his great speech. By 11 July he was presiding over the opening of the Triboro Bridge in New York, and then from 14 July he had been on a two week yachting vacation, cruising from Maine to the Roosevelt summer home at Campobello, New Brunswick.

Roosevelt had always been a keen sailor. On this occasion his son James had hired a 56-foot schooner, the *Sewanna*, which was owned by New York lawyer Harrison Tweed.[9] His companions were three of FDR's four sons—James, John and FDR Jr—and two professional sailors. They cruised for the two weeks, largely around Nova Scotia. Press photos show him relaxed at the wheel of the *Sewanna*, and there is little doubt that it was a most welcome break as he prepared for the forthcoming election campaign.

In fact FDR was at the centre of a small flotilla. In addition to the *Sewanna*, the group comprised the much larger Presidential yacht, the *Potomac*, the schooner *Liberty*, on which were based the press, an escort, the destroyer USS *Hopkins*, a minesweeper, the USS *Owl*, and a coast guard vessel, the *Pontchartrain*. The story put about was that the *Sewanna* would provide "greater comfort, space and privacy" for the President than the smaller yachts he had used for vacations in the past. It also provided great publicity shots and an opportunity to enjoy sailing per se. He often moved to the *Potomac* to eat or take a nap. On occasion he dropped into a friend's summer home. Sometimes he was a guest on another boat. Sometimes he entertained people to dinner on the *Potomac*.

It is clear, however, that although Roosevelt was technically on vacation at this time, he was kept informed of world affairs.[10] The naval vessels provided up to date telecommunications as well as protection. He knew what was going on in Spain and elsewhere. And he chose not to interfere.

Today at 2:15 pm, on the last day of his holiday cruise, the President hosted a picnic on a small island for his fellow travellers. He then gave a press conference at 4:00 pm, and this evening at 8:45 pm—well past midnight in Europe—he arrived at his beloved Campobello.

Above
15 July 1936: US team is farewelled from New York on board SS *Manhattan*

Left
US athletes; Eleanor Holm second from left, Dorothy Poynton-Hill second from right

Below
Avery Brundage

Thousands flocked to Berlin for the Olympics

Unter den Linden was always crowded with people

The Berlin Philharmonic played for the crowds *en plein air* ...

and Café Kranzler sparkled at night

Adolf Hitler was the centre of attention on the Opening Day of the Games

Hitler's entourage passing through the Brandenburg gate on its way to the Reichssportsfeld

Left
The Führer leading IOC members into the Stadium

Below
Hitler declaring the Games "open"

Jesse Owens was the star of the Games

in full flight...   in uniform...   ...and winning the 100 metres

US athlete Helen Stephens won the women's sprints

The Modern Pentathlon was created to test the skills of a military officer

Above
The shooting event

Left
Gotthard Handrick at the swimming

Below
Charles Leonard (US, silver), Gotthard Handrick (Germany, gold), Silvano Abbà (Italy, bronze)

Swimming Stadium

Japanese relay gold medallists (Yusa, Sugiura, Taguchi and Arai). The Japanese men dominated the swimming events in Berlin, as they had in Los Angeles four years earlier.

Hendrika "Rie" Mastenbroek of the Netherlands won three gold medals

Germany won five of the seven rowing events, but not the blue riband eights

Top
The victorious eight from the University of Washington

Middle
The finish of the eights: USA gold, Italy silver, Germany bronze

Bottom
The Italian eight won the sartorial stakes

The huge Maifeld at the Reichssportsfeld hosted polo and show jumping events during the Olympics. Post Olympics it was often used for Nazi rallies such as this reception for Mussolini on his 1937 State Visit

29 JULY

WEDNESDAY

When the International Olympic Committee met in Berlin today for its 35th Congress, the big agenda item was to decide which city would be granted the right to hold the 1940 Olympics. The venue for the Congress was the auditorium of Prince Heinrich's palace in the heart of Friedrich Wilhelm University on Unter den Linden.[1]

At first there had been nine competitors—Alexandria, Barcelona, Buenos Aires, Dublin, Helsinki, Rio de Janeiro, Rome, Toronto (or Montreal) and Tokyo.[2] The decision was due to have been made in 1935. Tokyo induced Rome to withdraw in February 1935 and, as a result, had become the favourite.[3] The IOC deferred its decision, however, until this Congress in Berlin. In the event, despite a late entry from London, Tokyo won the right to stage the 1940 Games with Helsinki the runner-up.

The next item was waived through without debate. It was a proposal that the IOC nominate Baron Pierre de Coubertin, the French founder of the modern Olympic Games, for the 1936 Nobel Peace Prize. De Coubertin was now 72 and living in reduced circumstances in Lausanne, and the Germans had been desperate to have him endorse the Berlin Games. Not only was he down and out and in poor health, de Coubertin had come to resent what he saw as a lack of recognition for his life's work.[4] He was reluctant to fully endorse the Berlin Games for a number of reasons; this was overcome, however, in late May 1936 when Hitler authorised the payment to him of 10,000 Reich marks and at the same time someone came up with the Peace Prize idea.⁵

One other agenda item attracted great attention. The USA had held three of the fifty plus positions on the IOC for some time. Avery Brundage, who had worked so hard to keep the Olympics for Berlin, had long aspired to fill one of the US positions. The long-standing incumbent members were William May Garland, a Los Angeles real estate developer who had been instrumental in winning the 1932 Olympics for that city, "General" Charles Sherrill⁶, a Yale-educated ex-diplomat who had recently lost his credibility because of the long letter he had sent to the *New York Times* in praise of Mussolini and Hitler, and Ernest Lee Jahncke, a 58-year-old New Orleans engineer and former Assistant Secretary of the Navy in the Hoover Administration.

Jahncke was the problem. He was a Republican with a conscience. He opposed US participation in the Berlin Games. On 25 November 1935 he had written a letter of explanation to the IOC president, Count Baillet-Latour:⁷

> *I shall urge upon my countrymen that they should not participate in the Games in Nazi Germany because it is my opinion that under the domination of the Nazi government the German sports authorities have violated and are continuing to violate every requirement of fair play in the conduct of sports in Germany and in the selection of the German team, and are exploiting the Games for the political and financial profit of the Nazi regime.*

Sigfrid Edstrom, the Swede who succeeded Baillet-Latour as IOC president upon Baillet-Latour's death in 1942, had written to Brundage as recently as 29 May: "As regards the third member of the Int. Ol. Com for the USA, your election is clear as soon as Jahncke resigns."⁸ But Jahncke would not resign.

Sherrill died on 25 June, so there was now a vacancy. But it was not enough for the IOC establishment to consider filling

29 July

this vacancy with Brundage; they wanted Jahncke gone. To that end, Garland moved a motion that Jahncke, his countryman, be removed from the Committee. This was achieved unanimously, 49–0, with Garland chivalrously abstaining from his own motion.⁹

Outside the genteel discourse of the IOC, swimmer Eleanor Holm had been talking. It had been just six days since Avery Brundage had expelled her from the US team, and Holm had been hired by her new friend WR Hearst Jr to cover the forthcoming Games for his *International News Service*. Hearst provided her with a ghost-writer, and she was now in Berlin as a novice journalist and private citizen. Brundage would soon understand that his decision to dump Holm had consequences. She let it be known that Brundage had a long-standing "zipper problem", that she had refused his advances, and that all her troubles since 1932 had been because of this.

The IOC took no notice. Brundage was appointed in Jahncke's place, not to fill the Sherrill vacancy. The resolution is explicit that Brundage was "*en replacement de M. Lee Jahncke*".

Count Henri de Baillet-Latour lacked the alleged charisma of his predecessor de Coubertin. He was a dour Belgian nobleman, a keen horseman with the well developed sense of self-importance seemingly required of all IOC members at the time; some self-importance might not be unjustified as, by 1936, he had been an IOC member for 33 years, having joined the Committee in 1903 aged just 24. In the wake of the Great War he had satisfactorily organised the 1920 Antwerp Games with just one year's notice, and he had been the unanimous choice to succeed de Coubertin in 1925. Once installed as President, Baillet-Latour centralised the administration by creating an Executive Committee that was authorised to run the IOC between Congresses. And, despite his aristocratic background and a ready acquiescence in the established order, he had "bottle". He would always defend the Olympics and Olympism. The "Jewish question" provides an example of his fortitude.

That racism and anti-Semitism were at the heart of Nazi Germany is unquestionable. Baillet-Latour himself held anti-Semitic views: "I am not personally fond of Jews and of the Jewish influence," he had written to a colleague on 3 November 1933.[10] But, as the President of the IOC, he would not let his prejudices or the Nazis' laws stand in the way of the Olympic Charter. Jews must be welcomed along with all others. Accordingly, Baillet-Latour required that, during the Games, Germany must eliminate any and all outward manifestations of prejudice against Jews; this meant any and all the offensive signs that were displayed throughout Hitler's Germany—"Jews not welcome here" etc—would have to go. After some brush offs and lies, in October 1935 Baillet-Latour finally fronted Hitler on this—and the Führer agreed to Baillet-Latour's requirements.[11]

So for the two weeks of the Berlin Olympics and for a week or so either side, there was an "Olympic pause" in the Third Reich's active anti-Semitism. The signs came down. ("... all signs posted in the fight against Jewry must be removed for the period in question.")[12] The hysterical anti-Semitic fortnightly *Der Stürmer* disappeared from the newsstands and newspaper reading-boxes. If selected, Jewish athletes competed freely (five won gold); kosher food was available in the Olympic Village; and Jews could visit a fashionable restaurant (such as the Cafe Kranzler on the Kurfürstendamm) safe in the knowledge that would not be presented with a silver plate and the dreaded note "You are not welcome here".

Today, the first of the planes Hitler had promised Franco arrived in Morocco.[13] Ten Junker 52s—a new tough utilitarian plane capable of serving as either transport for troops or a bomber—were sent as this first tranche of Nazi support. Disguised as civilian transport and carrying technicians and spare parts, nine flew directly to Spanish Morocco and landed safely; one blew off course, however, and landed in Republican territory. The Republic was starting to learn what it was up against.

29 July

Franco was thrilled with Hitler's new planes. He cabled Mola: "today the first transport aircraft arrives. They will go on arriving at the rate of two per day until we have twenty … We have the upper hand. Viva España!"[14] He was right, these ten Junkers plus the ten that would be sent by sea with the putative Condor Legion, would help turn the tide of the war.

A failed coup was quickly turning into what would become a prolonged civil war.

30 JULY
THURSDAY

Early this morning at the Elmas military airbase in Cagliari, Sardinia twelve planes were despatched for Spanish Morocco. They were Savoia-Marchetti S81 Pipistrello bomber/transports, a new 3-engined plane that was fast for the time and had good long-range capability, and they formed the first tranche of Mussolini's commitment to Franco.

Their capabilities notwithstanding, only nine planes made it to their intended destination, the aerodrome at Nador in Franco-controlled Spanish Morocco. Strong headwinds caused three to run out of fuel. One crashed into the sea thirty miles short of Morocco. Another crashed making an emerging landing and the third landed safely—these last two in French Morocco.[1]

The Savoia-Marchetti now impounded by the French authorities was manned by Italian airforcemen dressed in civilian clothes and the plane itself had its *Regia Aeronautica* (Royal Italian Airforce) colours painted over. This gave the French documentary evidence of Mussolini's intervention.

There were, however, no pilots among Franco's troops capable of flying the Savoia-Marchettis that had been delivered safely. The Italian pilots who had flown them to Morocco were quickly enrolled in the Spanish Foreign Legion. Franco now had nine Italian bomber/transports to add to the German fleet of Junkers already delivered or on their way. Together, these would provide the means by which Franco could airlift the Army of Africa to the mainland. It was to be the first airborne invasion in military history.

For the Olympics, Berlin was *en fête*. The weather had been beautiful these last few days. Visitors were arriving in their thousands from throughout Germany and from overseas. All was in readiness for the Opening Ceremony this coming Saturday, 1 August. The Olympic Family—that is the IOC, the National Olympic Committees, and the various International (sporting) Federations—and special guests of the Reich were accommodated in the best hotels. The Adlon, on Unter den Linden at Pariser Platz near the Brandenburg Gate and near the French and British embassies, had long been the centre of social activity. With its palm court, huge lobby and every possible amenity, it was the preferred venue of the elite. The Nazis themselves preferred the luxurious Kaiserhof—a few blocks down the Wilhelmstrasse on the old Wilhemlplatz, near to the old Reich Chancellery and Göbbels's Propaganda Ministry.

The city's great east-west axis, dubbed the Via Triumphalis for the Games, was stunningly decorated for the festival.[2] Huge banners decorated every building. The linden trees on Unter den Linden had been removed as part of the construction for a new subway. In their place of were 45 foot posts with flag banners, half Nazi /half Olympic, and beneath them sprouted lower masts, like branches of a tree, on which were hung 20 foot flags representing German towns. Everywhere there were miles of looped-up bunting and banners "such as might have graced the battle tent of a some great emperor."[3]

Over the course of July and August more than 1,300,000 overnight stays would be recorded in Berlin; half were German visitors, half foreign.[4] They flocked to the great department stores Wertheim and Kaufhaus des Westens ("KaDeWe"). On Unter den Linden the Berlin Symphony set up shop *en plein air*; contemporary photos show throngs of Berliners and their guests enjoying the entertainment.

Night clubbers had no end of options. For a few weeks it seemed as if the decadent days of the Weimar Republic had returned, as the authorities overlooked some of their more oppressive social policies. For the rich, the roof garden of the Eden Hotel on Kurfürstenstrasse beckoned: it was "Berlin's highest dance floor", Oscar Joost's dance orchestra played every night, the restaurant ran all day, the famously expensive bar served every fashionable cocktail—and for those so inclined, there was even a mini-golf circuit off to one side. Jazz was back, with Teddy Stauffer and his Original Teddies at the Delphi Palast again and Jack Hylton at the Mocca Efty bar.[5] The site of the world's first cinema, the Wintergarten in central Mitte, provided top variety entertainment for the Olympic visitors[6] ; all the theatres and cinemas were full, and the opera houses put on special out-of-season programmes.

And today saw the final run-through for the Opening Ceremony at the Olympic Stadium. The stadium was the best in the world. With a capacity of 100,000 it stood proudly at the centre of a sports complex of 425 acres—the Reichssportsfeld. In one corner was the Friesenhaus (where most female athletes were housed); this was next to the House of German Sports, with its own swimming pool—effectively a practice pool for the swimmers—and its own gymnasium. Tennis courts and the new tennis and hockey stadiums were closer to the eastern entrance to the Olympic Stadium, just north of the grand Olympische Platz. The new 16,000-seater swimming stadium was immediately north of and adjacent to the Olympic Stadium. Multiple playing fields, mini-stadia and equestrian facilities swept around the north of the Reichssportfeld to a huge flat field—the Maifeld—which formed the western boundary of the complex.

For the Olympics the Maifeld served as the polo playing ground and the venue for some equestrian events. At its edge stood a low-lying terraced platform, which housed the Langemark Hall, and above it rose a huge 250-foot bell tower—the Glockenturm—which itself housed a gigantic new bell, the Olympic Bell. These last mentioned buildings and the Maifeld might be designated "Nazi central", because the Maifeld and the viewing platform were ideal for political rallies. The Maifeld could accommodate perhaps 250,000 cheering adherents and the Langemark Hall which was built to glorify heroes of the Great War (at Verdun), flew regimental flags and shields and displayed martial inscriptions.

Across the Maifeld to the east was the Marathon Gate, the western entrance to the Olympic Stadium.

The stadium itself was made of grey-brown limestone, and its particular feature and success is attributable to March's inventive design. For while it was a handsome building when viewed at street level, the true dimensions of the arena cannot be envisaged from the outside. March had lowered the floor of the stadium a full 12 metres below street level, so that only on entering the arena was the huge dramatic oblong bowl of the Olympic Stadium disclosed.

None of this would have happened without Hitler's intervention. As late as 1932 he had thought the Olympic Games "a plot of Freemasons and Jews."[7] Then came the Los Angles Games, which were the first to promote a city and its lifestyle; de Coubertin was so struck by this aspect of the LA Games that he complained that they had been a "travel promotion" for Los Angeles.

The original plan for Berlin had been to expand, upgrade and refurbish the old 30,000 German Stadium which would have been the venue for the abandoned 1916 Olympics. With the advent of power in 1933, the Nazis changed their tune; they could see the advantages in being the centre of the world's attention for a few weeks. And so, on 5 October 1933 when Hitler came to inspect the work being done to the German Stadium, he had an apostasy.

The old stadium was within the Grünewald horseracing track and visitors reached it by tunnel. Hitler would have none of this. "Is the racecourse necessary?" he asked. It wasn't; there were two other racetracks in Berlin, and Grünewald made a loss.[8]

Hitler then gave the order:

> *This stadium must be demolished. A new one must be built in its place, capable of seating 100,000 people. It will be the task of the German nation! If Germany is to stand host to the entire world, the preparations must be complete and magnificent.*

And so the full force of the Reich was put behind the Berlin Games. Nothing was too much effort. All the required sporting facilities, not

> just the Reichssportsfeld, were requestioned and conveniently located nearby in the city's west.
>
> New railways lines were built, so that access to the Olympic Stadium and the Reichssportsfeld could now be gained from the huge new S-Bahn station to the south or the new U-Bahn to the northwest. Special timetables were introduced for the duration of the Games. Most importantly the Wehrmacht, Germany's burgeoning and efficient Army with its renowned logistics specialists, was harnessed to assist in organising all aspects of the Games.

Since its creation in the 19th century, just steps from the Arc de Triomphe, Paris' magnificent Salle Wagram has been the scene of many historic and gala events—from boxing (Georges Carpentier, Primo Carnera, Marcel Cerdan) to jazz and symphony orchestras. Although best known as the venue for right-wing gatherings, such as those of the racist and anti-Semitic Action Française, this evening it was the scene of a huge and most successful rally in support of the Spanish Republic—the first of any significance in the French capital. André Malraux, fresh from the battlefield, was the star attraction. He was joined by André Gide, Jean Giono, Louis Aragon and many others.

Together they raised their right fists in the revolutionary salute and sang the traditional *Marsellaise* and *La Carmagnole* and the new *La Jeune Garde*.[9] And then they formed a committee to provide food, medical assistance and money—but not military aid—to the Spanish Republic. The *Comité International de l'Aide au Peuple Espagnol* was the first major international support group for Spain.

> FDR had spent the day at Campobello Island, which is technically in Canada, and across the Bay of Fundy at Quoddy in Maine. The Bay of

30 July

Fundy has the greatest tidal shift in the world and scientists have long wanted to capture the power associated with the tides in some way; and today the President was inspecting one such project, since abandoned.

Spain would not have been high on his agenda. Nevertheless, by this time he would have known that Texaco was breaching the 1935 Neutrality Act. It was not illegal to sell oil to foreign combatants, despite its obvious strategic value. But it was illegal to give credit. And the pro-Fascist head of Texaco was doing precisely that, for Franco. As soon as the war broke out he had diverted a tanker to the rebels. What's more, he promised to provide all the oil they needed—on credit—for the duration of the conflict.[10]

At this point, FDR did nothing. He was concentrating on the upcoming November election. American Catholics, fuelled with reports of the clerical violence in Madrid and Barcelona, were vocal supporters of Franco and they formed a key constituency that Roosevelt wanted to keep on side.

This evening at 6:00 pm US time, approaching midnight in Europe, the President set off for Quebec in the presidential train; it was an overnight run from St Andrews, the small Canadian resort town up an inlet from the Bay of Fundy. FDR planned to spend the Friday in Quebec on official duties before travelling on by train, overnight again, to his family seat at Hyde Park on the upper Hudson River, New York.

31 JULY

FRIDAY

British reluctance to get involved in Spain was obvious. Foreign Secretary Eden had told the British Cabinet two days ago that "ordinary procedure" would be followed if either the rebels or the Spanish Government sought to buy arms from Britain.[1] He had already assured the Spanish ambassador that there would be no ban on the sale of civil aircraft and that any request for military materiel would "certainly be considered".

Today that changed. British PM Baldwin wanted Britain to stay out of the conflict. As a result, Eden announced a unilateral ban on all arms sales to Spain.

Members of the IOC are trained to accept fulsome hospitality. At lunch time today, the German Sports Minister and President of the German Olympic Committee, Hans von Tschammer und Osten, welcomed IOC members to his ex officio home overlooking the Havel river. It was hot but clear. Von Tschammer und Osten, a handsome 48-year-old front man from a landed family, was a Hitler toady; tall and clean-shaven with heavy dark eyebrows, he habitually wore the Wehrmacht uniform of brown riding britches, high leather jackboots and peaked cap.[2] His philosophy extended to the belief that sport was useful to "weed out the weak, Jewish, and other undesirables." The von Tschammer und Osten villa, which he enjoyed by dint of his position as Sports Minister, had a splendid view over this wide part of the Havel and would serve as a venue for many such luncheons over the course of the Games.

The two men most involved in organising the Games were the President of the Organising Committee, Dr Theodor Lewald and its Secretary-General, Dr Carl Diem. Lewald and Diem reported to von Tschammer und Osten, whose own immediate masters were in the Propaganda and Interior ministries and the Wehrmacht.

Dr Lewald, now 75, was of middling height, bald, with a bushy white moustache and a cheery, lively air. He had been a senior civil servant in both the Imperial Government and the Weimar Republic. With good language skills (French, English and Italian), he had been Reich Commissioner at the 1904 St Louis World's Fair, which incorporated the Games of the III Olympiad, and he had been an IOC member since 1924. Although the Lewald family had identified as Protestants for at least 100 years, Hitler had wanted him to stand down as President of the Organising Committee because of his ancient Jewish blood; Baillet-Latour defended Lewald, however, and he was allowed to continue as President of the Organising Committee, a role that would terminate when the Olympics finished, so long as he also agreed to resign from the International Olympic Committee post Olympics. Lewald was compromised; it was he who led the 1933–36 campaign within the IOC to retain the Olympics for Berlin, obfuscating the truth about the treatment of Jews and deceiving his colleagues.

Carl Diem was the brains of the Olympics. His life was sport. From an upper middle class professional family he had eschewed a conventional career. A good athlete, Diem became a truly great sports administrator. He had led the German Missions to the 1928 and 1932 Olympics. At 53, he had already been Secretary-General of an Organising Committee once—for the aborted 1916 Olympics, twenty years previously—and he was justly proud that he, more than anyone else, would be responsible for the Games' success. The Torch Relay was his idea, as were countless other innovations. Never actually a signed-up Nazi, Diem was an active fellow traveller; he had started to contribute articles to Nazi publications and gradually, over the coming years would become totally compromised by them.

This evening Dr Lewald, as President of the Organising Committee, entertained the IOC members and other members of the Olympic Family to a sumptuous dinner at the *Stadtschloss*, the former Hohenzollern palace on the Lustgarten. The Lustgarten is the most important square in Berlin and would be the venue for a grand ceremony when the Olympic Torch was scheduled to arrive tomorrow.

Within the Stadtschloss, the famous White Saloon had been made available for the Olympic participants. Covered in white marble with statues of Hohenzollern princes in the alcoves, a gilded ceiling and walls coloured with fine frescoes, it was a famously warm and hospitable site—arguably "the finest interior in Europe."

Tables were decorated with flowers and the flags of every participating nation. Of course the attendees had to suffer the usual platitudinous speeches—on this occasion from Lewald, the Minister for Foreign Affairs and Baillet-Latour—but then came the meal. It was over the top. The Kaiserhof hotel had prepared a feast:[3]

> *Consommé Julienne (accompanied by AR Valdespino amontillado)*
>
> *Black forest trout and salade Americaine (with a an Auslese riesling)*
>
> *Vol au Vent Toulouse (accompanied by Ch Mouton Rothschild '18)*
>
> *Saddle of venison with petits pois and salade romaine (ditto)*
>
> *Bombe Florentine (with 1929 Henkell sekt)*
>
> *Batons au fromage (presumably with any remaining Mouton)*

The only possible complaint could be the Henkell wine, albeit that this was Henkell's top sparkling product. Champagne would have catered to the IOC preferences, no doubt, but Hitler's

31 July

henchman von Ribbentrop was married to the Henkell heiress and was keen to make his contribution.

As the Organising Committee party broke up in Berlin this evening, a top secret project was reaching its climax in Hamburg, just 250 kilometres to the northwest.

For the last few days mechanics and engineers at the Junkers aircraft factory in Dessau had been disassembling ten Junker 52s and six Henkel He51 single-seater fighter biplanes. The disassembled elements had been conveyed to the Peterson dock in Hamburg.

During the day, the six Luftwaffe pilot volunteers had been bussed from the military base of Döberitz, next to the Olympic Village, to a Berlin railway station for travel to Hamburg. All were dressed in civilian clothes. By this time everyone knew they were going to Spain. Their superiors either didn't know that the pilots would soon be in combat or they misled them in this regard, because the pilots were explicitly told they would simply be protecting the Junkers that would be carrying Franco's troops from Morocco to the mainland.

General Milch himself was in Hamburg to greet the Luftwaffe pilots. About 100 volunteers, including the pilots, helped load 773 crates of "equipment" on to the Woerman Line cargo vessel *Usamaro*; it did not take long for the pilots, the vanguard of the future Condor Legion, to work out that the equipment included the six planes that they themselves would soon man.

And around midnight General Milch personally farewelled all of the volunteers as they sailed for Spain.[4]

1 AUGUST
SATURDAY

It was very cloudy and dull when, at precisely 8:00 am the bands of two infantry regiments played a grand reveille for the IOC members outside the Adlon Hotel.[1] By 9:30 am the IOC members and the Organising Committee, together with their wives (for there were no female members), set off to church. The choice was either the evangelical Berliner Dom (where Dr Lewald led the group) or the Catholic St Hedwig's (led by Count Baillet-Latour). Quite where this placed the IOC members from Japan, India and Egypt and others who might be presumed to be adherents of other faiths, or none, is not recorded.[2]

Next stop was the Zeughaus, a grand building that at the time accommodated a museum of Prussian military history on Unter den Linden, near the Lustgarten. And then to the War Memorial where, in front of a large crowd of bussed-in youth, Bailllet-Latour and entourage inspected a guard of honour at 11:00 am and placed a wreath. A marchpast by two battalions completed this ceremony, one battalion from the Luftwaffe and another from the Navy.

The weather remained a problem. It was overcast and threatened the day, and this was the big day—with the Opening Ceremony scheduled to commence at the Olympic Stadium, nine miles west, at 4:00 pm. Notwithstanding the weather, no visitor could miss the grandeur of the occasion. Olympic flags and the German National (Nazi) flag flew from every flagpole, one alternating with the other, and flags and bunting hung from windows and on every building. The airship Hindenburg hovered overhead, its constant hum adding to the atmosphere,

1 August

the Olympic flag displayed from its gondola and German flags from its tail fins.

Through the morning, on about 70 playing fields throughout the city, more than 100,000 schoolchildren celebrated the day with athletic events, football games and gymnastic displays. The Olympic Torch arrived at the Berlin city border at 10:48 am and wended its way through the streets to great acclaim and excitement.

Everything was to be centred on a Youth Celebration at the Lustgarten, the great public square at one end of Unter den Linden. The Olympic Torch was to be received in front of the grand Altes Museum. VIP stands were erected on two sides of the square, one in front of the Berliner Dom and another opposite. Joseph Göbbels's Ministry for Public Enlightenment and Propaganda organised 28,000 Hitler Youth and German Girls to come to the city centre; they arrived at six separate railways stations at about 9:45 am and marched four abreast through the city towards the Lustgarten.[3]

Hermann Göring welcomed the IOC and other dignitaries in the Oval Room on the top floor of the Altes Museum, and just after midday they came down to the museum steps to witness the dramatic arrival of the brigades of youth, who promptly filled up the square.

There were warm-up speeches from youth leader Baldur von Schirach and von Tschammer und Osten before Göbbels took his place on the podium in front of the museum. This was the 38-year-old Göbbels' great public moment of the Games. A temporary altar set up to receive the "Olympic Fire" stood in front and beneath this strange little man with his strange-shaped head and compelling voice. Göbbels then gave a fiery nationalistic oration, invoking German traditions and the wonder of German youth. Apart from Hitler, he was the Nazis' best speaker and he had developed a style somewhat reminiscent of his master's famous auto-intoxication performances; today's speech was one such, concluding with the shrill invocation: "Holy flame, burn, burn, and never go out."

With that the crowd could be heard to cheer the arrival of the Torch Bearer, a fair-haired youth from central casting. He loped down a large centre aisle between the exultant Hitler Youth and German Girls, and up to the temporary altar. There, to the continuing cheers of the crowd, the Torch Bearer lit the flame. He then returned down the centre aisle, through the crowd, running over to the Stadtschloss, where he lit the flame of a second altar; it would stay alight in the Lustgarten throughout the Games. The German National Anthem ("Deutschland über Alles") and the horrible Horst Wessell Song followed; since May 1933 the two songs had been twinned, by law, as a double anthem.[4] By this time there were perhaps half a million people on Unter den Linden. "Never did I see a whole town so carried away with enthusiasm," wrote the journalist from London's *Daily Telegraph*.

It was lunchtime. And Adolf Hitler was to be the luncheon host for the privileged few.

Meanwhile, in Paris, a second Cabinet meeting on the Spanish crisis had been underway all morning.[5] Cot argued that the policy of non-intervention in Spain that had been announced earlier in the week, on 25 July, had failed. The French now had proof of Italian intervention. (He made no mention of his own efforts in getting planes to Spain over the previous week.) President Lebrun counselled caution. Blum openly advocated assistance to Spain "whatever the consequences". Foreign Minister Delbos, an admirer and friend of his British counterpart Anthony Eden, argued "in consideration of the British position" that all parties who might aid one or the other of the combatants be approached to agree a formal pact of non-intervention.[6] It was an idea almost certainly dreamt up by foreign office chief Leger. When it was proposed that deliveries to Spain could continue pending such an

> agreement, Blum, both wanting to help Spain and always keen for an international solution, supported the solution.
>
> The French communiqué issued this evening disclosed the temporary solution:[7]
>
>> *The fact that one government has furnished war materiel to the rebels obliges France to reserve freedom to reconsider her position* [not to supply arms] ... *The Government has the double task of preventing an international dispute, and of maintaining friendly relations with the officially recognised Government of Spain which is fighting to restore order.*
>
> Paradoxically, the fear of an internationalization of the conflict had helped the anti-interventionists' cause. The communiqué showed their progress, when it went on to say that the French had invited "interested governments—Britain and Italy in the first instance—to participate in an agreement not to export arms to either side in Spain. However well-intentioned the initiative may have been, and it reeked of local French political imperatives, it was a disaster for the Spanish Government.

The IOC members and their spouses were driven to the Reich Chancellery on Wilhelmstrasse where Hitler greeted them at 1:30 pm. He wore his smart light brown jacket decorated with Nazi band on the left sleeve. Count Baillet-Latour, decked out in morning suit, with his similarly dressed colleagues circled behind him, delivered a saccharine—if fair—speech in which he congratulated Hitler for the organisation of the Festival (as the IOC chose to call the Games). Hitler thanked the IOC for granting the Games to Germany and, in a continuation of the fiction that there was some historic link between Germany and the ancient Olympics, announced that the excavations at Olympia which German archaeologists had discontinued in 1881 would now be completed.

One hundred and fifty guests sat down to lunch at 2:00 pm. A vast horseshoe-shaped table accommodated them with Hitler at the centre and Baillet-Latour and Lewald flanking the Führer.[8] Most were men. Such women as did attend were there as spouses of politicians or the Olympic Family. By 3:00 pm the cars taking the official party started leaving for the Olympic Stadium.

At 3:13 pm Hitler himself set off. The trip was scheduled to take 32 minutes.

Hitler would take the Via Triumphalis to the Olympic Stadium. It ran from the Alexanderplatz, over the Museum Island and the Lustgarten, along Unter den Linden, under the Brandenburg gate, through the Tiergarten, and then west down Bismarkstrasse Strasse to Adolf Hitler Platz (now Theodor-Heuss-Platz), along Heerstrasse in the direction of Hamburg (and the Olympic Village) to the Olympic Stadium. Crowds had gathered overnight and many camped there for today's great event.

The crowds were several deep along the Via Triumphalis. "Heil Hitler! Heil" was the common refrain. Hitler acknowledged the crowds to the left and the right, standing up in his open Mercedes, raising his arm in the Nazi salute. The loudspeakers along the route would announce on his approach: "He is coming. He is coming."[9]

> *At last he came—and something like a wind across a field of grass was shaken through the crowd, and from afar the tide rolled up with him, and in it was the voice, the hope, the prayer of the land. The Leader came by slowly in a shining car, the little dark man with a comic-opera moustache, erect and standing, moveless and unsmiling, with his hand upraised, palm outward, not in Nazi-wise salute, but straight up, in a gesture of blessing such as the Buddha or Messiahs use.*[10]

Many people wore an expression of ecstatic delight.[11]

Hitler arrived at the southern part of the Reichssportsfeld, at the Glockenturm, at 3:50 pm. He first inspected a battalion of honour. He then went into the Langemark Hall where, with War Minister Marshall Blomberg, he paid homage to the dead commemorated there;[12] and then he entered the flat expanse of the Maifeld.

Here were stationed the athletes, to the sides, waiting for the signal to march through the Marathon Gate tunnel and into the Stadium. Most had been there for more than an hour. Soft drinks and biscuits were handed out by uniformed German Girls but inevitably many of the athletes were getting restless. Heavy rain drops fell.[13]

Loudspeakers bayed the truism:

We await the Führer every moment. Never would this great field have been built except for the Führer. It was created by his will.[14]

Few of the athletes understood the broadcast as it, like so much that was to follow, was in German.

The Leader's party numbered about one hundred. They walked in silence through the field, acknowledging the athletes at their sides. IOC members, with Baillet-Latour and Lewald in front, accompanied Hitler. The IOC contingent wore morning suits and the new gold chains of office that Diem had ordered for them; Göring unkindly remarked that Baillet-Latour and Lewald looked like "flea circus directors".[15] Hitler, of course, led them all. He was now kitted out in a full Storm Trooper ensemble into which he had changed. Göring in the sky blue uniform of the Luftwaffe and Göbbels in a white suit followed.

As they approached the Marathon Gate, white-shirted Hitler Youth started the chant "Heil Hitler!" This was picked up by those on the Maifeld, and the cheers were transferred to and picked up by the 100,000 crowd in the Olympic Stadium.[16]

We can see the Olympic Stadium where 100,000 persons wait feverishly for the moment when the Führer will appear. We can well understand the expectancy of the 100,000 awaiting the moment when the Führer will enter the stadium. Achtung! The Führer now enters the stadium.[17]

Most foreigners only understood the "Achtung!" But the loudspeaker was soon drowned out by a trumpet fanfare that announced Hitler's arrival.

He strode down the steps of the Marathon Gate. To the accompaniment of Wagner's *March of Homage* the Führer and his ensemble started a march down the cinder track to his box, the Honour Loge. Half way along he paused to receive a bunch of flowers from Diem's flaxen-haired, five-year-old daughter; "Heil, mein Führer," she is alleged to have said.

The crowd had risen as one and saluted Hitler hysterically, Nazi style: "… you would have thought God had come down from heaven," reported one British athlete.

The Honour Loge, Hitler's box, stood proudly in the centre of the southern stand. Behind it there was a reception area and several private rooms including a personal dining room for the Führer.[18] Today Hitler was making a very public entrance; for the rest of the Games he gained access to the loge via a subterranean tunnel.

No sooner had the Führer taken his seat in the Honour Loge than all stood for the German National Anthem and the Horst Wessel Song. The *Olympic Fanfare* by Herbert Windt followed, and next came the command: "Hoist flags!" At this point the flags of all 50 participating nations were raised around the top rung of the arena.

There was a moment of silence. And then the Olympic Bell started to sound gently, gradually increasing in volume. This was the sign for the athletes to enter the stadium. The bell was the symbol of the Games. It was enormous. Weighing nearly 17 tonnes it had been specially manufactured at Bochum, near Cologne and its ten day transportation from there to Berlin—more than 500 kilometres—in January 1936 had itself been something of an event, not unlike the Torch Relay.

Entering the stadium first up, by tradition, was the team from Greece; Spiridon Louis, the marathon winner back in 1896, carried the flag. Martial music played as each team came into the stadium and formed up on the athletic field. The crowd were not to know, but the management of each team had faced a dilemma: how should they acknowledge Hitler and the dignitaries as they passed Hitler's loge? For years there had been an Olympic Salute which was almost indistinguishable from the Nazi Salute now ubiquitous in German civilian life. (The Olympic version had the hand held higher with the palm turned outward and downwards.)

The crowd received each team according to their perceived observance of Nazi protocol. Australia gave a simple eyes right and dipped the flag; there was "almost, well, complete silence."[19] The French received a huge cheer for their salute, which was actually the Olympic version.[20] The British—Great Britain alphabetically—were less well received for their simple eyes right. Italy, which gave its own "Roman Salute"—identical to the Nazi version—was roundly hailed and dipped its flag. And so on, until the Americans came past; the men placed their boaters and the women their hats over their hearts[21]—but they did not lower their flag, and were consequently received quietly. Immediately thereafter came Germany's huge team, bringing up the rear. The crowd lapped up their fellow countrymen, decked out as they were in white uniforms and snappy caps; of course the Germans saluted "correctly" and dipped their flag—and the Olympic Orchestra reprised the German National Anthem and the Horst Wessel Song.

With all the teams assembled, de Coubertin's voice was then

scratchily broadcast over the audio system:

L'important aux Jeux Olympiques n'est pas d'y gagner mais d'y prendre part; car l'essentiel dans la vie n'est pas tant de conquerir que de bien lutter.

It was his familiar refrain and it appeared in English translation on the announcement board:

The important thing in the Olympic Games is not winning but taking part; the essential thing in life is not conquering but fighting well.

Dr Lewald was next up, and he would have benefited from a translator and an editor. He spoke for far too long and most of the visiting athletes couldn't understand a word he said. Had they understood it, however, they would have heard the nonsense about Germany's "blood ties" to ancient Greece:

In only a few moments now will appear the torch-bearer, who will bear the Olympic fire aloft to the tripod from which, during these festive weeks, the Olympic flame will ascend to the sky. He is the last of over 3,000 youths, belonging to seven nations, who for thousands of miles have followed one another in the greatest relay race which the world has ever seen. From the altar of the temple of Zeus in ancient Olympia, through Hellas and Bulgaria, Yugoslavia and Hungary, through Austria, Czechoslovakia and Germany, the flame has been carried. Over mountains and valleys, on hard or dusty roads, through rain and darkness, in the heat of the noonday sun and through the coolness of the nights, in order to create both an actual and a spiritual bond of fire between our German fatherland and the ancient Greek shrine, founded nearly four thousand years ago by settlers from northern lands.

Notwithstanding Dr Lewald's indulgence, the show was ahead of time. And so, just before 5:00 pm, Adolf Hitler, Führer und

Reichskänzler to give him his official title, opened the Games with a single sentence:

I proclaim open the Olympic Games of Berlin, celebrating the Eleventh Olympiad of the modern era.

Hitler was the star, and he knew it.

The ceremony wound down. The weather had held off. A giant Olympic Flag was hoisted by sailors in the centre of the field. A twenty-one gun salute was fired by an artillery detachment. Hitler Youth released twenty thousand carrier pigeons from their cages; some swept over the Americans and voided their bowels. The *Olympic Hymn*, specially commissioned for the Games but not one of Richard Strauss's better works, was played—with Strauss himself conducting.

And then the 3075th torch bearer of the 3075 kilometre Torch Relay appeared at the top of the steps of the Eastern Gate. Fritz Schilgen was a 29-year-old former athlete of distinction; he was tall and muscular, the picture of German youth, and, his physical appearance apart, he had apparently been chosen because of his graceful athletic movement—a quality he demonstrated amply as he strode the full length of the stadium, through the serried ranks of athletes midfield, up the steps of the Marathon Gate to the bronze tripod altar at the top of the steps. There Schilgen paused, raised the Torch high one last time, and dipped it into the altar to light the Olympic Flame.

But there was more. Spiridon Louis presented Hitler with an olive branch from Olympia. The flag bearers then assembled in a semi-circle and dipped their flags while Rudolf Ismayer, a German gold medallist from Los Angeles, took the Olympic Oath on behalf of all the competitors:

We swear that we will take part in the Olympic Games in loyal competition, respecting the regulations which govern them, and desirous of participating in them in the true spirit of sportsmanship for the honour of our country and for the glory of sport.

It was 5:30 pm, exactly on time. The teams marched out to Handel's *Hallelujah Chorus* as the voices of 3000 white-clad choristers concluded a magnificent ceremony.

> Imagine removing more than 100,000 people from the Olympic Stadium—some by car, some by public transport—heads of state, the best athletes in the world, the rich and famous, some humble citizens and even some poor. And then returning a similar number to the Stadium, all in less than two and a half hours. That was the task ahead, because this evening the Organizing Committee had scheduled the "Festival Play".
>
> It was a job for the logistical skills of the Wehrmacht.
>
> Baron de Coubertin had asked that Beethoven's *Ode to Joy* form part of the opening ceremony. Diem and Lewald were not of a mind to do so. They planned, and in particular Diem planned, something much more ambitious. Diem wanted a separate theatrical event that would complement the official ceremony. It should feature youth and have music. And it should not exceed one and a half hours in length. The resultant Festival Play was to provide the template for all future opening ceremonies.
>
> For eighteen months they worked on it. "[The] task was not so much of a poetic piece as of a rhythmic creative nature ... Diem himself designed a festival play in which in a loosely constructed series of several pictures showed youth of various ages in playful and sportive movements, concluding with ... the final movement of the Ninth Symphony."[22]
>
> It was called "Olympic Youth", and it had four parts or pictures: Children at Play, Maidenly Grace, Youths at Play and in a Serious Mood (yes, that's the full title), and finally a rather unfortunately named series of dances—Heroic Struggle and Death Lament. Despite the pretentious titles of the parts (and perhaps that has something to do with the

English translation), it worked.

The music was by Carl Orff and Werner Egk. Diem engaged Hanns Niedecken-Gebhard, a former stage manager of New York's Metropolitan Opera, to work with Egk. They were conscious of the constraints of a stadium, and of the opportunities.

Most would see the performance from a bird's eye perspective. The scenes needed to be enjoyed from all parts of the stadium. And they needed to move from one scene to another without unnecessary disturbances. This is where lighting came in. As one scene ended, it being night time, the lighting could be extinguished and a new scene appear in another part of the stadium. The performers who had finished their scene disappeared into the night.

Thousands of girls and boys were employed. More often than not they were clothed in white. Primary colours were used to provide contrast. One movement moved to another; circles moved from one corner of the stadium to another; the Olympic Rings appeared; gangs of children ran in and out, all in formation; there were flags; the children sang. There were constant changes of space, dance formations, light effects and music. The narrator's words may have helped at times but they were ultimately unnecessary for the enjoyment of the visuals.

The Festival Play had opened at 9:00 pm with the invocation "I summon the youth of the world", with the Olympic Bell softly ringing, and it concluded before 11:00 pm, again with the Olympic Bell tolling gently, and 1500 male and female voices belting out *Ode to Joy*. A ring of lights circled the stadium and the flags of each nation emerged through pink and blue theatrical smoke, the flags carried aloft by white-clad boys. Seventeen searchlights from the Reichssportsfeld swept the skies until they moved in unison to form an arch over the Stadium which gradually fell into darkness.[23]

There had never been anything like it before.

2 AUGUST
SUNDAY

An innocent coming upon the scene at the Döberitz military drill grounds in the early hours this morning might have concluded that a high-level cavalry exercise was about to take place. Army officers were everywhere.

In fact what our hypothetical innocent was witnessing were the preparations for the first stage of the Pentathlon, the equestrian cross-country race. It was overcast and warm, and misty. A 5000 metres course had been marked out over the vast Döberitz military base south of the Olympic Village and on the other side of the Berlin–Hamburg highway. The course had great variety—open country, woods and thickets, a water barrier among twenty obstacles such as fences and jumps—and it would prove to be a very difficult test for the competitors. Sixteen countries had entered the Pentathlon, most with three competitors.

This had always been Sweden's event. A Swede had won the first competition in 1912 and a countryman had won at every Games since. The winner had always been a military officer. This should not be a surprise in that the five elements were designed to reflect the skills (and virtues) of an officer and a gentleman: riding, fencing, swimming, running and shooting. Baron de Coubertin claimed origination of the event, although the alternative claimant, Viktor Balck, is a more likely author; he was the head of the Organising Committee for the 1912 Stockholm Olympics, when the Modern Pentathlon[1]—to give the event its correct title—was first held.

2 August

The War Ministry had been seconded to organise three of the five stages of event: today's equestrian part, the shooting and the final cross-country run. The event was to be run over five days.

Horses came into the paddock at 7:00 am. At 8:00 am the participants drew lots for the horses, no competitor being allowed to bring his own. They were truly magnificent animals, specially trained by Army experts—but inevitably the horses could not be of equal quality. The competitors had fifteen minutes to acquaint themselves with their assigned horse, and at 9:00 am the first rider set off. There was a five minute break between each of the forty-two competitors.

It took until 1:30 in the afternoon for all riders to complete the course. Twenty five of them did so without any penalty. After this first stage, Italian cavalry officer First Lieutenant Silvano Abbà was in the lead, closely followed by a Belgian and then the German hope, Luftwaffe First Lieutenant Gotthard Handrick. The gold medallist in 1928, Swedish army officer First Lieutenant Sven Thofelt, a fencing specialist, loomed close by. For the USA, infantry officer Lieutenant Charles Leonard, was well back at the close of this first stage.

Francisco Franco was unhappy with the progress of his airlift across the Straits. Fewer than 5,000 had arrived in Seville, the staging point for a planned march on Madrid. Most would think this satisfactory, indeed unprecedented, but Franco was impatient for the march to get underway.

Accordingly, today he flew with a small party to inspect the situation.[2] It was a brief visit—he would stay overnight—and he was not impressed with the preparations. Nor was he impressed with Quiepo's self-aggrandisement and vanity: huge portraits of the local warlord were hanging from major buildings in Seville; Quiepo's face was reproduced on mugs and vases, ashtrays and mirrors—and a photograph of

> the general was mandatory on any household where "reds" had lost a family member.³
>
> Franco put Quiepo's personal indulgences aside for the moment and concentrated on the war. To that end, he authorised the advance of the first column northwards. The goal was Mérida, 200 km to the north and about a third of the way to Madrid.

Meanwhile, at the Olympic Stadium, the first track and field events were underway. There was no rain but it remained overcast.

The 100 metres heats started at 10:30 am, but as there were ten heats, the last—with Jesse Owens—did not finish until noon. Notwithstanding the enthusiastic reception he had received in Hamburg and Berlin on arrival, Owens was apprehensive as to what his reception might be at the Stadium. And indeed, strangely, this morning his reception and the reception for everyone was somewhat cool. Perhaps it was the weather; perhaps it was because these were "just" heats. In any event, Owens did not disappoint: he won his heat in the World and Olympic record-equalling time of 10.3 seconds!

The crowd had warmed up by the second round at 3:00 this afternoon. Owens was greeted with what would become something of a war cry: "Yessay! Yessay! Oh-vens! Oh-vens!"

He had rushed back to the village for a sandwich, a round trip of more than an hour. Slight rain started to fall. Again, Owens did not disappoint. Running in that controlled, seemingly short step, with his shorts hitched up to his waist, Owens skimmed across the track in 10.2 seconds; only a tailwind prevented it being a new world record.

Sprinters invariably run through a finish. Had Jesse Owens done that today he would have landed in one of the pits Leni Riefenstahl had created so as to get her desired camera angles, dug deep into the turf at the end of the straight. It was dangerously close to the finish of the outside lane—but Jesse elegantly stepped around it.

Hitler had missed the first Gold Medal of the Games, a victory for German Tilly Fleischer in the women's javelin. But he was there for the second. German SS officer Hans Wöllke beat the American favourite Jack Torrence in the shot put. As soon as his winning shot was announced, Wöllke turned to the Führer's loge and snapped to attention with a Nazi salute. It is all there on Riefenstahl's film.

Hitler ostentatiously called Wöllke and Fleischer to his box and publicly congratulated them. He did the same with the three Finnish 10,000 metre runners, they finished 1–2–3, soon after 6:00 pm.

The men's high jump had been going all day: eliminations at 10:30 am were followed by semi-finals at 3:00 pm. The final itself started at 5:30 pm and, as is the way with the high jump, it dragged on. After almost three hours of competition, the final was down to three Americans, two of whom were black, and a Finn. Hitler had left the stadium by the time Cornelius Johnson, one of the blacks, finally prevailed, beating colleague David Albritton into second place.

King Edward had sent standard good wishes to the British team before the start of competition:

> *I send my best wishes to the members of the British team taking part in the Olympic Games where I am sure they will maintain the tradition of British sportsmanship.*[4]

He and Mrs Simpson had spent the weekend at Fort Belvedere. He loved the place. Set on a hill, Shrubs Hill, overlooking Virginia Water in the extreme south of Great Windsor Park, it was "a child's idea of a fort."[5] As Prince of Wales he had first secured a lease from the Crown

Estates in 1929. "What would you possibly want that queer old place for?" asked his father, the King, "Those damn weekends, I suppose."

Indeed he did. The Fort had became his redoubt, somewhere he could retreat from the intrusions and pressures of being Prince of Wales and now King. "Here I spent some of the happiest days of my life," he wrote, "London was only 22 miles away so that I could, and did, travel back and forth almost daily."[6]

He built a swimming pool and a tennis court, installed central heating and en-suite bathrooms for the six bedrooms. The enlarged and improved Gothic revival structure, with towers and castellated belvederes, had become a hodge podge of comfort. The King was a keen gardener—the estate had about 60 acres—and Edward would spend weekend afternoons pottering among his roses dressed in bright shorts and a white jersey;[7] weekend guests were encouraged to muck in.

Once Wallis moved in—their bedrooms were separated by a newly created dressing room, thereby allowing the lovers uninterrupted access to each other [8]—she took over the running of the house. Table decorations, food, flowers and the general household routine were her domain.[9] She was an accomplished hostess. Her style was new to the English upper crust; to their eyes it was casual, even democratic: at the Fort the King and his consort typically didn't "dress" for dinner. She gave the chef and butler their orders.[10] At dinner, she wittily moved light conversation along. Her menus were inventive. The King loved it all; he "watched her happily as she joked, talked, spread her strong expressive hands in acute, sharply defined gestures ... [and] would be restored to his old bouncy self."[11] Cards and dancing to the gramophone would follow dinner, and the guests would play into the night. Sometimes he would play the bagpipes for them.

When "David" and Wallis were alone he would attend to his peculiar hobby of needlepoint. Wallis was happy. Just yesterday she had written a chatty letter to her Aunt Bessie. This would be the couple's last full weekend at the Fort for more than a month—because in a week's time the King and Mrs Simpson would be off to the Dalmatian coast for their summer holiday.

3 AUGUST
MONDAY

"Today is dull and cloudy and will probably rain," wrote Australian swimmer Evelyn de Lacy in her diary. "It's always raining here."[1] This was unfortunate since, in the weeks leading up to the Games, Berlin's weather had been more often than not fine and clear.

The track and field competition in the Stadium started up again, as scheduled, at 9:00 am. The pentathlon fencing started at the same time, the venue being the nearby Cupola Hall in the House of German Sport. And the wrestling continued in the magnificent Deutschland Hall less than 4 kilometres away.

The proximity of the various venues, one to another, was a feature of the Berlin Games. For the women, housed as they were in the Reichssportsfeld, it was particularly convenient. Evelyn de Lacy, for example, records practising her stroke today at 9:30 am in the pool in the House of German Sport, and then going over to the Olympic Pool at 1:00 pm for a training swim, both venues being within a few hundred yards of her accommodation.[2]

At some point during the morning Dr Karl Ritter von Halt called upon Hitler. A Nazi sports administrator and a former Olympian, Ritter von Halt was in charge of the Games' track and field events. His visit to the Führer was at the behest of Baillet-Latour who was concerned that while Hitler had publicly congratulated the German and Finnish gold medallists yesterday, he had not congratulated Cornelius Johnson. Obviously Hitler could not be present to congratulate all winners. Equally obviously it is unlikely he would want to be seen congratulating a black American. Baillet-Latour's message was that if he could not congratulate all winners in public it would be better if he congratulated none. This Hitler accepted.³

After lunch, Evelyn de Lacy went over to the Stadium.⁴ Like everyone else she wanted to see Jesse Owens run.

Leni Riefenstahl had made great demands upon the Organising Committee for her planned film. The Government had granted her a huge budget, one she constantly exceeded, and she had Hitler's backing. Göbbels was her titular boss and she and the Propaganda Minister did not get along. In order to get the camera angles she wanted, she had made all number of requests of the organisers—camera pits, camera tables, camera towers and so on. One was to have a camera mounted on a rail that followed runners down the Stadium straight, such as for the 100 metres final that was to be the feature of today's program. It was all too much for Ritter von Halt and his colleagues; so exactly a week ago, on 27 July, the International Amateur Athletic Federation issued the following strict guidelines:

The IAAF has carefully studied the filming of the track and field week during the Olympic Games. We took into consideration the fact that all has to be done to produce a model sport film of the Olympic Games of 1936. Therefore, we (the directing officials for athletics in the Organizing Committee for the XIth Olympiad), are glad to inform you, in the name of the IAAF, that:

1. You may use 2 pits for the camera-men taking pictures of the high jump at the high-jumping site, and another pit, 5 metres from the starting line of the 100 metre dash. One at the side of the finishing tape. One at the end of the 100 metre course. One at the southern side of the southern jumping course.

2. The following towers will be permitted: 3 towers in the center of the field during the longer races. One tower behind the start of the 100 metre course. A sliding rail behind the protecting grid for throwing the hammer during the qualifying tests. The towers must be removed immediately after use.

3. The following are forbidden on principle: The taking of motion pictures directly in front of the contestants in the races as well as in the throwing and jumping contests. All cameramen must operate sitting or prone. North of the northern jumping course and south of the southern jumping course, pictures may be taken from the lowered passageway only with the exception of the pits on the southern side.

4. In the throwing contests, the broad jump, and the hop, step and jump, only the first attempt (in the qualifying test, preliminary and final) may be photographed. In the men's high jump, photographs may be taken of the qualifying test only up to a height of 1.80 metres, of the final up to a height of 1.85 metres, in the women's high jump, up to a height of 1.40 metres in the qualifying test, and to 1.50 metres in the final. In the pole vault, up to a height of 3.60 metres in the qualifying test, and up to 3.80 metres in the final.

5. Immediately after the try-outs the camera-men must return to the lowered passageway. From there pictures may be taken without restrictions. The boundaries are the same as for photographing:
a) Pictures may be taken only from outside the running course. Boundary: grass.
b) Throwing and jumping boundary at least 3 metres on each side, marked by a yellow line.

6. The number of camera-men should not exceed 3 for throwing and jumping. The use of noiseless cameras is desirable.

7. If a competitor does not desire to have his picture taken, his wishes must be complied with immediately.

8. After the finals, the winners and those placing in the field events can be filmed during one trial each, provided that this does not disturb other contests.

9. The number of the daily identification cards for the Olympic Film and the News Reel camera-men will be fixed at
6 for the inner field
9 for the sunken passageway.

> *Cameramen taking each other's place must exchange their arm-bands behind the enclosure at the Marathon entrance.*
>
> *The use of a catapult camera on sliding rails cannot be allowed on the 100 metre track, since that would not comply with the Regulations of the International Amateur Athletic Federation. Permission cannot be given for the use of a special camera car for the Marathon Race. However, reverting to the desire of your company, formerly expressed, we should gladly admit one of your camera operators with a portable moving picture camera into the third car of the judges for filming the competitors in the race. Along the course we shall make all possible provisions for assisting the filming, especially near the control stations and the canteens.*
>
> *The IAAF calls your attention to the fact that competitors in the Olympic Games may not take part in any public performance for filming purposes. The IAAF is convinced that the agreement made yesterday and this letter cover all the possibilities for filming the track and field events in a manner not possible at former Games.*
>
> *Very respectfully yours,*
>
> *[signed] S. Stankovits, Bo Ekelund*
>
> *IAAF*
>
> It wasn't what she wanted, but it was enough. Apart from being a brilliant and beautiful film in and of itself, Riefenstahl's *Olympia* was to become the original case study on how to film sporting events.

As people made their way to the Stadium for the afternoon's events, a polo match was underway on the Maifeld. Polo was an example of the sort of "gentlemanly" amateur sports—such as tennis, shooting, fencing and horse-riding—that were much favoured by the IOC establishment. They did not always resonate with the general public and while polo had been played at the Olympics on and off since the 1900 Paris Games, this was to be its last appearance at an Olympic Games.

3 August

The polo competitors played on through a heavy shower that passed over Berlin about 2:00 pm, and the crowd started to build for the first of the track events due at 3:00 pm.

At 3:30 pm Jesse Owens waltzed through his semi, recording 10.4 seconds on the damp and heavy track. His countryman Frank Wykoff, competing in his third Olympics, and the Swede Strandberg, both on 10.5, provided the placings and they too qualified for the final. The crowd knew their favourite: "Oh-vens! Oh-vens!" was once more heard throughout the arena.

Ralph Metcalfe of the USA won the second semi. He won easily in 10.5s, running away from the Dutchman Osendarp in 10.6 and the local hope Borchmeyer in 10.7. We now had the six qualifiers for the final.

Metcalfe, who had grown up in Chicago and was a graduate of Marquette University, was black and 26-years-old. He had lost the LA Games final in 1932 to Eddie Tolan in controversial circumstances. Both recorded 10.3 seconds, with the tall and elegant Metcalfe probably breasting the tape first and the squat and bespectacled Tolan probably crossing the line first; crossing the line was deemed to be the determinant. After two hours review, Tolan was given a new world record, and Metcalfe (as second place), who the crowd thought had won, was denied it. Metcalfe had won the US championships that 1932 Olympic year and he was the fastest in the world for the next few years—during which period he equalled the 10.3 world record. It was in 1935 that Owens started to beat him. The final today would be decided between the two, and there was every reason to believe that Metcalfe had been foxing to this point.

The heats of the women's 100 m provided an interlude. These showed that the American favourite, Helen Stephens, was a street ahead of her competitors.

At 5:00 pm sharp the six male finalists were called by the starter to the line. There were no blocks; in order to secure their start, runners were provided with small trowels to dig holes in the cinders. The six dug their holes and went through their ritual preparations. Owens was on the inside lane, nearest the athletic field, Metcalfe on the outside, nearest the southern stand. Two black men flanked the four white men. The six were under starters orders, and the stadium was electric.

Auf die Plätze! ... Fertig! ... Riefenstahl's camera moved in closely on Owens. He was a picture in concentration, and relaxation. With the sound of the starting pistol the Stadium let off a terrific roar.[5] Metcalfe stumbled at the start then challenged Owens—before Owens took over at about 70 m, and sailed serenely away to a clear metre or so win.

If there ever had been any doubt, Jesse Owens was now the star athlete of the Games.

In due course there would be much conjecture about Hitler "snubbing" Jesse Owens today. Certainly, he did not congratulate the champion. But we know that, after the first day, he had given an undertaking not to publicly congratulate any winner if he could not congratulate all.

There is little doubt that Hitler now welcomed that undertaking. Baldur von Schirach, the leader of Hitler Youth, was in Hitler's box when Owen's won; much later he reported that the Führer had said "The Americans should be ashamed of themselves, letting negroes win their medals for them. I shall not shake hands with this negro."[6] Then, the story goes, when Tschammer und Osten pleaded with Hitler to meet Owens "in the interests of sport", Hitler shouted at von Schirach for the first time in their eleven year acquaintanceship: "Do you really think that I will allow myself to be photographed shaking hands with a negro?"

Whatever took place in the Honour Loge this afternoon, the one person who could feel aggrieved was Cornelius Johnson. He was on his way to winning the high jump yesterday when Hitler left the Stadium before the conclusion of the first day's events and before Hitler had giv-

> en the undertaking. Obviously it would have been good form to wait to see the result. It was therefore Johnson not Owens who was snubbed.

In Moscow, two hours behind Berlin, the Soviet Government had let the Spanish genie out of the bottle. A huge crowd—variously estimated at 120,000 to 150,000—marched into and through Red Square expressing solidarity with the Spanish Government.[7] They came in their thousands as soon as the factories closed. It was a hot evening, still 97°F (36°C), and perfect weather for a demonstration.

E. Bystrova, identified as a woman from the "Red Dawn" factory, told the demonstrators why they were there:

Our hearts are with those who at this moment are giving up their lives in the mountains and streets of Spain, defending the liberty of their people. We send our greeting of fraternal solidarity, our proletarian greeting to the Spanish men and women workers, to the Spanish wives and mothers, to all the Spanish people. We say to you: remember that you are not alone, that we are with you.

The well-crafted banners read WOE TO THE TRAITOR REBEL GENERALS OF SPAIN and HAIL, SPANISH PROLETARIAN FIGHTERS. The All-Union Council of Trade Unions announced that a "voluntary" contribution of 0.5% of every worker's pay had been unanimously agreed to in every workplace, and that this would be donated to the Spanish Government as soon as it could be collected; the levy would raise $5 million for the cause.

Spanish PM Giral had been waiting nine days for a response to his telegram to the Soviet Ambassador in Paris. This was undoubtedly it. Not a formal response, of course, but undoubtedly an official one.

The Executive Committee of the Communist International had met on 23 July to discuss Spain. It had met again today and had directed International Red Aid to "immediately undertake a wide campaign of solidarity." As the Spanish Ambassador to the Soviet Union sagely pointed out to his head office, "public opinion" in the Soviet Union is "absolutely directed and controlled"—and this evening's spontaneous demonstration was a reliable guide to official thinking.

Back at the Stadium, after a heavy shower about 7:00 pm, the organisers put on a reprise of the Festival Play. Again it was a triumph. Whatever Carl Diem's shortcomings, this idea—the children, the music, the lights—was an enduringly good one. With the full dress rehearsal last week on Thursday the 30th, then the principal performance two days ago immediately after the Opening Ceremony, this reprise, and two further shows scheduled for 18 and 19 August after the Games were closed, the Festival Play was performed five times. More than 500,000 people saw it live.

4 AUGUST
TUESDAY

Once more the weather was overcast in Berlin.

The weather did not deter attendance at "KdF City" in Berlin. Kraft durch Freude ("Strength Through Joy" or "KdF") was a huge leisure organisation created by the Nazi regime as soon as it came to power in 1933. By 1936 KdF had grown to a claimed membership of 30 million. The purpose of Strength Through Joy was to provide cheap and accessible leisure activities to all Germans, regardless of age and class; inevitably it involved a degree of control, and certainly influence, over the leisure activities of a large part of the working population—and this was its further purpose. Seven million Germans partook of some form of KdF activity in 1936—concerts, day trips, plays, cruises and skiing holidays formed the basis of the menu—and these seven million probably reflected the active membership of the organisation. Whatever the number of members, it was the world's largest tour operator.

Five large wooden halls were set up to create KdF City near the Funkturm, the prominent radio tower in west Berlin.[1] Decorated in a rustic style representing traditional German country peasant or folk life, the establishment was barely 4 km from the Olympic Stadium. A temporary S-Bahn station brought up to 20,000 members to KdF City every day, on twenty to thirty special trains. Once at KdF City they enjoyed gallons of beer, bratwurst, brass bands, dance and other performances—even high wire acts. Bus tours of Berlin were put on too. Those who could afford tickets to events at the Stadium could make the short walk via Adolf Hitler Platz.

Over at the Stadium, an unspoken star was gaining a following. Franz Miller, the starter of the track events, was a large man from Bavaria—and quite the most competent and entertaining person anyone had ever seen in that very public role. He was competent because he did his job, getting the race under way—without grandstanding, as so many in that position are wont to do—and getting it under way *fairly* for all those under his control. And he was unintentionally entertaining in the way he went about it.

Herr Miller was punctilious. Every start was the same. Dressed in white from head to foot, shoes included, he'd call—

Auf die Plätze ("on your marks"), and on the *auf* he would dip his knees; then, about two seconds would pass before—

Fertig ("set"), and on the first syllable of the two syllable fer-tig the knees would dip again;

finally, after a break of unpredictable length, with the .380 pistol held high in his right hand, he would fire the gun—for a perfect start.

Everyone loved Herr Miller.

Lining up for the start of the women's 100 m at 4:00 pm were six women. Three attracted great attention, and they were the favourites. Stanislawa Walasiewicz, or Stella Walsh as she was widely known, was the defending champion from Poland; it was reported that she'd run 11.6s in Warsaw in her final competition a week or so ago, before the Games.[2] A US resident since the age of three months, Stella Walsh had been brought up in the Polish section of Cleveland, Ohio. She was now twenty-five and, since her victory in Los Angeles, had spent much time in Poland where she was now celebrated as a local hero. Stella had continued to win races in Europe and also when visiting the USA. Unable to become an American citizen before she was 21, which is why she had represented Poland (albeit as a stateless person) in LA, she had the opportunity to do so for the Berlin

Games—but, on the cusp of doing that, she chose to explicitly take out Polish citizenship. Decidedly masculine in appearance, with a square jaw and dark bushy hair, she was stocky and dark, and ran with a determined, if agile, gait. Stella Walsh was by every measure a formidable competitor, something her opponents knew well.

The local champion was Käthe Krauss. She was joined by two German colleagues in the final, but Krauss was their superior. Krauss was dark and very tall—indeed considerably taller than even the US hope, six-foot Helen Stephens. Now 29, Krauss had beaten Stella Walsh once in 1934 and had been the German champion since that year.

The one to beat was Helen Stephens. Only 18 years old, a farm girl from Fulton, Missouri, Stephens held the world record of 11.6s. She hadn't been beaten in the tens of races she'd run since her classic victory the previous year over Stella Walsh; on that occasion Walsh derogatively dubbed the 17-year-old Stephens "that greenie from the sticks", which meant that all their subsequent races were grudge matches.[3]

Tall and flat chested, with a deep voice, Stephens—"the Fulton Flash"—was a dominant presence. She had blitzed the first round heats and her semi final. Her times of 11.4 and 11.5 would have been world records had they not been wind assisted. The best time recorded by her competitors was Krauss' 11.9 behind Stephens in their semi-final.

There were repeated false starts by nervous competitors. It was the first occasion anyone had seen any annoyance from Herr Miller. Once they were off, however, it was no contest between Stephens and the rest of the field. She beat Walsh by a big margin with Krauss well behind; the official times for the placegetters were 11.5s, 11.7 and 11.9.

A bizarre event was to follow.

Hitler had arrived for the women's 100 m final, and he asked to meet Helen Stephens. After giving some press interviews, Stephens and her coach were ushered into a room behind the Honour Loge.[4] A dozen SS officers then entered and distributed themselves around the room. Hitler appeared and gave Stephens and the coach a Nazi salute. Stephens reciprocated with "a good old Missouri handshake." "I put extra pressure on it," she reported, "and that gave him the wrong message because he immediately began to hug me and pinch me and squeeze me and see if I was real."

Stephens asked Hitler for an autograph and, while he was signing her book, a camera flash lit up the room. "Get him! Destroy the evidence!" someone cried. Hitler slapped the photographer around the face with his leather gloves, the camera was dropped and kicked away and the photographer manhandled away.

According to Stephens, Hitler again turned his attention to her, now replacing the face of utter fury with a benign smile. "He wriggled his body as if to shake himself back to composure." Hitler suggested that she should run for Germany, after all she was "pure Aryan". Stephens thanked him for this, but declined. Hitler then asked her if she liked Germany, to which she politely replied yes. Next, through the interpreter (who was no less than Nazi No. 3 Rudolf Hess), Hitler made a bizarre offer:

> *You would like to spend the next weekend with Chancellor Hitler at his villa in Berchtesgaden?*

At this point Stephens' coach intervened to observe that she would be required to run the relay at that time. Nothing would stop the Führer, though, because he then included the coach in the invitation. "Thank you, but no," she replied, "I too cannot accept your kind offer." With that reply in English, which Hitler obviously understood, he wished Stephens well. Finally, reported Stephens, the Führer und Reichskanzler "reached behind me, pinched me, then saluted us both, and marched out."

4 August

The final event of the day was the long jump. Here, the German champion, Lutz Long was a real chance to beat Jesse Owens. Owens had had a very busy and tiring day, with the heats of the 200 m having taken place at 10:30 am, the same time as the long jump eliminations, the semi-finals of the 200 m at 3:30 pm, quickly followed by the semi-finals of the long jump at 4:30 pm. And it was now 5:45.

Long and Owens were a great contrast. Long was a fine example of German youth: 23 years old, tall, blue-eyed, flaxen haired, the lot. Owens was black, sleek and charmingly modest. Long had the classic jump with arms flung high in the air. Owens run fast and hard and jumped low with a strange kick mid-flight.

Much has been made of the sportsmanship allegedly shown by Long today. It is part of folklore that, with Owens having fouled twice in the morning elimination round and therefore facing elimination if he did not qualify with this next jump, Long advised Owens to take off short of the foul line. The qualifying distance was 7.15 m, something Owens could probably make running backwards. (His world record was 8.13 m.) Certainly they talked. Indeed there is a famous set of photos showing the two athletes—black and white—lying on the ground engaged in friendly chatter. What makes the story almost certainly apocryphal, though, is the fact that every schoolboy athlete knows that to avoid a foul you adjust your run-up.

But Long, was indeed a great sportsman. He never headed Owens in the semi-final or the final. By the semi-finals Long was just 3 cm behind Owens—7.87 m to 7.84 m. In the final round Owens fouled on his first jump, and then Long came up to Owens, equalling his 7.87 m. Owens immediately topped this with 7.91 m. Leni Riefenstahl's *Olympia* shows Hitler on the edge of his seat. But a victory for Germany it was not to be. Long fouled on his last attempt, and then Owens jumped a new Olympic Games record of 8.06 m.

It is what came next that is important. Long rushed to congratulate Owens. To the crowd's now familiar chant of "Yessay Oh-vens" was added "Long! Long! Long!" And the two walked arm-in-arm around the Stadium, taking in the crowds' cheers, and they went off to the dressing rooms together.

5 AUGUST
WEDNESDAY

After his visit to Seville on Sunday, Franco returned to Morocco two days ago, on the Monday. He was concerned that the build up of troops in Spain proper, by means of the German and Italian transport aircraft, was taking too long.[1] Against the advice of his colleague Yagüe and some naval officers, who thought it too risky, Franco resolved to try to break the Republican naval blockade across the Straits. To that end he assembled about 3000 troops at the rebel-occupied Spanish enclave of Ceuta. At dawn the troops boarded four merchant navy ships and at 7:00 am they started a 41 km dash across the Straits to Algeciras, the mainland city near Gibraltar.

Franco's man in Algeciras was General Alfredo Kindelán, a 57-year-old royalist and the most senior airforce officer to defect to the rebels. Kindelán had a well-established relationship with the British authorities in Gibraltar. Indeed, as early as 19 July they had already shown their sympathies with him and the rebels by placing at his disposal telephone lines upon which he could speak without passing through any Spanish exchange. This enabled Kindelán to be in direct contact with Franco in Morocco (and Alfonso XIII, and Italy and Germany).[2]

Franco was aware of the Republican Navy's lack of direction and reckoned also that they would be intimidated by the German warships that were patrolling the Moroccan coastline. Moreover, twenty-two German and Italian aircraft were now available to provide cover for his convoy.

When the loyalist-commanded destroyer *Lepanto* was bombed by Kindelán's aircraft and suffered serious damage, it naturally sought refuge in Gibraltar. On Franco's suggestion, Kindelán telephoned his friends in the British Navy there, asking them not to give aid or refuge to the Republic's vessel. The British obliged! Only the dead and the wounded were allowed to disembark. The damaged vessel was duly ordered to leave port, and at 7:30 am it limped off to its base at Malaga.

The British foreign office under Anthony Eden had already shown its hand. They had allowed BOAC to sell four aircraft to the rebels last week, on 29 July; in so doing the British Government announced that they would not interfere in a "civil, commercial transaction".[3] As we have seen, two days later, now five days ago, Eden announced a unilateral ban on all arms sales to Spain— whether the prospective purchaser was the Spanish Government or the rebels. And now, in Gibraltar, they explicitly sided with the rebels in. Perfidious Albion was at work.

In Berlin, while his new friend Franco was trying to get his Moroccan troops across to Algeciras, Hitler was making a morning visit to the Reichssportfeld. As usual, every move of the Führer was choreographed. Somehow the word got around that he would be travelling along the Via Triumphalis at this time, and the crowds gathered along it to glimpse and herald him.

Hitler had come today to the swimming stadium to see the swimming stage of the Pentathlon. Gotthard Handrick was in the lead after three stages. On Monday the German had come second in the fencing with Sweden's Thofelt, a fencing specialist, finishing only equal fifth. Yesterday, in the shooting, the American Charles Leonard had scored an incredible perfect score of 200 bullseyes; Handrick came fourth with a score of 192. The result was that Handrick now stood with a clear lead on 8 ½ points, Thofelt second on 20, Leonard with 26 and the Italian Abbà on 26½.

> The Olympic swimming stadium was open to the weather and rankings would be determined by the time each athlete recorded over 300 metres. It was cold and wet, the temperature gradually rising from 15.5° to about 18°; the pool temperature was higher, it always being kept at a steady 21°. The fastest time of 4m 15s went to the German Lemp. Thofelt (4:35), Leonard (4:41) and Handrick (4:52) all did well too. Abbà swam the distance in 5:13. So at the end of the fourth day, Handrick was still clear on 17½ points, Thofelt on 23, Leonard on 32 and Abbà on 40½. As noted, Sweden had always provided the gold medallist: Thofelt had won in 1928 and was a close fourth in 1932. Leonard and Abbà were the best runners. All would now depend on tomorrow's cross country run.

In the Stadium itself, the pole vault eliminations started at 10:30 am. It was a lousy day for the thirty competitors; it rained, quite heavily at times, it was cold—just 14° to 16°—and it was windy. And pole vaulting is an incredibly complex event, requiring great strength and agility. So it was a surprise that only five athletes were eliminated at this first stage. The semi-finals were scheduled for 4:00 pm.

Next up was the men's 200 m sprint. With the temperature only up to 17°, the competitors emerged about 2:30 pm. Jesse Owens was of course the favourite. His world record stood at 20.3s. Given the weather, though, this would not be a day for world records.

The 200 m is only a sprint in name. No one can maintain top speed for the entire distance and, in any event, the event starts on a curve. It involves both technique—hugging the inside of the lane, leaning into the curve, using centrifugal force—and tactics. Competitors are habitually run down in the straight when lactic acid kicks in and it is difficult to maintain effort. Top runners try to get a good start, then accelerate, then float and relax as they hold onto as much speed as they can sustain.

Owens' only real competition could come from his fellow black American, Mack Robinson. Robinson, tall and poor, was just 22. He was the third of five talented children who had moved with their mother from Georgia to middle class Pasadena, California in 1920. The youngest, Jackie, was born in 1919. It was he—Jackie Robinson—who would break the "baseball colour line" when he turned out for the Brooklyn Dodgers at first base in 1947.

At 3:00 pm, in pretty awful weather, Robinson won the first semi-final in 21.1s. Owens won the second semi in 21.3s.

Back on the field, the pole vault semi-finals took the attention of the crowd from about 4:00 pm. Pole vaulters are typically tall with good sprinting capacity, upper body strength and flexibility; they are competing in the most technical of all athletic events. An athlete has to choose a pole that is the right length with the strength to carry his body weight. Holding the pole horizontally, he will probably employ a bounding or bouncing gate, hold his hips high through ten or more strides as he accelerates towards the box for the pole, then lower the pole to engage it in the box, drive with his leading leg, swing up, hang, and then push up on the pole and turn—and hope to clear the bar.

It was still cold and blustery this afternoon, and the weather—together with inevitable tiredness after competing for nearly six hours—started to take its toll on the pole vaulters. Twenty competitors were soon eliminated.

The temperature was down to 13° as the "Yessay Oh-vens" chant announced the appearance of Owens for the 200 m final. They were on their blocks at 6:00 pm and under Herr Miller's orders. Owens was in lane 3, advantageously inside Robinson who was in 4. The weather threatened but the wind fell. Owens then blitzed the field, scuttling away to a clear victory over Robinson. Owens was elegant, almost dainty in his running style. There was none of the arm-pumping power which is so much

5 August

a part of the technique of modern-day sprinters, and one can only wonder if such an amendment to his style might have given Owens even better times. Whatever, he looked terrific, and was timed at 20.7s—a new Olympic record.

The final of the pole vault immediately followed the 200 m. It was a lesson in self-control. There were just five competitors left—three from the USA and two from Japan. They started late at 7:00 pm and ended in darkness at 10:30 pm, the vault apparatus itself lit by floodlights and highlighted against a black sky. The event had already taken more than twelve hours, and was yet to find a winner.

Two great friends from USC, Bill Sefton and Earle Meadows, and two Japanese—Shuhei Nishida and Sueo Oe—eventually fought a pitched battle to find a winner.

Sefton, Nishida and Oe all cleared 4.25 m but could not make 4.35 m. Meadows cleared the 4.35 m on his second attempt. and so won the gold. A complicated countback and possible jump off resulted in Sefton placing fourth, Nishida second and Oe third. So respectful had the Japanese become, one to the other, however, they refused to engage in a jump off—and later cut their medals in half, soldering them into two bespoke half silver/half bronze specials.

Leni Riefenstahl's *Olympia* captures the drama of the long day beautifully and her inventive camera angles explore and explain some of the athleticism required for this marvellous event; it is, though, like the Japanese medals, a reconstruction. Riefenstahl persuaded the athletes to restage those elements of the event where her extensive live footage did not meet her exacting standards, and then wove the new footage into her masterpiece.

Propaganda Minister Goebbels had not had such a happy day. He noted in his diary:

> *We Germans win a gold medal, the Americans three, two of which are won by niggers. This is a scandal. White humanity should be ashamed of itself.*[4]

Back in the Mediterranean, Franco's convoy from Ceuta had been forced back by fog. Late this afternoon, however, they set off again. And this time, with the Republican naval vessels harassed from the air, Franco's troops got through to Algeciras. The rebels now had 8000 Moroccan troops on the mainland. They would soon assemble in Seville for the march on Madrid.

The convoy's successful crossing was a triumph for the rebels. Franco's people had broken the naval blockade. In rebel propaganda it became the "Convoy of Victory", which was perhaps not an exaggeration. From this point troop ships and war matériel started to flow relatively freely across the Straits.[5]

6 AUGUST
THURSDAY

Wannsee, at the western edge of Berlin—beyond the Olympic Stadium, the Grünewald and the Olympic Village, and adjacent to Potsdam—is the great lung of the city. Part of the Havel River system, it comprises two lakes—Grosser Wannsee, and across a bridge, the much smaller Kleiner Wannsee. Within this water wonderland of swimming, sailing, canoeing and the like, is the Strandbad Wannsee—the largest lido in Europe, fully 1.3 kilometres in length with about 80 meters of sand—the beautiful former imperial possession, the *Pfaueninsel* ("Peacock Island"), and the Wannsee Golf Club. The Golf Club was the centre of attention for many this morning.

Almost every member of the IOC, President Count Baillet-Latour included, was coming to the Golf Club. They arrived well before 7:00 am because this morning they would witness the ultimate stage of the Pentathlon—the cross country running race. Baillet-Latour was the President of the *Comité International du Pentathlon Moderne Olympique* and his colleagues may well have turned up out of respect for him. The German military leadership turned up too: War Minister—yes, that had been his title since 1935—Field Marshall Werner von Blomberg, the chief of staff of the Army, General von Fritsch, and the same General Milch from the Luftwaffe—its #2 man—who had secretly seen off the future Condor Legion to Spain just six days ago.

The race would be over 4000 metres, and it was a difficult course. Open fields followed deep gulleys, woodlands flowed into ravines, and the final kilometre was largely uphill.[1] The competitors were sent off at one minute intervals. Given the distance, though, the better runners would likely pass the lesser ones; the best might do 13 minutes or so and the top runners could expect to finish within 15 minutes. Points would be awarded according to one's finishing place; i.e. the fastest would get 1 point and last place—there were still 39 competitors—would be awarded 39.

The American Leonard ran the race of his life, recording 14:16; he had passed the champion Swede Thofelt who blew up and finished in 15:16. It now looked to be between Leonard and Gotthard Handrick. They were 14 ½ points apart. Handrick, who "would rather drive" than run[2], proved that he was a fine runner, finishing the course in 14m 42s. Leonard had recorded the equal seventh fastest time compared to Handrick's fourteenth, a 6½ point gain.

Gotthard Handrick therefore emerged the clear winner, with Leonard second. This was a great event for the German military, and Gotthard Handrick became a hero of the Third Reich. Hitler personally promoted him one rank in the Luftwaffe—a practice he employed for all military personnel who won Games medals.

An important goal of German foreign policy was the detachment of Britain from its alliance with France. The 1935 creation of the Anglo-German Fellowship by British sympathisers had provided a vehicle for promoting German interests in the UK. Several members of the Fellowship made visits to inspect and report upon the "New Germany" in the days and months leading up to the Games. In late May and June, 1936 Joachim von Ribbentrop, who was a German Ambassador-at-large, had been in England specially to hand out invitations to the Olympics.

Two of the Mitford girls, Diana (the soon-to-be wife of British Fascist leader Sir Oswald Moseley) and Hitler-obsessive Unity, were members of the Fellowship. They received invitations from Ribbentrop, as did the press barons Rothermere and Beaverbrook. Another was the Tory MP "Chips" Channon, an American-born socialite married to a Guinness heiress.[3]

The Channons had arrived in Berlin yesterday, thereby missing the first few days of events. They were put up in a "magnificent set of rooms" at the Hotel Eden.[4] If the Channons thought they were magnificent, they were. Last night, having taken in the vast crowds on Unter den Linden, they were guests of Prince Otto von Bismarck, the chargé d'affaires at the German Embassy in London; von Bismarck put on a party for fifty on the Eden's roof garden, and the Channons had retired, ultimately, at 2:00 am. Today, after rising at 12:30 pm, they eventually made it to the Reichssportsfeld, where they saw Hitler for the first time (which excited Chips immensely), and watched "hurdling and running, which bored us."[5]

The Mitford sisters were no better. They were staying at Göbbels' country house at Wannsee, and were chauffeured at their whim to and from the Reichssportsfeld. They found the sporting events tedious, so more often than not they preferred to stroll around the complex—socialising with fellow Brits and drinking nips of gin from a handy flask.[6]

In fact, these sports philistines had been witness to one of the great running races of all time.

Twelve athletes had qualified for the final of the 1500 metres, the first three placegetters from each of the four heats which had been completed yesterday. Many had been foxing. Luigi Beccali of Italy, still only 28, was the defending champion. Glenn Cunningham of the USA was the favourite. And the dark horse, literally in that he ran in the distinctive all black colours of New Zealand, was Jack Lovelock.

Cunningham, known as the "Iron Horse of Kansas", had an amazing history. At the age of eight he had survived the explosion of a fire heater in his remote Kansas school. His elder brother died in the fire. Cunningham lost all the flesh on his knees and shins and all the toes on his left leg; doctors wanted to amputate the leg and only his dire protests deterred them. With great effort and support from his parents he was walking again within two years. At the University of Kansas he had been not just a champion athlete—big, strong and determined—he also topped his class. Kansas being at the centre of the Bible Belt, it should be no surprise to learn that Cunningham was a keen Christian; indeed, he attributed his recovery and successes to his faith. Cunningham had finished fourth in LA and, coming into these Berlin Games, was the holder of the world mile record. He was now 27—having celebrated his birthday the day before the heats—and was universally well liked.

Compared to Cunningham and the Swede Eric Ny, who was also a finalist, Jack Lovelock was tiny. He was just 9½ stone or 60kg. The child of English immigrants, he had been a success in all sports. After studying medicine at the University of Otago he won a Rhodes Scholarship to Oxford in 1931, where he completed his medical studies. Lovelock had come seventh in LA. He had won the Empire Games mile in 1934, and held the mile world record for a time before it was bettered by Cunningham. Now an intern at St Mary's Hospital in London, Lovelock had intellectualised running or at least his own qualities—the tactics of a race, of course, but also the physical characteristics and the potential of himself and his competition. He had come to conclude that he only had one supreme effort in him per season. To that end, he had held back in his heat and finished just third, the last qualifier from it.

The weather had been better today. Evelyn de Lacy reported it "dull".[7] The official report says it was overcast with a dry ground, 17.8° and little wind.[8]

Herr Miller set them off at 4:15 pm. Cornes, an Englishman

who had finished second in LA, led the twelve men through the first lap. There are four laps in the 1500 m. Cunningham soon took over, his imposing hulk a contrast to the neat Lovelock who was shadowing him. Ny challenged Cunningham and settled into second; together they fought out the middle two laps, Ny even forcing Cunningham to step onto the field at one point.

These two big men were dominating the race, and going into the last lap Ny was looking good; he was well ahead and pulling away. Suddenly, the blond kinky-haired Lovelock pounced. With 300 metres to go he raced past Ny. Cunningham tried to stay with Lovelock but could not. Ny fell back through the field. As they rounded the turn to the straight, Cunningham—the Iron Horse of Kansas—came again and bore down on the little New Zealander and seemed ready to overpower him. "I put in another little effort as a second response to dishearten and choke off a further attack," Lovelock later recalled immodestly. His arms and legs working like a machine with his "little effort", Lovelock looked back to make sure he had shaken the American off. And he crossed the line in a new world record of 3:47.8.

Cunningham too broke the world record. Defending champion Beccali, who had always been in contact, came third and broke his own Olympic record. Everyone who knew anything about athletics thought it one of the greatest races they had ever seen.

The evening's entertainment were much more to the Channons' taste. This was the official reception for the Reich's guests of honour, the Ehrengäste. There were obvious qualifiers for an invitation—the IOC, national Olympic committees and so on—but fully 2000 guests were invited and in attendance from 8:00 pm. The venue was the Staatsoper—the State Opera House—a prominent neo-Palladian 19th century masterpiece, set back slightly from Unter den Linden, which had been decommissioned for the evening.

Tens of footmen dressed in pink velvet and powdered wigs marked the entrance steps, holding glass lanterns high. Göring, as Prime Minister of Prussia, hosted the evening. Decked out in a huge and splendid white uniform and loaded down with decorations, he—and his "tall, handsome and seemingly almost naked" wife Emmy—greeted guests in the foyer.[9] Women had come in their evening dress finery, with competitive jewellery; the men wore white tie and decorations. After hors d'oeuvres and drinks, the guests moved into the opera theatre itself.

The auditorium had been renovated extensively in 1928, but for this gala event it had been reworked by an architect imported specially from Munich. Just for this evening, the auditorium had been made into one great festival hall by removing the seats and raising the floor to the stage level. This new grand arena was now decorated in "Pompeiian" red with special white velvet festoons. No end of expense had been incurred. Certainly it was the intent of the Government that this should be the "culminating feature" in a series of Olympic festivities.[10]

Nazi dignitaries sat in the boxes—Göbbels, his wife, and his top guest Crown Prince Umberto of Italy, to the right of the proscenium, and the host, Prime Minister Göring, and Frau Göring, to the right. Crown Prince Gustaf Adolf of Sweden and King Boris III of Bulgaria—King Boris seemed to show up everywhere during the Games—were seated with Göring. The guests themselves sat at round tables in the new level arena. "[The] food was good, and the wine flowed";[11] dinner was accompanied by the voices of opera singers on high, and after dinner members of the opera house's corps de ballet danced among the tables.

"Berlin has not known anything like it since the war," wrote Channon; they were showing the world "the grandeur, the permanency and the respectability of the new regime."[12]

7 AUGUST
FRIDAY

The SS *Usaramo* arrived in Spanish waters from Hamburg last night. It stood at anchor, and then early this morning docked in Cadiz.[1] A specially commissioned train now took the complement of more than one hundred Germans the 125 km to Seville. There, the pilots and other officers were accommodated in the excellent Hotel Cristina. Ground personnel were quartered in local pensions, and the mechanics were sent straight to the Tablada airfield on the outskirts of the city.

Flushed with the success of the "Convoy of Victory" and with his first troops safely in Peninsular Spain, Franco left Morocco behind. He flew to Seville this morning to establish his new headquarters.

In Berlin, the weather had lifted. "Today is beautiful," reported Evelyn de Lacy, "just like spring. The sun is shining, all flowers in bloom and a gentle breeze comes over green fields …"[2]

Over the next two days the Decathlon would decide who was the best all round track and field athlete in the world. Of the ten events, four would be on the track (100 m, 400 m, 1500 m and 110 m hurdles) and six in the field (long jump, high jump, pole vault, discus, shot put and javelin).

In fact, one of the favourites would not be competing: the former world record holder, 27-year-old Hans Sievert from Germany had injured himself during the summer. Germany had a fine replacement, in Erwin Huber. Huber was a "veteran" of the Olympics, having competed in the 1928 Amsterdam Games (where, as a 21-year-old novice, he came 15th), and again in LA (where he came fourth). Huber was the epitome of Aryan manhood, so much so that it is he who is used by Riefenstahl in the opening sequences of *Olympia*: the ancient Discobolus statue of Myron transmogrifies into a human Adonis, the near-naked human Huber.

And there were three Americans—Glenn Morris, the favourite and new world record holder, Bob Clark and Jack Parker. They were all young, although Morris, at 24, was the eldest. He had been a star athlete at Colorado State College and had continued his athletic career after graduation while working as a car salesman. At first Morris thought his best chance for the Olympics was the 400 meter hurdles, but gradually he and his coaches came to see that he was in fact a superb all rounder. Although he was the world record holder, having broken Sievert's record at the US Olympic trials, Morris had actually only ever completed three decathlons.

Bob Clark was 23, a recent graduate of University of California at Berkeley, and was a crack long jumper. Jack Parker was the baby, not yet 21, a farm boy from Iowa; he had been snapped up by talent scouts and was attending Sacramento State College. There must be an optimal build for decathletes, because all three Americans weighed 185 lbs (84 kg) and were 188 or 187 cm tall.

Two events would be contested this morning and three after lunch; the same sequence would apply tomorrow. Scoring for the decathlon is based on existing world records for each event; thus, if one equalled the world record for 100 metres (10.3s) one would be awarded 1000 points. Less than the world's best and you get fewer points according to a predetermined scale.

First up, as always was the 100 metres. There were twenty-eight competitors and, as ever at these Games, the ten heats started promptly on time at 9:00 am. The Germans were keen fans of *zehnkampf*, as they called the decathlon. Glenn Morris was well known to them by reputation and he had featured on the cover of the Olympic Program. The stands were filling fast; this despite the fact that the early stages of the

7 August

decathlon would be the only events in the Stadium until 4:00 pm this afternoon.

Clark won the 5th heat in 10.9s; this gained him 872 points. He was not happy with his time and reported to his colleagues that the track was slow. Morris beat Huber in the ninth heat, recording 11.1s (814 points) and 11.5s (710 points) respectively. Since Morris had run 10.7 at the US trials, he too concluded that the track was slow. It did not augur well for any records.

Clark nailed the long jump when it started at 11:00 am. He had come sixth in the individual event three days earlier—just 20 cm behind Lutz Long—and today he jumped only 6 cm less than that effort. He earned 977 points to Morris' 796; as a result Clark had a handy lead after two events.

The Honour Loge may have been empty but the fans were lapping it up. Everyone seemed to be taking down the scores of their favourites. There would now be plenty of time for them to compare notes, because everyone—athletes and audience alike—had a couple of hours to kill before the start of the afternoon's events, the first of which would be the decathlon's shot put which was not due until 3:00 pm.

Quiepo did not like the idea of Franco taking over. He enjoyed being top dog in Seville, and contemptuously declined to meet Franco on his arrival in the city. It was an unwise decision as it could only alienate Franco further, thereby hurting any chance he might have of promotion under Franco's inevitable rise. Either Quiepo didn't understand where he stood in the emerging hierarchy or he didn't care. Perhaps he (correctly) assumed that Franco would be moving on towards Madrid in due course, and that this would leave Seville to his care and exploitation.

For the moment, though, their rivalry was of secondary importance. The first priorities for Franco were to assemble his troops and put together a general staff. Seville was the largest city under rebel control. and the bridgehead from which he could command the occupation of the rest of the Peninsula. It was the landing point of the *puente aéreo* ("airbridge") for the Army of Africa—as noted, the first troop airlift in military history—and would now also be receiving troops who could arrive by sea.

Quiepo was headquartered in the adequate and very comfortable Hotel Simon. Franco showed him who was boss by moving into a sumptuous palace offered to him by the Marquesa de Yanduri. Franco was no camp bed general like Napoleon; this future caudillo preferred the comforts of a luxurious palace when he was on campaign. Consistent with these preferences, Franco enjoyed the exquisite rooms and gardens of the Palacio Yanduri for the next three weeks.

Franco could not compete with Quiepo in the ashtray, vase, mug and mirror departments—at least not for the moment—but he did insist that his huge portrait should hang alongside those of Quiepo on all major buildings in Andalusia. These were put up over the coming days.

On the resumption of the decathlon competition at 3:00 pm, Glenn Morris won the shot put. Between events he was all action, constantly practising what needed to be done.[3] Everyone was transfixed by his energy, not least Leni Riefenstahl, who seemed to have a camera constantly trained on the handsome American. Some thought the attention was not just one way, and that he was playing up to her too.

The weather stayed warm and bright. A Dutchman, Reindert Brasser, jumped a superb 1.90 metres in the high jump to win that event—from Morris and several others who cleared 1.85 metres. Morris was now closing in on Bob Clark.

The final event for this day was the 400 metres, held at 5:45 pm. There were five heats, the two fastest being the third—won by Clark in 50.0s—and the fifth, won by Morris in 49.4s. As a result, Clark was

> still ahead at the end of the first day of competition—by 2 points: Clark had earned 4194 points, Morris 4192, Parker 3888, Brasser 3873, with Huber only 10th on 3593.

FDR was still at Hyde Park. He had quite a busy schedule, meeting various government officials and political associates who had come to his family home, and he would not return to Washington DC until the coming Sunday night. No one could be in any doubt, though, that he was in touch with all affairs of state.

At noon, US East coast time, Roosevelt gave a press conference in his study at Hyde Park. It was the usual affable stuff, although very early on he received this question:

Mr President, the newspapers are full, as you are well aware, of stories of war and rumours of war, and we are wondering whether you would have anything to say at all in relation to America's foreign policy in relation to what's going on over there.

He understood the somewhat tortured question, and answered:

I don't think so. There is no news.

But there was. The French had been very busy. Their ambassadors had visited their counterparts in Rome and Berlin, promoting the idea of a European non-intervention treaty. "Non-intervention" has a specific meaning within the sophistry of diplomacy; for a civil war it boils down to an absence of interference by a state in the internal affairs of another state—with or without the consent of the state where the war is taking place.

The British had already publicly committed themselves to

non-intervention. The agreement in contemplation was to be one among European powers. Three days ago, on Tuesday 4 August, the French discussed their proposal with US Secretary of State Cordell Hull, explaining their wish for a parallel embargo from the USA[4]. The State department was divided between "realists" (as they would have it) and "idealists" (as the "realists" saw them); the vigorous debate was ultimately resolved in favour of the realists such that, two days ago, Cordell Hull let it be known, unofficially and without any public announcement, that the US Government favoured non-intervention.[5]

Today, the French ambassadors in Berlin and Rome presented to the German and Italian governments a draft declaration of non-intervention that had already been accepted by Britain, Belgium, Holland, Czechoslovakia, Poland, and Russia.[6] And in Washington DC, Acting Secretary of State William Phillips announced that the US would "scrupulously refrain from any interference whatsoever in the unfortunate Spanish situation."[7]

The Spanish could fight it out among themselves. No matter what treaties or agreements had been solemnly sworn before the 18 July army rebellion, no matter what common decency itself would demand, the popularly-elected Spanish Government was soon to be alone; if the French non-intervention proposal was agreed and implemented (and supported by the United States), the Spanish Government would not be able to use its own funds to buy arms from any major power.

8 AUGUST
SATURDAY

For most sports followers the track and field events are the centrepiece of the Olympics. But there is of course more. Wrestling would continue through the weekend; it had already been going for a week. The pentathlon had been completed. Fencing—where there are any number of variations: foil, sabre, épée; individual and team—had been running through the week and would continue for another. Field hockey, too, would run throughout the Games fortnight. The weightlifting was over. Both football (soccer) and yachting had been underway since the start of the week, and they too would have another week to reach their conclusions.

The polo would reach its climax today with the final between Argentina (of course) and Great Britain; the Argies prevailed 9–0. Shooting would finish today. Handball had started in the last couple of days, as had cycling and canoeing; these events would be completed over the weekend.

All the athletics events would be completed by tomorrow, with the marathon and the relays. For the coming week basketball, gymnastics, boxing and equestrian events would be decided. For many, though, the feature events of the second week would be in the swimming pool and on the rowing course. The rowing would not start for another few days but the swimming started today—at 9:00 am in cold overcast weather, with the heats of the men's 100 m.

> In the Olympic Stadium, today's second and final day of the decathlon would comprise the 110 m hurdles at 10:00 am and the discus at 11:00 am; then, at 3:00 pm the decathletes would compete in the pole vault, at 4:30 pm in the javelin, and finally at 5:30 pm in the 1500 m run. As always, completing the ten events would be incredibly demanding.
>
> Being a hurdler, Glenn Morris could be expected to do well in the hurdles. He did. His 14.9s in the last heat was well ahead of Clark's 15.7. At last this put him in the lead, 126 points ahead of Clark, with four events to come.
>
> The discus put Morris further ahead. He now lead Bob Clark by 236 points and Jack Parker by 439. The apollonian Huber was well behind, although his best events were still to come.

While the Germans and Italians were delivering their new aircraft to Franco's rebels on a daily basis, getting planes and war materiel into Spain from France was a haphazard affair. By today about seventy aircraft had found their way to the Republican government, with perhaps forty or fifty of these coming from the French Government.[1] Others, private individuals such as André Malraux, delivered the other twenty or so. None were of the latest design and capabilities.

Now, today, the new Spanish Ambassador to France signed a contract with a private group "for the purchase in France and other countries of all products".[2] The commission of 7.5% showed his government's desperate need.

But then, keen to ingratiate himself with the British and reversing the decision of 2 August, Prime Minister Blum today suspended further arms sales to Spain as well as sales of any civilian aircraft.[3] As a result, six ammunition trucks destined to supply the defenders of the Basque country against Mola's rebels were immediately stopped at the border.[4]

Much has been made about the exclusion of two Jewish athletes from the successful US 4 x 100 m men's relay team.

The US Olympic trials had been held at Randall's Island, New York over the weekend of 11/12 July 1936. (They could not be held in the South because black athletes might not be allowed to compete.) On the Saturday, the result of the 100 m was:

1. Jesse Owens
2. Ralph Metcalfe
3. Frank Wykoff
4. Foy Draper
5. Marty Glickman
6. Sam Stoller
7. Mack Robinson

This meant that Owens, Metcalfe and Wykoff would be entered for the individual event. And, because the US had recently adopted the strange practice of not selecting its fastest runners to form its relay team, the next four finishers—Draper, Glickman, Stoller and Robinson—could expect to form it. Glickman and Stoller were Jews. They were not the only Jews on the US team of course—Sam Balter, won a gold medal in the basketball, Adolph Kiefer won gold in the swimming—but they were the only Jews on the track squad.

On 27 July, the *LA Times* reported head track coach Lawson Robertson saying in Berlin that he will "postpone final selection of the relay teams…until 4 August, in order to pick the best conditioned combinations." Things developed. Mack Robinson's name disappeared from the likely list. Then, four days ago, on 4 August, Robertson announced that Owens would not be on the team because he had done "just about enough in one Olympics."[5] The *New York Times* speculated that Glickman, Stoller and Foy Draper were "certainties on the basis of trials the last few days" and that Frank Wykoff would probably be the fourth man.

At 9:00 am this morning, Glickman and Stoller—along with Owens,

> Metcalfe, Draper and Wykoff—were summoned by Robertson and the other track coach, Dean Cromwell, to a bedroom in the Olympic Village. Sitting on the beds and standing where there was space, the athletes were told that the team would be Owens, Metcalfe, Wykoff and Draper—the four fastest at the trials.[6]
>
> So at 3:00 pm this afternoon, the US team won the first heat in 40.0s, equalling the world and Olympic record. The second and third heats were won in 41.3s and 41.4s. Unless they dropped the baton, everyone knew the US would win the final tomorrow. There is little doubt that they could also win with Glickman and Stoller rather than the chosen team; Glickman—but not Stoller—claimed the two runners had been excluded on the basis of anti-Semitism.[7]

While the heats of the relays got underway at 3:00 pm, so did the decathlon's pole vault. Morris was not confident in the event. Clark could be expected to do well and Huber better. Although rivals, there was good camaraderie among the Americans—and indeed between them and Huber. The Americans were taken to spreading a towel on the ground where they rested between and during events.

Everyone had noticed Leni Riefenstahl's interest in Glenn Morris. Her cameras hovered over him at every opportunity. Before the start of the pole vault, as all three Americans were companionably resting, Riefenstahl asked Erwin Huber to introduce her to Morris. "With a towel over his head, Glenn Morris lay relaxing on the grass, gathering strength for the next event," recalled Riefenstahl. She was wearing her trademark baggy white trousers, matching jacket and a headband. She took a handkerchief and brushed back Morris' hair, as if to arrange it for the camera. Then she did it again. Leni later wrote: "When Huber presented Morris to me, and we looked at one another, we both seemed transfixed. It was an incredible moment and I have never experienced anything like it."⁸

Riefenstahl's recollection may well be fanciful. Certainly the handkerchief on the hair was real; this is recorded in photographs. Many had already noticed, however, that there seemed to be something going on between them well before this time. Riefenstahl was certainly a fantasist. It is no fantasy, though, to record that they developed a physical relationship at some stage during the Games and that it continued for a few weeks afterwards.⁹

Notwithstanding Leni's attentions, the athletes completed the pole vault satisfactorily. Huber was the best of the competitors, Clark next and Parker and Morris behind them. Morris' lead over Clark was reduced to 153 points. In the javelin, which followed at 4:30 pm, although Huber and Parker bested Morris, Morris was now 217 points ahead of Clark and 401 ahead of Parker. The final event, the 1500 m run would determine the winner.

The 1500 m was due to commence at 5:30 pm. A gymnastics demonstration delayed the start of the three heats. Morris would be in the last with Huber. It was getting colder and the light was fading when the first heat got going. Parker came last in the first heat with a time of 5:07.8; it was not a good result and put his prospective bronze medal in danger from Huber. Clark did well in the second heat—clocking 4:44.4, thereby securing a near certain second place. Morris would be the winner if he ran a safe race.

Safe was not in Morris' psyche. He would need to run sixteen seconds better than his personal best to break the world record. And, with Hitler in the stands, cheering on this American Aryan, Morris set out to do just that. It was not a pretty sight. Morris was a sprinter and a hurdler, and very good at everything else, but he did not like this last gruelling event. With all the determination he could muster, however, and grimacing in a tortuous run towards the end, he did it. He finished his heat first, in 4:33.2—and a new world record for the decathlon.

The British Embassy had booked this evening for its party. It was not a success.

The Ambassador, 60-year-old Sir Eric Phipps, was a dour and earnest man with little sympathy for the German (and more particularly, Nazi) cause of undoing the agreements that had wound up the First World War. The head of the Foreign Office was 58-year-old Sir Robert Vansittart. Phipps was moustachioed in the British military style; Vansittart was tall and elegant. They were married to sisters. Both men were fluent in French and German. They also shared a common native tongue—that dialect of English spoken by Old Etonians. Vansittart had resisted Ribbentrop's official invitation to the Olympics; he had come to Berlin in a private capacity to support Phipps, on what he later described as a "busman's holiday"[10].

Vansittart was a leader of the anti-appeasement forces in Britain. Accordingly, the Germans took every opportunity available to influence and impress him. Hitler himself would entertain the Vansittarts in the coming days. Tonight, however, it was the Vansittarts and Eric Phipps who were in the vanguard because Lady Phipps was unwell. Lady Vansittart stood in for her sister as official hostess.

The embassy was the venue for the reception. It has always been on the Wilhelmstrasse, near Unter den Linden and around the corner from the Adlon Hotel. Every German leader turned up tonight, save Hitler. There were more than 1000 guests, which was too many. Göbbels reported that "it turned into a massive reception. A thousand people and a thousand idiotic conversations."[11] Channon agreed: "The Embassy reception was boring, crowded and inelegant."[12]

During the evening Göbbels thought he was making some progress with Vansittart: Vansittart had "opened up a lot" since they had met a few days earlier. Back then Göbbels had written "He is a gentleman who is too highly-strung, and whilst clever, he is not energetic."[13] This assessment was a miscalculation and misunderstanding; Vansittart was in fact impatient, analytical and forceful. Writing up his earlier conversation, Göbbels went on: "I work on him for an hour ... He gains a new understanding of the issues … [and] understands the German position. He leaves impressed. I have turned on a light inside him."

While Vansittart found Göbbels "the deepest of them all" and "found much charm in him—a limping, eloquent, slip of a Jacobin," and even that he was "a man with whom one might do business", there is no reason to believe he had resiled from his initial assessment of Hitler's Germany, made more than three years ago on 6 May 1933:

The present regime in Germany will, on present form, loose off another European war just as soon as it feels strong enough … we are considering very crude people, who have very few ideas in their noodles but brute force and militarism.

9 AUGUST
SUNDAY

The weather had turned for the better in Berlin. "The sun shines brightly and everything is gay and beautiful," wrote Evelyn de Lacy.[1] The temperature would be 22° or 23° throughout the day. The only people unhappy with the new warm day, prospectively hot as it was, were the marathoners—who would start in the feature event this afternoon.

> In Seville the sun was baking. At the airport, the German contingent started to put together the six single-seater Heinkel fighter aircraft they had brought by sea from Hamburg.[2] The workshop at the Tablada airfield was rudimentary and poorly equipped. Nevertheless, the specialist ground personnel and the six pilots set out to get the job done—"breaking open the crates, raising aircraft fuselages, attaching wings, fixing bracing struts".
>
> There was some friction between the Spaniards and the Germans at Tablada. The Germans were set on their work at hand. The Spaniards who, to be fair, had been subjected to constant attack from Republican aircraft were annoying the Germans; they seemed to be standing around, monitoring the assembly progress, and asking unnecessary questions about the aircrafts' capabilities. Despite the intense heat and the annoying Spaniards, the Germans would complete the assembly of the first Heinkel by tomorrow night.
>
> A week ago, on his initial visit to Seville, Franco had authorised the first of the rebel columns to move north towards Mérida. There were now five such self-contained columns on the march—each compris-

ing about 1500 men, both legionnaires and Regulares. They moved in lorries that had been requisitioned in Seville, carried 75 mm artillery and were provided air cover by the Italian Savoia-Marchettis (piloted by Italians, now in Spanish Legion uniforms) and the German Junkers (piloted by Luftwaffe officers).[3]

Franco's troops made great progress. He had put his bloodthirsty colleague, Yagüe, in overall command. Yagüe was a terrifying sight: "Chunky, tall with a leonine mane [of grey hair] and the look of a hunting animal—a short-sighted one—he was an intelligent man but led, at times blinded, by his temper. A bully and a rebellious braggart, he often suffered cyclical depressions … which made his actions inconsistent and incoherent."[4]

The rebel troops made progress because of their superior arms, training, tactics—and terror. Local Republican militias were no match for the Moroccans. The loyalists' arms were shotguns, old blunderbusses, knives and hatchets. The Moors were experienced in sweeping across open plains and scrub; moreover, the rebels had local command of the air. When they came to a city their lorries would halt. Mussolini and Hitler's aircraft would then bomb it. Next came a call over their German-supplied loudhailers that all doors and windows were to be left open and a white flag hung from every house.

Invariably what followed was a slaughter, whether there was a surrender or not. Anyone who could be associated with a defence militia was shot. No prisoners were taken. Anyone who had been an official of the Republican government, elected or otherwise, was likely to be executed. The Moors—los Moros—had been the savages in Spanish folklore ever since the Reconquista, and now they proved that reputation valid. As each town fell, and the advance's speed and success could be reasonably compared to Hitler's coming 1940 blitzkrieg, the occupying troops raped working-class women and looted houses.[5]

By this evening Yagüe's troops were on the outskirts of Mérida, 200 kms north of Seville and a third of the way to Madrid. It had only been a week since the first of their number had set out from Seville.

A diverse group of fifty-six men came into the Olympic Stadium at about 2:30 pm. They were members of that strange freemasonry, the marathon runner. Typically small in stature, they were hard men who could endure great pain and psychological stress for the 42 kilometres of the marathon. The crowd's favourite was Juan-Carlos Zabala from Argentina. He had won in Los Angeles and, although he had not run a marathon since, had been training hard in Berlin for months. Training in the Grünewald forest, which would form part of the course, he had recently become a familiar and popular figure—to aficionados and the general public alike—with his white teeth and signature floppy linen hat.

The three Finns would be a threat; everyone expected them to use their classic tactics, running as a team, swapping the lead amongst themselves, swooping around a competitor, speeding up and slowing down in unison—and driving their competition to distraction. There were others too, but the competitor most feared was the Japanese runner, Kitei Son. He had been reported to have run some amazing times in Japan.

The Germans knew the race as *der klassische lauf*—the classic race. For many it was the most important event of the Games. It has been estimated that as many as one million spectators lined the route today; we do know 160,000 people came in to Berlin by train today, and it seems likely that most were in the city for *der klassische lauf*.

Hitler and his entourage arrived at the Stadium just before the start.

At 3:00 pm the competitors set off to the sound of blaring trumpets. Many were wearing hats to protect themselves from the bright sun. Kitei Son sported a peculiar running shoe which separated his big toe from the others. Zabala led them out of the Stadium.

More than forty-two kilometres stood between the runners and the finish line. They would meander through the Grünewald forest, much of the time running beside the bucolic Havel river. Then they would cut over to the dead straight Avus raceway whose hard concrete surface would run for about 10 km to the raceway's finish at Avus Nord near the Deutschland Hall (where the weightlifting had been completed, the wrestling would finish this afternoon and the boxing would kick off tomorrow). This was the half way point, and the runners would then retrace their steps.

In the Stadium, three relay races were next on the agenda, the men's and women's 4 x 100 m and the men's 4 x 400 m. First up was the men's 4 x 100 m.

The Germans had a team in the race and could reasonably expect a medal, but it was the Americans that the crowd had come to see—most importantly their "Yessay Oh-vens". The familiar chant rose throughout the arena. Owens did not disappoint. "I never missed any of his races," wrote Evelyn de Lacy, and in a sentiment shared by many, she said "he ran with such beauty and grace, he was beautiful to watch."[6] Owens ran the first leg, giving Ralph Metcalfe a four metre lead; Metcalfe stormed so fast down the back straight that his changeover to Foy Draper, with the US team now seven metres in front, was only just inside the handover boundary; Draper and the final runner Frank Wykoff maintained that lead to the finish. They ran 39.8s, a new world record.

Italy came second in 41.1 and Germany third in 41.2. The US team's world record would stand for twenty years until another US foursome bettered it at the 1956 Melbourne Olympics. Ironically it was Metcalfe's first and only Olympic Gold; he was the second best runner in the world in 1936, had held the world record for several years previously and in the period 1932–1935 had been the best runner in the world. It says something about the US practice of not selecting their fastest runners for relays, albeit abandoned on this occasion and for every Olympics since, that for Frank Wykoff this was his third Olympic Gold—all in relays.

The women's 4 x 100 m relay followed. Germany was expected to win having broken the world record in the heats. Leading into the final changeover, however, and with a good lead, they fumbled the baton and dropped it. Hitler had been on his feet anticipating a great victory for his team. He sat down, twice slapped his knee with his gloves and said something to Göbbels beside him and to the person behind. The eight meter lead would almost certainly have been too much for Helen Stephens to catch up—but that was now academic; Stephens stormed over the line for a US win, albeit 0.5s slower than the Germans' new world record. Hitler called the German girls to his box, where he comforted them and, in the words of his propaganda mouthpiece *Der Angriff* "must have eased their sorrow and pain."[7]

A rare victory for the British was to follow. Their 4 x 400 m relay team beat the Americans. It was one of those classic 1600 m relay races where the lead changed several times. Harold Abrahams, the British 100 m champion from the 1924 Paris Games, described Godfrey Rampling's leg, in which he received the baton behind the US runner and finished five yards ahead as "the most glorious heaven-sent quarter-mile I have ever seen."[8] Runner-up in the individual event Arthur Brown took that final changeover in the lead and increased it to win well, a full 2.0s ahead of the USA. Perhaps it is churlish to note that, consistent with the practice abandoned for the 4 x 100 m half an hour earlier, the US did not include in their team their two best runners—Archie Williams and Jimmy Lu Valle, both black, who had finished first and third respectively in the individual event. Archie Williams has since said their omission "was nothing but racism."[9]

While all this excitement was taking place in the Stadium, periodical reports were coming through from the marathon. Zabala had set off at a cracking pace. The Finns were holding back. Kitei Son established a rapport—he spoke some English—with a tall 34-year-old English miner, Ernest Harper. They ran together; Son later said "Harper kept telling me not to worry about Zabala but to let him run himself out. So we paid no attention to him or any other runners and set our own pace."[10]

As they came out of the Grünewald on to the Avus, at 12 km, Zabala was 90 seconds ahead. He was still ahead at the half way point, at the turn. Son increased the pace and Harper came with him. By 28 km they drew level with Zabala—and at 31 km Zabala was broken; he took off his hat to dip his black curly hair in the cooling water station, stumbled, and retired from the race, exhausted.

It was now just the little Japanese, showing no emotion whatsoever, competing head-to-head with the taller Harper. Son started to get away from Harper at about 33 km, where he led by twenty-five seconds. It was cruel that the runners now had to pass the cooling waters of the Havel, where spectators were quenching their thirsts with steins of beer.

By the time he reached the Stadium, Kitei Son was nearly two minutes ahead. He sprinted the last 100 metres, abandoning the rolling bandy-legged gait he had shown for 42 kilometres—and finished in a new world record of 2:29.19. Harper followed; he had fought off a fast finish from the other Japanese runner.

The Japanese in the crowd, easily the best dressed and always among the most excitable at these Games, went wild. "We've been preparing for this victory for twenty-four years," one said. "Now we can hardly believe we have won. It's a big moment for Japan."[11] Göbbels, perhaps in anticipation of the imminent Axis agreement with Japan, was equally thrilled: "A Japanese wins the marathon!" he wrote in his diary, "What a nation, what a race!"[12]

Except Son was not Japanese. He was Korean and his correct name was Sohn Kee-chung. Not yet 24, he was a keen Korean nationalist; he hated the Japanese occupation of his land which had been a fact all his life—since 1910, two years before he was born. Accordingly, in Berlin, he had ostentatiously signed all his autographs with his correct Korean name—and always appended a small map of Korea.

He graciously thanked Harper for his help: "Much credit for my victory must go to Mr Harper of England," he told journalists, "Please say Mr Harper is a very fine man for telling me about Zabala."[13]

When they received their medallions in the award ceremony, both Sohn and his fellow "Japanese"—in fact fellow Korean Nam Sung-yong—hung their heads as the Japanese anthem was played. Sohn held the young oak tree given to winners close to his chest, thereby covering the Japanese flag on his uniform. He later told reporters that he bowed his head in silent "shame and outrage" over Japan's occupation of Korea.[14] A Seoul newspaper *Dong-a Ilbo*, published a training photo of the two Koreans with the headline "Korean Victory in Berlin"—and air-brushed out the Japanese rising sun flag from Sohn and his colleague's track suits. Ten members of the newspaper's staff were immediately arrested and the newspaper was closed for nine months.[15] Japan banned Sohn Kee-chung for life, and he never ran again.

In Paris, in the wealthy commune of St Cloud, about 10 km from the city centre, nearly 100,00 people assembled for a peace rally. Prime Minister Blum was careful not to mention Spain, yet he was cheered.[16] A captivating speaker, he spoke of peace and the importance of using the League of Nations in the promotion of peace. (This, notwithstanding the League's failure to invoke its own protocols and the Treaty of Locarno when Hitler had reclaimed the Rhineland in March and its unwillingness to support Ethiopia against Mussolini.) Other speakers had not avoided the subject of Spain, and the crowd wanted their views known. They cried out "Viva l'Éspagne!" and, in response to the recent cabinet decision, "Des avions pour l'Éspagne!"[17].

Overhead an airman traced out "PAIX" in the smoking entrails of his aeroplane's exhaust. There was no peace in Spain, of course and the display reeked of irony.[18]

It would become an actuality that for Blum, Spain's holocaust and the Popular Front's inadequate responses to Spain's plight would haunt him for the rest of his life. It has been said that the policy of non-intervention "broke the heart" of his government.[19] It is well documented that Léon Blum had wanted to resign when he could not get his cabinet to support the Spanish government; he was only persuaded to stay by colleagues who argued that he was needed to hold the government together and by the Spanish ambassador who had hope that he—and perhaps only he—could reverse the decisions.

And while Blum was speaking at St Cloud, the counsellor of the German Embassy in London was officially informing the British Foreign Office that "no war materials had been sent from Germany and none would be."[20] Of course it's entirely likely that he did not know of the German planes and airman already in Spain. In contrast and contradiction, however, at the same time as this official misinformation was being conveyed to the British, his colleague, the German consul in Seville, was asking the Wilhelmstrasse to ensure that the German military contingent in Seville did not appear in public in their uniforms.

10 AUGUST
MONDAY

It was no secret to the thousands of villagers who had come to the small Dalmatian port of Sibenik this morning that the man travelling as the Duke of Lancaster was in fact the King of England. Nor indeed were they in any doubt that one of his guests, Mrs Simpson, was his lover. Yet it would have been news to the vast majority of Britons and the King's subjects throughout the Empire that he had an established lady friend.

The Times reported it thus:[1]

THE KING ON HOLIDAY

ON BOARD THE NAHLIN

Belgrade, 10 August

King Edward, who is travelling as Duke of Lancaster, arrived at Shibenik, where the steam yacht Nahlin awaited him at 8.45 this morning. His Majesty was met by Commander C.L. Firth, of H.M. Destroyer Grafton, commanding the naval escort in attendance on the yacht. The Yugoslav commander in Shibenik, the mayor, and other dignitaries were also at the station, while the shores of the harbour were thronged with people, who loudly saluted his Majesty.

A salute of 101 guns was fired by ships of the Yugoslav Navy to mark the arrival of the King. After having taken breakfast in the train, his Majesty went aboard the yacht, which put out to sea at 11.15 am.

10 August

The King's aide, Jack Aird, had followed the instructions given him by Edward in Calais just two weeks ago to the letter. The King wanted a big comfortable yacht in tip top condition—and he got it. This was the steam yacht *Nahlin*, a huge vessel—250 feet at the waterline—which had every amenity, a maximum speed of eighteen knots and a cruising speed of fifteen. It was owned by the widowed and enormously rich Lady Yule. She hated publicity, and her captain and crew were habitually sworn to secrecy. (The captain, when asked, was given to reply: "We have come from nowhere and are going nowhere".)

The *Nahlin* had sailed from Portsmouth ten days earlier with a crew of fifty-eight. Progressing down the Atlantic coast it had encountered "two sinister looking shapes stealing inshore" at Cape Trafalgar; they were destroyers, probably the Spanish loyal navy, which they lost before entering the contested Straits of Gibraltar.[2]

Once it got into the Adriatic the *Nahlin* was joined by a Royal Navy destroyer, HMS *Glowworm* from the Mediterranean fleet. The *Glowworm* provided an escort for the rest of the journey to Sibenik. This morning at 5:30 am they met up with another destroyer, HMS *Grafton*, which was already moored at the Sibenik quay. Over the coming month the two destroyers would provide protection for the sovereign, emergency contact and deliver his official papers.

Two days ago the King had been driven from Fort Belvedere to a private aerodrome at "Heath Row", whence a large plane from the King's Flight took him across the Channel to Calais.[3] In Paris he was joined by Wallis and some of the cruise party; here they boarded the Basle express, which took them through France and Switzerland, then on by other trains to Austria (where Edward and Wallis incautiously strolled together along the Salzburg train platform) and into the Balkans. Although lent the Yugoslav Prince Regent's own Pullman carriage for the final leg of their trip, this did not satisfy the King: "I subjected myself to an indescribable night journey by train into Yugoslavia with a clanking and jolting such as I had never before experienced."[4]

It seems likely that the King would want to show his future wife just what she could expect as his consort. He would have wanted her to enjoy and see the fruits of his office—the luxury, the fawning attention, and the cheering crowds. Surely the twenty thousand odd "peasants in bright costumes [swarming] around them, shouting glad greetings" at Sibenik provided a good start. And there, on this bright sunny day was the *Nahlin*—gleaming white, huge and stately, with its distinctive red and orange funnel. The 101 gun salute would also have impressed her.

A party of eleven—seven guests, including Wallis and Edward, plus their four maids and valets presented themselves to the *Nahlin* at about 10:00 am. They had much baggage which the King's valet, Crisp, set about organising with the assistance of Naval bluejackets from the destroyers.

The tone of the voyage was set by "Poots" Butler, wife of the King's former equerry Major Sir Humphrey Butler MC and herself a former girlfriend of the King, who immediately asked: "Could I have a martini, Crisp?"[5] Henceforth ten o'clock became known as Martini Time.

The *Nahlin* had everything. (Wallis had vetoed the King's first suggestion that they might borrow the Duke of Westminster's splendid yacht *Cutty Sark* on the basis that it was insufficiently comfortable.[6]) There was a dance floor, a library, gymnasium, sitting rooms and a large dining room, decks and all the comforts of a country house. The décor was not to Jack Aird's taste, albeit that he had procured the vessel; he thought it was "furnished rather like a Calais whore-shop."

Eight grand staterooms each had their own en-suite bathroom; two master's suites were in the bow—these were assigned to Edward and Wallis—and six suites were in the aft.

The books were taken out of the library ("not wanted on voyage"), the shelving removed and the space converted into a "state room" where Edward could attend to official business and where he could be with Wallis in private.[7]

> *The special charm of a large yacht,*

wrote Edward,

> [is] *that it enables presumably responsible people to combine … a beachcomber's milder irresponsibilities with the comforts of the Waldorf-Astoria Towers.*

Edward and Wallis' party sailed north through the dazzling string of islands off Zadar, into the Gulf of Kvarner. The King was a clotheshorse. He had come off the train in Sibenik dressed as an English gentleman: "lounge suit, bareheaded, a white flower in the lapel of his jacket, the bright sunshine glinting on the light brown hair."[8] No sooner had the vessel left Sibenik, however, than Edward was out of his suit and into shorts. He was on holiday.

Over the coming weeks the cruise's guest list would change from time to time. Guests usually came for a week or so as the *Nahlin* sailed up and down the Dalmatian coast, past Albania to Corfu, through the Corinth Canal, to Athens and the islands of the Saronic Gulf, through the Dardanelles to Istanbul; from there the remaining party came home by train via Belgrade and Vienna. Apart from the King's aides, who were a picture of rectitude, the guests naturally comprised the King and Wallis' cronies.

Hugh Sefton and Helen Fitzgerald had travelled with the King and Wallis by train from Paris and boarded the *Nahlin* at Sibenik. They were long-standing friends of Edward. Sefton— Hugh William Osbert Molyneux, the 7th and last Earl Sefton— not yet forty, was a landowner and what would be called in his circle a "sportsman" or "sports enthusiast", by which is meant he ran racehorses and was active in "field sports" such as fox hunting and shooting. His companion was Helen Fitzgerald, a Canadian-born society beauty of some note; her sister was married to Lord Beaverbrook, and she was estranged from her much older husband of nearly thirteen years—Hon Evelyn Fitzgerald CB, a 62-year-old stockbroker.

They were joined by Humphrey and Gwendolyn ("Poots") Butler, who too were key members of the King's circle. Together with the King's equerry, Jack Aird, they made up the initial party.[9] Another aide, Alan "Tommy" Lascelles, who was not on the trip, reproachfully wrote: "Outwardly [they were] as respectable as boatload of archdeacons ... but the fact remains that the two chief passengers (the King and the Earl) were cohabiting with other men's wives."[10]

By 2:30 pm, after a leisurely cruise at about 13 knots, the King's party arrived at Port Tajir in the bay of Tilashnitza—way up in northern Dalmatia near Istria.[11] Dress was to be very casual during the day. More often than not Edward sat around bare chested. The men followed the King's casual lead, albeit rarely shirtless. The "ladies"—after all, that's what they were—wore casual outfits during the day. Wallis' ensembles were the height of resort wear fashion. Helen Fitzgerald was a chic dresser too; to some she appeared to ape Wallis as her fashion clone.

What Mrs Fitzgerald couldn't clone was Wallis' exquisite diamond bracelet of Latin crosses. A gift from Edward, it had been created by Cartier the previous year and each cross represented a significant event in the couple's life together. (There were four or five such crosses in 1936.) Wallis wore the bracelet throughout the Nahlin cruise, even while swimming, and she would wear it again on their wedding day.[12]

In the evening the King was likely to kit himself out in a white naval uniform and the women would dress up accordingly. Dinner was invariably taken in the yacht's dining room, after which the party would move to the softly lighted "guest deck" where a huge somewhat racy jigsaw featuring a bare-breasted mermaid was set out. After dinner games were likely to go on into the early hours. Protocol required everyone to stay up until the King retired, often about 2:00 am.

In the United States, FDR had left Hyde Park by the Presidential train for Washington DC at midnight, i.e. 5:00 am in Europe. By 8:45 am Washington time he was at the White House. His meetings today included one with Assistant Secretary of State Sumner Welles at noon US time; Welles was an "idealist" or supporter of the Spanish Government.

Over the previous days, since Cordell Hull's non-announcement on Friday that the US favoured non-intervention, the President had been faced with a practical issue on the Spanish question. The Glenn L Martin Company of Baltimore wanted to sell eight bombers to the Spanish Government and had asked the State Department to give it some guidance.[13] Acting Secretary of State William Phillips drafted a response which simply reiterated the United States' general position of non-intervention. Roosevelt wanted it to be stronger, then he had second thoughts, before finally agreeing to a letter sent today which said that the proposed sale of bombers would contravene "the spirit of the Government's policy" of a "moral embargo" on arms to Spain.[14]

It was a carefully worded statement and it meant that the US would join Britain and France in embargoing any assistance to the Spanish Government, even arms-length commercial transactions. It was a critical decision, one which would have an important impact on Spain's future—and a decision the President would come to deeply regret.

One might have thought that, with their events at an end, track and field athletes might be allowed to enjoy the second week of the Games as spectators. Not so for the US track stars.

Yesterday at 4:30 pm, in the changing rooms immediately after the victory ceremony for the relay, Jesse Owens was fronted by the Secretary-Treasurer of the American Athletic Union, Daniel Ferris; he told Jesse that he was expected to run in a demonstration meet in Cologne the next day, today.[15] By the time he got back to the Village, Ralph Metcalfe told Jesse to quickly grab his spikes and a bag—because they had to catch a train to Cologne.

There were to be two US troupes and they would appear at different meets in various European cities over the coming week or so. This was not a complete surprise, Brundage had made casual reference to such a plan on the boat over. The athletes knew the US Olympic Committee needed money and that their appearances would help in that. Even so, the haste and lack of consultation surprised and disappointed them. They had had no time to enjoy Berlin and their successes; there would be no nights on the town. Moreover, they had no opportunity to rest or lap up and enjoy the comforts of the Olympic Village, to say farewell to their teammates and new-found friends. They were being put to work.

So at 6:00 pm this evening Jesse and Ralph Metcalfe and others, having arrived in Cologne late last night, did their bit. The 35,000 seat Cologne stadium was full to capacity, and the AAU would get 15% of this evening's gate because Jesse was there; it would have been 10% without him.

Everyone was tired, physically and emotionally. Owens himself had lost weight. Nevertheless, in the 100 m run he and Metcalfe were splendid. Jesse was leading by two metres at 80 metres when he slowed down to let his pal win; Metcalfe equalled the world record of 10.3s. It's possible that by that friendly act Jesse Owens let pass another world record.

But the athletes were expected to do more. Although he was scheduled to catch a plane to Prague tomorrow at 8:30 am, Jesse was required to attend a reception in Cologne this evening. He did just that, dutifully fulfilling the expectations of the AAU—

and fawning admirers kept the exhausted hero up until midnight.

Back in Berlin, those athletes who were given some time off could enjoy a propaganda evening at the Stadium. It was organised by the Strength Through Joy movement and included a brilliant military display. Evelyn de Lacy, who was resting between her two swimming events, described it thus:[16]

After dinner we went over to the stadium, where there was a youth festival on. The stadium was packed out and we eventually got seats in the distinguished visitors part. First there was an address by their leader and the performance was called 'strength through joy'. Then in came the soldiers with spades, men with accordions and great logs of wood. They sang songs and gave a flag display and the men with logs threw them around as if they were sticks. Then they marched out. Then came soldiers with lighted flames making it look like a stream of tiny stars pouring into the arena. Then all the surrounding countries poured onto the ground and gave folk dances and songs. Finished up by a band of eight hundred men. Oh, a marvellous night. Very tired, so home to bed.

11 AUGUST
TUESDAY

When the Roman Emperor Diocletian decided to retire in AD305 he had travelled the western world and had anywhere in the Roman Empire to choose as the place to see out his days. He chose to build a palace—really a fortress—on a small town first colonised by the Greeks at what we now know as the city of Split. It was the heart of ancient Illyria on the Dalmatian coast, today's Croatia. The natural beauty of the region is self-evident, even with modern development: islands float off the coast and nestle in bays, the sea is clear and bright and blue and still, low lying mountains flow down to the sea, in its hidden coves traces of Roman, Venetian and Ottoman history appear among the quaint old towns; vineyards, cherry orchards and olive trees populate the hillsides.

The Duke of Lancaster may have been on a private holiday, but all the world knew he was in the Adriatic sailing along the Dalmatian coast—somewhere. The King's party was hardly anonymous. The grandest private yacht in the world and two RN destroyers could not disappear, and for the duration of the cruise the *Nahlin* flew the flag of the Admiral of the Royal Yacht Squadron.

Lady Diana Cooper and her husband Duff, a Conservative MP and Minister for War, were to join Edward's party in a few days and were on another vessel coming down the coast from Venice; Lady Diana wrote:

The other passengers were madly excited about the King's

11 August

journey, all eyes scanning horizons. The Captain saw three ships long before any of us did. They were sailing obliquely ahead of us and were soon out of sight again. The destroyers Grafton and Glowworm look a bit too militant, you know, but stirring to English hearts.[1]

The King very much enjoyed the deferral to his rank and the respect (and affection) he received as sovereign. He expected his privileges and was good at playing the public role of king. He did not enjoy the administrative duties that came with his new role, though. And he felt entitled to enjoy his privacy. But it was a fine line, and Edward often overstepped it.

No matter how discrete Lady Yule's crew had been trained to be, this cruise was not comparable to a country weekend at some grand house where long-standing retainers habitually turned a blind eye to the comings and goings of the upper classes. As noted, there were fifty-eight crew on the *Nahlin*; in addition, both destroyers had a complement of about 140 officers and crew. So Edward's private cruise was in fact a flotilla of vessels housing hundreds of participants—with the King and his party at its centre.

One guest noted that the staterooms and their disposition were so arranged as to invite "a certain amount of unsanctioned pairing."[2] The sleeping arrangements cannot have been lost on the *Nahlin's* crew and must have become known to the naval crew and officers. And, as former PM Ramsay Macdonald wisely opined: "The people of this country do not mind fornication but they loathe adultery."[3]

Jesse Owens' plane was delayed this morning at Cologne airport. He was scheduled to be meeting a number of other athletes, including Glenn Cunningham, in Prague. Such was the lack of support given by

> Brundage and his AAU brigade to their champions, however, Owens had no spending money and had to rely on a fellow traveller to buy him a sandwich and a glass of milk. It must have occurred to him that had he been back in the Village—like Glenn Morris, for example—he could have enjoyed a full range of delicious fare in the US team's dining room.
>
> Arriving in Prague at 4:30 pm, Jesse went straight to the stadium. As usual he was the star—albeit that his efforts today were only of his own schoolboy standards. Over the three hours from 6:00 pm, he ran a heat and then won the final of the 100 m, and he won the long jump. The crowd was thrilled to see him, Jesse was his courteous self, and Avery Brundage and the American badgers got their pound of flesh.

Late this afternoon at 4:30 pm, in this quiet northern corner of Dalmatia, still up in the Bay of Kvarner, the *Nahlin* pulled into the small town of Rab on the remote island of the same name. Some photographs show the King's party aboard a motor boat arriving at what they dubbed "Paradise Island"; one widely-circulated photograph has Wallis intimately resting her hand on Edward's wrist and the sovereign turning solicitously to hear what Wallis is saying. It caused an outrage when seen in Britain; the intimacy of the scene was bad enough, but one does not touch the sovereign's person!

The King was recognized—"Cheerio!" they cried out, as crowds did everywhere, that being their idea of the quintessential British greeting—and his party was soon surrounded by a scrum: "We went ashore for sightseeing, " wrote the King, "[where] we were overwhelmed by a crowd of German and Yugoslav tourists. All but mobbed, we fled back to the Nahlin."[4]

As Edward later wrote: "The American press had by this time begun to comment on Wallis' presence among my party and was following my yachting holiday with more attention than

11 August

I considered necessary."⁵ The King's cruise had in fact aroused an "epidemic of curiosity"⁶ along the Dalmatian coast, even into its most undeveloped enclaves like Rab—and overseas. That curiosity was about to be intensified, because Edward and Wallis' recreational plans for tomorrow would forever put the island of Rab on the tourist map of Croatia.

Back on the *Nahlin*, the party would have soon found comfort in a cocktail or two. Typically, they toyed with the huge jigsaw featuring the well-endowed mermaid, practised their golf swings, drank martinis and whisky sours, danced and listened to the wireless. Wallis' preferred tipple was whisky and water. Edward came to find a local substitute for the then fashionable cocktail, the Cloverleaf (gin, grenadine, mint, egg white and lemon). It comprised:

two jiggers of gin

Dalmatian chartreuse

Dalmatian champagne

dash of lime juice

a teaspoonful of sugar

a strip of lemon peel, and

one olive.

It was a great success on the languorous cruise. Perhaps you had to be there, as they say, because when translated to London with real chartreuse and champagne—and beyond the aura of the King and the romance of Illyria—most imbibers found it quite the worst cocktail they had ever tasted.

No one seemed to have a kind word for Joachim von Ribbentrop. Tonight, as the Ambassador-designate to the United Kingdom, he and Frau von Ribbentrop gave a "supper"—as it was described in the Games' official Report—in the garden of their smart villa in the fashionable suburb of Dahlem.[7] Supper was for six hundred.

Von Ribbentrop was forty-three. He and his wife Annelies had been married for sixteen years and, since 1932, both had been enthusiastic members of the Nazi Party. He had married well: Anna Henkell belonged to the Weisbaden family that owned the huge Henkell wine business, and they were immensely wealthy. The villa to which their guests would arrive this evening, 7–9 Lenzeallee, Dahlem—had been a wedding gift from her parents. Von Ribbentrop had learnt French and English in a peripatetic childhood and in his early career; he had served on the Eastern Front in the First World War (winning an Iron Cross) and had became a successful wine salesman for his wife's company. When in 1925 an aunt adopted him, he was entitled to add the aristocratic "von" to his name.

Hitler liked him, presumably because von Ribbentrop supported the Führer absolutely. Von Ribbentrop rabbited Hitler's ideas and was totally loyal to his leader. Most found von Ribbentrop arrogant, icy and unjustifiably haughty. The old-timer Nazis really disliked him: "Von Ribbentrop bought his name, he married his money, and he swindled his way into office," as Göbbels would have it. Nevertheless, he was now near the top echelon of the Nazi hierarchy.

The supper was ostensibly for the IOC, the National Olympic Committees and "a number of guests of honour." In fact it was for the von Ribbentrops and about the von Ribbentrops. Von Ribbentrop had convinced himself that there was a prospect of some inchoate Anglo-German alliance; thus, all the people von Ribbentrop had deemed important when he had come to England in May and June were invited. So too top Nazis Göring, Hess and Himmler and their wives, the top diplomats—Phipps, Vansittart and France's François-Poncet, among them—the Prinz von Lichtenstein and countless other Eastern European aristocrats, even the Hitler-besotted Mitford sister Unity.[8]

Chips Channon reported that the villa "had been transformed into a scene of revelry."[9] The guests were presented with a thick pamphlet listing them and the seating plan. A vast marquee was erected to cover the tennis court and the lawn in their substantial garden; von Ribbentrop remembered that his wife had "turned our garden into a veritable little fairground … at night it all looked like fairyland: the beautiful lawn, of which we had always been proud, the swimming pool covered with water lilies, the gorgeous rhododendrons, and the festively laid tables. My wife had surpassed herself."[10]

After dinner a violinist entertained the guests and there was "some very good singing". Dancing followed about midnight; the dance floor was the tennis court covered with an unfortunate form of matting which constrained the steps of the more ambitious and exuberant dancers'. Hermann Göring impressed Chips Channon, who wrote: "he really is a most disarming man." François-Poncet was impressed with the fine French wine: "Champagne flowed like water; it was the best Pommery, a brand for which [von Ribbentrop] had long been salesman and agent."[11]

The Channons stayed until three in the morning: "I enjoyed myself quite wildly," wrote Chips, "The lovely evening, the fantastic collection of notabilities, the strangeness of the situation, the excellence of the Ambassador's (or more correctly Frau von Ribbentrop's) champagne, all went somewhat to my head." Von Ribbentrop noted that the Vansittarts stayed the longest: "they danced a lot and seemed very happy—was this a good omen?"

It wasn't. Ambassador Phipps found the future Ambassador to the Court of St James "a lightweight (I place him near the bottom of the handicap), irritating, ignorant and boundlessly conceited."[12] Vansittart himself found von Ribbentrop "shallow, self-seeking and not really friendly."

12 AUGUST
WEDNESDAY

At dawn a firing squad executed rebel General Manuel Goded. He was 53, and was despatched in a courtyard of Barcelona's Montjuïc castle. Goded's surrender to the Barcelona militias on 19 July had hurt the rebel cause; worse still—in the rebels' eyes—was his radio broadcast that evening in which he suggested the putschists should lay down their arms. In these circumstances it is unlikely that his reputation could ever have been restored among the coup leaders. Yet he was an original co-conspirator with Mola, and the truth is that—until the Barcelona surrender—he was one of the few generals who could have challenged Franco for the leadership of the uprising.

It had been less than four weeks since Goded's surrender. He can have been in no real doubt as to his fate. He had led the rebellion in Majorca and then flown to Barcelona to take charge of the uprising there; on arrival in Barcelona, he had attempted to "arrest" colleagues who had remained loyal to the Republic. By any measure that is treason. At first he had been imprisoned at Montjuïc. After a few days he was transferred to the comparative comfort of the *Uruguay* in Barcelona harbour. It was on board that naval vessel, yesterday, that the rebel general faced a court martial. Charged with treason, he was found guilty and sentenced to death.

> J. Cooper, a crewman on board the Nahlin, wrote in his diary:
> *I should explain that many of the places visited are small bays snug-*

gled amongst the hills and mountains and generally approached by a tortuous channel…It is obvious that these anchorages have been chosen to ensure that the Royal party shall have, as far as possible, the privacy and quietness essential to the enjoyment of their holiday.[1]

Kandarola Bay is just such an enclave. Located on the southern side of the wooded Franj peninsular opposite the town of Rab, it is a small sheltered cove with shallow turquoise water leading up to a pebble beach where large rocks populate the foreshore. It is the picture-perfect private bay. For some years prior to this day it had been known as a place where a discrete skinny dip could be taken without disturbance. The story is that Edward and Wallis did just that today. Their naked romp is celebrated by naturalists as the historic event that forever liberated the Dalmatian coast for the hoards of naked German and Scandinavian tourists that now flock there. And, in recognition of the royal imprimatur, Kandarola Bay is now often known as English Bay.

The celebrants are almost certainly wrong. Not that Edward and Wallis swam naked together on the Dalmatian coast. No, that is probably true—but the naturalists have almost certainly got the wrong site. An inspection of the *Nahlin*'s log and Cooper's diary shows that the King's party never got near Kandarola Bay. The *Nahlin* left the town of Rab at 6:00 am today and sailed 45 miles north through the Planinski channel. After four hours they reached the Novigradsco sea: "[a] beautiful anchorage, a natural basin surrounded by huge towering mountains," according to Cooper's diary. He went on:

> *It is arranged here that the party go picnicking. I am in the crew required to work the two launches and, towing a dinghy, our little flotilla sets off. We have a provender for the day. We leave the basin by a narrow channel, flanked on either side by towering cliffs. Following this for about 2 miles we emerge into a large lake, I should say about 10 miles long by 5 in breadth.*
>
> *… a search is made for a convenient landing. A search is made at a point where there are some shrubs and small trees to provide a little shade. The party are transported by means of a dinghy, the luncheon*

baskets landed and off we go some little distance ... Some few hours are pleasantly passed.[2]

Wherever the site or sites of their frolics, the King of England swimming naked with another man's wife is of note—and overtly sexual.

Before the King left on holiday, Buckingham palace had requested Fleet Street to respect his privacy, as was usual. This was agreed to without dissent. As a result no major news source in the UK (or the Empire) made any reference to Wallis' presence on the cruise. Even so, *The Times* hinted at something—when it preached that a sovereign "should be invested with a certain detachment and dignity."[3] Of course they knew about Wallis. It's most unlikely, though, that they knew about the skinny dipping.

Edward was not a big man. He was just 5'5" or 1.65 m tall, and slight. Thelma Furness affectionately called him the "little man". When she was dumped she let it be known that he was little in all respects[4]. There must be some doubt as to the veracity of this innuendo. Given that there is no record of his being modest or awkward when naked with others—to the contrary—it seems entirely likely that the King was equipped with standard issue wedding tackle and had nothing to be ashamed of.[5]

There can be no legitimate doubt as to Edward's sexual orientation either. Whatever hope doe-eyed photographs of the young Prince with "buttercup yellow" hair might have given homosexual admirers, such portraits were par for the course in those days; what's more, that's the way he actually looked. And the camp uniform imposed upon him for his 1911 investiture as the Prince of Wales was most certainly not his choice. Once he belatedly lost his virginity—at the age of twenty-two[6]—Edward became a keen heterosexual swordsman. He picked up with Mrs Dudley Ward as soon as he could, and that was undoubtedly a physical relationship. As was his long-standing association with her successor Thelma Furness.

Not that the Prince was entirely faithful to his mistresses. His extensive tours of the Empire post 1919 were punctuated with opportunistic sexual encounters. In 1927 it all became too much for his censorial aide

> Tommy Lascelles, who wrote: "[Edward] in his unbridled pursuit of wine and women, and of whatever selfish whim occupied him at the moment, was going rapidly to the devil and would soon become no fit wearer of the Crown."[7]
>
> Once he acquired Fort Belvedere in 1929, though, Edward seemed to settle down into a kind of privileged domesticity. High points were the nightclubs in the West End, of course, his weekends at the Fort and with friends at their stately homes. It was a form of self-indulgent domesticity, albeit non-marital, mixed with the high life of high society. When Wallis succeeded Thelma Furness in 1934, Edward's life continued with business as usual. Speculation surrounded Wallis' particular hold on him, of course, the most salacious rumour suggesting that Wallis had learnt "oriental" sexual techniques[8] during her stay in China and that these had cured Edward of his alleged tendency towards premature ejaculation.

Adolf Hitler was the centre of attention throughout the Games. He was not the star, in the sense that Jesse Owens or Glenn Morris or Germany's own Gotthard Handrick were stars, but everyone, *everyone*, wanted to know where he was and whether he would he be attending this or that event or another.

Of course there were many Germans, perhaps most, who opposed Hitler—but he was a constant source of fascination. Crowds gathered outside the Chancellery on the Wilhelmstrasse. "No one is allowed to walk in front of it," reported Chips Channon, "and sentries motion one to cross to the other side of the street; there is always a crowd waiting in hope of seeing the Führer. The guards, picked SS men, wear black breeches, unlike the Storm Troopers, who wear brown."[9]

The opening ceremony had taken place eleven days ago. For many—with the track and field events decided—the Games were winding down. "Berlin is still very crowded," wrote Chips

Channon, "and everyone goes to the Olympic Games all day: we pretend to, and don't, as they are very boring, except when Hitler arrives."[10] Berlin was *en fête* and, for the visiting dignitaries, the evenings were filled with gala social events. Tonight Chips—"us well-dressed 'elegants'"—went to dinner at the old Bristol hotel on Unter den Linden. There is little doubt he would have preferred to have been invited to Hitler's reception.

Eleanor Holm was one of the guests at Hitler's soirée tonight.[11] She was invited to all the parties. Her work for the Hearst newspapers was largely done by ghost writers. Eleanor's former team mates had sent her a box of handkerchiefs with a note saying "Keep your chin up"—and that she was determined to do.

The Vansittarts' fortnight in Berlin would finish tomorrow, and this evening they were the principal guests for the Führer's reception. It was the first dinner Hitler had hosted in the new State Dining Room complex (the *Festsaal mit Wintergarten*) that had been constructed in the expanded Old Reich Chancellery over the previous year.

As the one hundred and sixty guests were ushered into an anteroom they were announced by a black liveried and knee-breeched major domo. Several commented on the contrast between the dull khaki uniforms of most German guests and the smart evening dress with decorations of the foreigners, not least the kit sported by the tall handsome guest of honour, Vansittart. Hitler himself wore evening dress, albeit—according to Lady Vansittart—ill-fitting, with the tailcoat slipping off his shoulders.[12]

The guests moved into dinner and were placed in a horseshoe, Hitler at the centre with Lady Vansittart to his right. The room was brilliant; it featured dark red marble pillars, supplemented for the evening with tall gold candlesticks on the dining table, a blue and gold ceiling in a mosaic of squares, a grand Gobelin tapestry at one end with the other end leading out to the marvellous new conservatory which was gradually lit up as the gala evening progressed. Guests included several members of the Anglo-German Fellowship; one such, Lord Rennel, on his return from the Games, applauded the Führer's "good taste" in a letter to *The Times*: "that remarkable man of vision … had shown his perceptive feeling in the remodelling of his official residence."[13]

In his earlier private meeting with Hitler Vansittart had got nowhere in seeking the Führer's support for a new five power conference; he was proposing a "new Locarno" to establish a basis for maintaining peace among the European powers. On that occasion all Hitler would talk about, though, was the war in Spain.[14] This evening Hitler took a different tack. He charmed Lady Vansittart with his manners: on introduction he gave a formal kiss on her hand, and he took her arm when he escorted her to the table. There he ordered spinach and a poached egg; he took no wine. Lady Vansittart showed her breeding by ordering the same simple fare and drinking water. They struggled to make conversation as neither had much knowledge of the other's language; even so, Hitler found an opportunity to laugh loudly at her wit—so loudly, it was a guffaw, most everyone looked up to see what was going on. Lady Vansittart noticed how extraordinarily smooth his skin was.[15] And then, after dinner, to her surprise, he escorted her to his study for a private conversation.

Sitting knee to knee, with only an interpreter present, Hitler picked up the peace theme that was ubiquitous (and so obviously false) in several Nazi propaganda pieces at the Games. Reich War Minister Field Marshall von Blomberg, a guest at the dinner, had been widely quoted:

> *This Europe of ours is too small for a war, but it is large enough to contain a field of combat upon which the youth of the world will win a decisive battle for the cause of peace. To cooperate in the solution of this task is the sincere and sacred wish of the entire German nation.*[16]

Baldur von Schirach, the Hitler Youth leader, decked out in his quasi-military uniform, had carried a similar message at the Youth Rally in the Lustgarten when the Olympic Torch arrived on 1 August: "We serve no warlike aims but those of peace. My comrades, consider the Olympic Games a safeguard of peace."[17]

And now, Hitler put it to Lady Vansittart: "You saw all the young men in the stadium today. Do you think I'd let them die in battle?" Lady Vansittart responded that it was always the youngest who die in wars. And with that they returned together to the dining room.

The German overtures had not moved Vansittart himself either. He summarised his thoughts on their fortnight in Berlin:

These tense, intense people ... will want to do something with this stored energy ... These people are the most formidable proposition that has ever been formulated; they are in strict training now, not for the Olympic Games, but for breaking some other and emphatically unsporting records, and perhaps the world as well.[18]

Fort Belvedere, c.1936

SY *Nahlin*

Edward and Wallis in leisure mode on the *Nahlin*

Edward in naval rig, dressed for dinner on the *Nahlin*; mermaid jigsaw in foreground

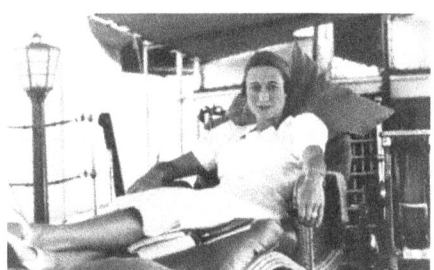

Wallis wearing her bracelet of Latin crosses on board the *Nahlin*

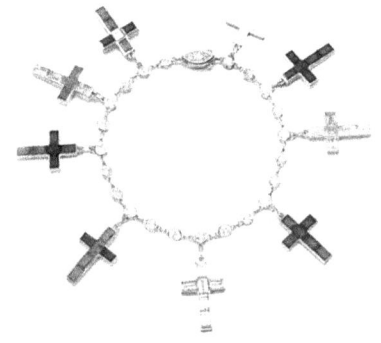

Wallis' bracelet

Edward wearing matching chain

Edward's chain

The King's party were mobbed whenever they stepped ashore from the *Nahlin*

Swimming and boating on the *Nahlin* cruise

Wedding Day,
3 June 1937

August 1953: The Duke and
Duchess of Windsor on holiday
in Rapallo, Italy

13 AUGUST
THURSDAY

While Hitler's guests from last night could enjoy the comfort of the clean sheets in the Adlon or the Kaiserhof, Jesse Owens and Larry Snyder had spent a cold night on mattresses in an empty hanger at the south-west London airport of Croydon. They had arrived just before midnight after a bumpy flight by small plane from the German city of Bochum. Jesse and Snyder, his coach and mentor from Ohio State, had met up yesterday in Bochum. Jesse had come from Prague and Snyder, who had been with the second athletic troupe in Dresden and Hamburg, had been sent to Bochum to look after him there.

Yesterday's Bochum exhibition would be the third day in a row that Jesse had been expected to perform, each time in a different city. He had not eaten for twenty-four hours when he first had a decent meal at 4:00 pm. By 6:00 pm he had lost the long jump to an unknown. And then at 6:00 pm he ran the 100 m in 10.3—equalling his world record! The locals (and the AAU) had certainly got their money's worth.

Snyder and Owens' well-earned sleep in that dank Croydon airport hanger was interrupted by the arrival this morning of thirteen colleagues. Glenn Cunningham, Ralph Metcalfe, Jimmy LuValle and Dave Albritton were among a cohort who had travelled overnight from Hamburg; their trip had taken eighteen hours, including a "nightmare trawl" across a stormy English Channel.[1]

Everyone was tired, cold and broke. Stale sandwiches was

breakfast this morning for these heroes of the Berlin Olympics. Today and tomorrow, however, they would be put up in a central London hotel and, at last, they hoped to be able to play tourist. Two days hence, on the Saturday afternoon, they would be putting on an exhibition—"USA v British Empire"—at the White City, and there was hope that they could go home next week.

Mérida fell to Yagüe's forces two days ago, on 11 August. Consistent with the rebel aim of "[smashing] the cruel rabble with a great hammer blow that would paralyse them,"[2] and also to create a wave of fear as Franco's troops advanced on what they proudly called the March of Death, the usual reprisals followed the town's capture. Erstwhile defenders were shot; no prisoners were taken. Women were sexually humiliated. The Spanish Foreign Legion and the Regulares mutilated casualties—cutting off ears, sexual organs and heads. To identify leftists, a liberal Republican physician, Dr Temprano, was walked through the streets by one of Yagüe's men. Those who greeted the doctor were arrested; Yagüe's man then shot the doctor.[3]

Today, Quiepo ingenuously told the London *Daily Mail* correspondent that:

Except in the heat of battle or in the capture by assault of a position, no men are shot down without being given a hearing and a fair trial in accordance with the rule of procedure of our military courts.

It was a deliberate lie. Even so, it was working. The widespread destruction and desecration of churches by the Republic's supporters, the humiliation and murder of priests and other religious, together with the execution and humiliation of the seemingly rich and those deemed rightist sympathisers—all this had been given extensive coverage by the foreign press. But the first casualty of war is truth. Those atrocities undertaken in the Republican zone were largely reported accurately. That is, the reports were true. What they lacked was balance and completeness.

The Republic had no central policy that promoted the violence and killing; it had simply lost control of law and order, and it would take months to get it back. On the other hand, until now, nearly four weeks into the uprising and with Yagüe's March of Death well under way, the rebels' own atrocities had been left largely unreported—yet they formed an essential part of the generals' centralised policy of oppression and elimination.

But there was more. It was not simply in the reporting of the behaviour of the warring parties that "history stopped in 1936", as George Orwell put it:

> *In Spain, for the first time, I saw newspaper reports which did not bear any relation to the facts ... I saw great battles reported where there had been no fighting, and complete silence where hundreds of men had been killed ... I saw newspapers in London retelling these lies ... I saw, in fact, history being written not in terms of what happened but of what ought to have happened ...*[4]

Franco had met with Yagüe the night before Mérida fell. With Mérida now in rebel hands the territory held by Franco's Army of the South was united with that of Mola's Army of the North. The rebels now held a contiguous stretch of territory from Navarre in the north east, sweeping west (and south of the Basque country and the big industrial cities of Bilbao and Santander, which were still in the Republic's hands) through the conservative cities of Burgos, Valladolid, Segovia and Salamanca north of Madrid, over to the north west and down to Seville and much of Andalucía. Madrid was the obvious next point of attack.

Badajoz was the capital of the region with a population of about 40,000. Bordering Portugal, on the Guadiana river, it is 60 km south west of Mérida. It held no strategic importance in the war but it was still in Republican hands, an inconvenient redoubt on the Portuguese border. Franco instructed Yagüe to take it. Accordingly, this afternoon, a rebel plane flew over the city dropping thousands of leaflets. The leaflets carried a message from Franco:

> *Your resistance will be pointless and the punishment that you will receive will be proportionate. If you want to avoid useless bloodshed, capture the ringleaders and hand them over to our forces ... Our triumph is guaranteed and, to save Spain, we will destroy any obstacles in our way. It is still time to mend your ways: tomorrow it will be too late.*[5]

In fact there had been little violence against rightists in Badajoz. The Guardia Civil unsuccessfully tried to ferment an uprising in support of the rebels a week ago, on 6 August, and from 7 August the city had been subjected to rebel bombings. Yet the Right's casualties were limited to ten reprisal killings—including two Guards and a man who had been on a rooftop signalling to the rebel planes. The local bishop, who had been evicted from his palace, had been allowed to continue to take the Holy Sacrament; he had even been provided with a bodyguard.

In the circumstances, the holocaust that was about to be visited on the people of Badajoz was entirely disproportionate.

While Jesse Owens and his colleagues were on the road earning money for the AAU, the second week of the Games was still underway. Swimming was at its heart, and at least three stars emerged from the events—17-year-old Dutch girl Rie Mastenbroek, US diver Dorothy Poynton-Hill and the Japanese men's team.

The Japanese men were a collective galaxy of stars because they were clones of each other: apart from their individual facial characteristics, they all looked alike and acted the same. Each swimmer was tallish, slim with light musculature, dark-haired, intensely competitive and impeccably polite.

They kept to themselves, but there were cultural issues. Pat Norton, an

Australian swimmer reported: "One day we were at the training pool when the Japanese male swimmers arrived to train. They immediately began to undress at the poolside—which made us three modest Australian girls let out a yelp and dive for cover! We were only just getting used to men wearing topless costumes. When this was explained to the Japanese trainers they undressed in the rooms provided."[6]

At Los Angeles, the USA had seen the glory days of Johnny Weissmüller and his colleagues washed away. The Japanese "boys"—they averaged only seventeen years of age in LA—had dominated the swimming, winning five of the six men's events. In Berlin, the Japanese dominance continued: they won four of the events—and when they didn't win they came second and or third. Again, you could barely tell one swimmer from another.

Dorothy Poynton-Hill was something else. Today she won the high dive. And every move—on and off the diving board, in the air, in the water—was worth watching. Barely twenty-one she was already a "veteran"; she had won silver in 1928 and today's win from the platform was a reprise of her 1932 triumph in Los Angeles. But winning was just part of the show. Poynton-Hill came from Pasadena in California and comported herself like a movie star. She wore high heeled shoes on the pool deck; she wore water-proof lipstick, she plucked her eyebrows and sported chic swimsuits: her smart checked number was only topped by the gold lamé one.

In *Olympia*, Leni Riefenstahl captures much of Poynton-Hill's magic and puts paid to the assertion that Riefenstahl was only prepared to celebrate male beauty. The diving sequence in the movie redefines motion, time and space. Dorothy Poynton-Hill is silhouetted against the sky, she moves in true time and is slowed down; she is seen from above and from below—in and through the air and the water.

The second final of the day was to start at 5:10 pm. Three days ago, on the Monday, Rie Mastenbroek had won the 100 m in a fabulous thrashing finale; "the finish she puts in is a marvel," wrote Evelyn de Lacy[7]. Mastenbroek had been the fastest in the heats and semis, but was behind in the final until her dramatic final effort; that win in itself had made her a star. But there was more. Judging by her form in the heats of the 400 m she was looking good to win that (as she did), and the Dutch girls were favourites to win the relay (as they did).

This afternoon, though, would be a challenge for the Dutch champion. It was the 100 m backstroke final—Eleanor Holm's event. Rie Mastenbroek held the world record but over the last couple of days her 16-year-old colleague Nida Senff had twice broken Holm's Olympic record, in the heats and a semi-final. The weather had gradually turned from bright to overcast during the day and it was now just 17.4°C. The water itself was always kept at a comfortable 70°F or 21°C, which was perfect for racing.

Eleanor Holm Jarrett was there.[8] Smartly turned out in a rose-coloured dress and a picture hat, she was making an almighty racket as the girls came out to the start. "Come on, Alice! C'mon!" she cried in support of the American hope, Alice Bridges.

Nida Senff took the lead from Mastenbroek. Disaster struck when Senff didn't touch the wall with her hand at the turn; so she did it again. "C'mon, Alice!" rang through the stands. "C'mon!" Rie looked the goods, though—until Senff, coming from behind, took her countrywoman on the line. Alice Bridges was a close fourth. It was the only event Rie Mastenbroek would lose; she finished the Games with three gold medals, and was the outstanding performer in the swimming events.

The times speak for themselves. Senff was outside Holm's old Olympic record in the final—but then she'd done two turns. Romantic a notion as it was, it's difficult to believe Eleanor Holm could have won "her" event—unless she'd given up the champagne and improved upon her best efforts. But who knows?

13 August

Hermann Göring was the second-most powerful man in Germany. At 43, his official titles were Reich Air Minister and Prime Minister of Prussia. A huge man, he was a voluptuary given to much extravagance and display. He had a galaxy of grand uniforms tailored to engulf his vast girth; they were varied according to daily preference, and invariably the chosen ensemble was enhanced with an array of medals and decorations. Göring was vulgar with a huge appetite, but many found him amusing. He may have seemed comic to some; in fact he was a most effective and steely right hand man for the Führer, to whom he was totally loyal. Tonight it was his opportunity to entertain.

The official Report of the Games, published in 1937, reported:[9]

On August 13th the Prime Minister, General Göring, and his wife, gave a particularly charming party at their home. Artistic hands had changed the garden into a festive place of rare beauty. The Prime Minister and his wife received their guests in front of a tea pavilion. A special feature of the evening well worth mentioning was a fine exhibition of artistic dancing performed by members of the State Opera Ballet. Joy and happiness among the guests rendered the evening an outstanding success.

The Göring "home" was in fact the huge Ministry of Aviation, built in 1935 and 1936. It stood on the corner of the Wilhelmstrasse and Leipzigerstrasse, within a block of the Reich Chancellery, and was one of the regime's prestige projects. The building was "far larger and more elaborately fitted out than the White House in Washington," according to US Ambassador William Dodd.[10] Chips Channon, who knew from personal experience about opulence, wrote that "the Görings live in theatrical magnificence."[11]

Eight hundred guests came to the "charming party." Search lights traced the sky from adjacent buildings, thereby ensuring that those who were not invited knew something important was taking place and those who were invited felt that they were part of that something important. Fairy lights lit up trees on the Wilhelmstrasse and Leipzigerstrasse. Göring and his attractive wife, former actress Emmy Sonnemann, did indeed greet the eight hundred in front of a tea pavilion; ensconced on a divan, Göring in a bright white uniform with gold braid and medals, the Görings were genial and attentive hosts.[12] (With Hitler a single man, Emmy Sonnemann had become the Nazi's de facto "first lady.)

Lights illuminated a giant lily pond, through which swans floated. As dinner concluded the corps de ballet from the Berlin Opera danced in the moonlight.[13] By this time, according to Channon, it was already agreed by the dazzled guests that the Görings had outdone the Ribbentrops. But there was more.

"The end of the garden was in darkness, and suddenly, with no warning, it was flood-lit and a procession of white horses, donkeys and peasants, appeared from nowhere and we were led into an especially built Luna Park," recorded Channon. Göbbels, who was in many ways a rival of Göring's and was planning his own event two days hence, did not enjoy the evening: "So many people," he wrote, "A little formal and cold."[14] Perhaps he left before the horses and donkeys arrived, because what Channon saw "was fantastic, roundabouts, cafes with beer and champagne, peasants dancing and 'schuhplattling,' vast women carrying pretzels and beer, a ship, a beerhouse, crowds of gay, laughing people, animals, a mixture of Luna Park and White Horse Inn. Old Heidelberg and the Trianon … Reinhardt could not have done it better. The music roared, the astonished guests wandered about."[15]

French Ambassador André François-Poncet reported Goring "rode the merry-go-round until he was breathless."[16] The party went until dawn. Acrobats appeared; clowns leapt to and fro. A German air ace even put on a stunt show overhead.

Eleanor Holm was there, fresh from seeing her Olympic title disappear that afternoon, and Emmy Göring adopted her: "My poor lamb! ... Just for a glass of champagne! My dear, you are so lovely. They should be drinking it out of your slipper ... We will help you forget those terrible prudes![17] The Chief Prude, Avery Brundage was also a guest. "... I was at all these important functions," Eleanor Holm told *Sports Illustrated*, "I would ignore him, like he wasn't even alive. I really think he hated the poor athletes."[18]

For Göring's stepson Thomas von Kantzow, the son of Göring's first wife, Eleanor was the highlight of the evening. Von Kantzow reported:

> *I went downstairs to the swimming pool. The underwater lights were on and there was a single girl slowly swimming up and down, occasionally pausing to fill a glass of Champagne from a magnum on the side. She was naked (and) ... very lovely ... I recognized her as the American swimmer Eleanor Holm. Then I noticed that I was not alone. In the shadows at the side of the pool, Hermann and Emmy were sitting together, his arm around her shoulder, watching the beautiful American sliding through the blue and gold water.*[19]

14 AUGUST
FRIDAY

It's strange how seemingly unimportant events can influence people's attitudes to one another. Last night, a simple impromptu gesture from Edward endeared him greatly with the crews on his flotilla.

While Göring was entertaining his fancy guests in Berlin, Edward's party was at Brgulse Bay, off the small and quiet Dalmatian town of Builje. Yesterday they had travelled the 44 miles from Planinski in a little more than four hours, arriving off Builje at about 2:30 pm. After dinner, as was often the case, Mr Fletcher, the King's piper (who was also a second valet), was playing the pipes on the main deck. This was always much appreciated by Edward's party—and indeed the crews of the *Nahlin* and *Grafton* and *Glowworm* ("the nanny boats"), many of whom were Scots.

Last night, however, they were in for a surprise. Mr Fletcher was joined on the pipes by the King. Everyone was thrilled when Edward tuned up his own pipes and led Mr Fletcher around the *Nahlin*; along the starboard alleyway, across the foredeck and down the port side they went—and around again. According to crewman Cooper, many a complimentary remark ensued:[1] "Aye, he's a piper alright," said one man who had played quite a lot himself. "Well, if he's no a Highlander, he ought to be, " said another Scot. Apparently the loyal Scots were still talking about it when they went to bed.

The happy crew drew anchor this morning at 6:00 am. The

14 August

Nahlin would be sailing for a little more than six hours today, 85 miles south to Trogir, in the bay near Split. His Majesty was not an early riser.[2] For breakfast he favoured grapefruit, tea, toast and marmalade—and he would take breakfast in his suite. Wallis rarely emerged before 11:00 am. Both were likely to miss Martini Time.

Edward was always keen to keep trim. To achieve this he exercised and missed the occasional meal. One of his favourite forms of exercise was rowing, and the cruise offered him the opportunity to do some. The *Nahlin*'s dinghies were rather heavy so a light dinghy was commandeered from one of the destroyers.[3] Edward's rowing outings on the dinghy would often include a circumnavigation of one or both of the destroyers, when he would jokingly cry out to the sailors: "I am reviewing the Fleet!" For some reason, his detectives felt obliged to take to the water too; the detectives would then engage some unfortunate rating to undertake the thankless and red-faced work of carrying them all a discrete distance behind the exercising sovereign.

Keen recreational rower that he was, Edward would have enjoyed the Olympic Regatta. Rowing was important at the Berlin Games. It was a traditional event, a gentleman's sport, and the Germans were good at it.

The rowers were not housed at the Olympic Village. Like the sailing competitors—all men—who competed at Kiel and had special accommodation there, the rowers had their own accommodation. It was in Köpenick, an ancient village in the south eastern corner of the metropolis, about 16 km from downtown Berlin. A complex of buildings, including a fine palace, had been commandeered for the duration of the Games; it provided comfortable accommodation for the rowers and canoeists, in most respects comparable[4] to the Olympic Village—but with the advantage of being within a small cobblestoned town that had handsome old buildings, bakeries and delicatessens, restaurants, even beer halls.

The rowing course itself was located a short distance away from Köpenick, down the Dahme river (a tributary of the Spree) on the relatively sheltered Langer See at Grünau—a corner of that wonderful complex of rivers, including the Spree and the Havel, which wind through the city of Berlin itself and to its south.

The course was a spectator's dream. Stands and enclosures could comfortably house a crowd of 30,000; there was even a temporary covered stand for 6,000 which actually sat in the river at the finish. Another feature was a special Olympic Flame which blazed brightly on top of the Müggelberg mountain about a mile away. A race caller let the crowd know via a public broadcast system just what was going on and where the teams were placed.

For the competitors the course was perfect. An enormous sign "ZIEL" meant and marked out the finish. Unless there was a headwind or a crosswind, in which case there were decidedly preferable lanes, it was a fair course. When there was a wind, those closest to the shore were protected while those out in the Langer See were not.

The regatta had started with heats and later repechages three days ago. Today was finals day. Unfortunately the weather was dreadful. There were seven events—pairs and fours with coxswain and without, single sculls, double sculls and the eights—all to be contested over 2000 m.

It had rained steadily throughout the morning. The temperature was a miserable 14° or 15°. Had the prospects for the German competitors not been so good—Germany had won no rowing events in LA—people would undoubtedly have stayed away. In the event, though, the stands were full and tens of thousands more lined the banks of the Langer See, packed shoulder to shoulder and protected from the elements by umbrellas and rainwear. Hitler had turned up too for what everyone knew was going to be a great day for Germany.

First up was the coxed fours at 2:30 pm. The Germans won. And they won the next four finals too: pairs without cox, single sculls, pairs with

14 August

cox, fours without cox and then double sculls. The Germans had won every race to this point. Disciplined, brilliantly fit athletes from the Third Reich had done their duty. Hitler and his Nazi entourage—almost all of the leadership were there—were rightly proud of their men, and they showed it. In the penultimate event, however, the British pair of Jack Beresford and Dick Southwood rather spoilt the German monopoly with a big win in the double skulls; the Germans were runners up.

And so to the last event—the Blue Riband event—the eights. There not being any true sprints in rowing—sprints are for canoeing (also known as kayaking)—the 2000 m race for eights is the event every team wants to win.

The USA was represented by the college eight from the University of Washington. It comprised eight raw-boned young men, the oldest being just twenty-one, plus a spunky little Jewish cox. A number of the crew came from quite humble circumstances and had scrimped and saved to stay in college.

To get to the Olympics the Washington crew had beaten all the established crews from the East Coast as well as their perennial rival, the University of California (Berkeley). In late 1935 their usually taciturn coach, Al Ulbrickson, had boldly opined that the Washington crew would win the Olympics. This was before he had even decided on his final crew in Seattle. It put enormous pressure on his final choices; they were the anointed ones from whom everything was expected. But it was a great motivator. Nothing was going to stop them winning.

The crews from the USA, Hungary and Switzerland won their heats and this put them straight into the final. Germany, Italy and Britain—the three teams the Washington crew most feared—had since come through the repechages to the final.

Meanwhile, a looming problem for the Americans was the health of their stroke—the key to the rhythm of any crew—who was ill. Put to bed for twenty-four hours, Don Hume was not expected to row.

The weather was awful. Rain was coming down hard. The Langer See was rough, dark and gloomy. (Not that bad weather per se was a problem for a crew that had trained through the Seattle winter.) And there was now a serious crosswind.

Ulbrickson put up a terrific protest when he learnt that, in conflict with the usual protocols whereby the best performers in the heats were given the best lanes, his team had been awarded the outside line, lane six, in the middle of the course. With the crosswind whipping up, this was a decided disadvantage.

The start was set for 6:00 pm. The Italians certainly won the fashion stakes; they all sported white bandanas to accompany their usual silky azure blue tops and dark blue shorts. The Germans were slick in all white. The Americans came decidedly last in the fashion department; they kitted themselves out in old sweatshirts and shorts—preferring, apparently, to keep their uniforms pristine for posterity. And for the first time the crew imposed their will on their coach, insisting that Don Hume take the stroke's seat (something he was prepared to do), no matter how ill Hume might be.

The British and the Americans missed the start. The Swiss took the lead, but with several of the crew having already competed in other finals could not maintain it. The Americans lagged behind. Italy and the Germans, protected from the wind until the last 400 metres, soon seemed to have the race won between them. Gradually the Americans rallied. With 200 metres to go they were in front. The Italians and the Germans came at them. There was nothing between the three boats. And then, finally, as they had done so often before, the University of Washington crew summoned up everything—this time rating higher than ever before—and just won. Italy was second, Germany third. After 2000 m there was less than a second separating the three placegetters.

Olympia records the event magnificently—from cameras on a dolly running along the course with the crews, and overhead from a zeppelin. All the drama and physicality and teamwork is on show, as is the desperate interchange between the competing coxes and their strokes— not least because, in the coming days, Leni Riefenstahl induced the men to recreate certain aspects of the race for her cameras.

14 August

In London this afternoon, as had seen the case in the days previous, Jesse Owens was receiving overtures to cash in on his notoriety by one means or another. The lucrative offers came from Eddie Cantor and Al Jolson and Joe Louis' promoter Mike Jacobs; each was for tens of thousands of dollars. Other proposals came from less reputable or at least less readily identifiable sources, but Jolson, Cantor and Jacobs were all parties to be taken seriously.

Jesse was now the toast of London town and, as everywhere, the centre of attention. Sadly there was nothing in it for him other than the adulation. He had had plenty of that over the last few weeks. The *New York Times* reported him saying: "Somebody's making money somewhere … and we can't even buy a souvenir of the trip." Opportunities beckoned at home. He was tired and had lost weight. And he wanted to go home.

This afternoon a person who Jesse and Larry Snyder had never met previously appeared—and gave them airline tickets for what they were told was to be an exhibition in Stockholm on Monday night. The man told them it was to be the start of a "week long Scandinavian tour."[5] It was all too much. Snyder gave back the tickets. "We're going home," he said.

Back in Berlin, Glenn Morris had not been tapped for either of the troupes that Brundage had required tour the four German cities and Prague this past week. For a track and field athlete the best advice may have been to go into hiding.[6] Morris had been happily resting up in the Village, taking in some of the remaining Olympic events and hanging out with Leni Riefenstahl.

This evening, after an enjoyable afternoon at the rowing regatta, he and his roommate returned to the Village. They found this notice was slipped under their door:

UNITED STATES MEN'S TRACK AND FIELD
MEETS—UPDATED

Mon, Aug 10—at Cologne (COMPLETED)

Mon, Aug 10—Dresden (COMPLETED)

Tue, Aug 11—at Hamburg (COMPLETED)

Tue, Aug 11—at Prague, Czechoslovakia (COMPLETED)

Wed, Aug 12—at Bochum (COMPLETED)

Sat, Aug 15—at London

Mon, Aug 17—at Glasgow, Scotland

Mon, Aug 17 and Tue, Aug 18—at Helsingfors, Finland

Mon, Aug 17—at Prague, Czechoslovakia

Tue, Aug 18—at Vienna

Wed, Aug 19; Thu, Aug 20; Fri, Aug 21—at Stockholm, Sweden

Thu, Aug 20—at Joensuu, Finland

Thu, Aug 20, Fri Aug 21, and Sat, Aug 22—at Oslo, Norway

Sun, Aug 23—at Karlstad, Sweden

Sun, Aug 23—at Paris, France

Mon, Aug 24—at Helsingfors, Finland

Tue, Aug 25—at Hamburg, Germany

Wed, Aug 26—at Oslo, Norway

RETURNS

Wed, Aug 19—ss President Roosevelt from Hamburg

Wed, Aug 26—ss Manhattan from Hamburg

Thu, Aug 27—ss Manhattan from Havre and Southampton

SEE INDIVIDUAL MEET ASSIGNMENTS AND DEPARTURE SCHDEULES ON FOLLOWING SHEETS

Glenn had already heard the rumour that he was likely to be called upon to do the three day meet in Stockholm, and that was confirmed in the attached schedules.

The attacks on Badajoz—bombing and artillery—had started

at dawn today. This lasted through the morning. By the early afternoon the full-scale assault was on. It failed at first, driven back by the defending militia's machine guns.[7] Yagüe's legionnaires tried a second, almost suicidal attack.[8] This time, driven on by their mad regimental hymn which invoked their bride to be death, they prevailed.

An orgy of violence ensued. As always in war there was much confusion. A fifth column of defenders went over to the rebels. The Legionarios and the Regulares summarily killed anyone they suspected of supporting the city's defenders. Even those who threw down their arms and raised their hands were executed.[9] Militiamen were bayoneted in the aisles and on the high altar of the cathedral. One man was shot dead by a rebel-aligned priest in the confessional box.

Hand-to-hand fighting meant the streets literally ran with blood. Piles of corpses created a sight of "desolation and dread".[10] Once they had prevailed, Yagüe's troops—Legionarios, Regulares and Falangists alike—looted the city. They did not discriminate between their supporters and the Republican defenders. Justifying the confiscation of anything portable, even from their own supporters—watches, radios, jewellery, typewriters, bales of cloth and the like—a rebel officer explained: "It is the war tax they pay for salvation."[11]

But the defenders of their city suffered most. Falangist patrols stopped men at random. They ripped open their shirts to see if there was a bruise that might be interpreted as a wound from a rifle recoil.[12] If not, were you a Socialist, anarchist, middle-class Republican or simply a labourer who did not support the Army rebellion? In which case you were shipped off to the bullring—where, this afternoon and evening, eight hundred men and women were machine-gunned to death in batches of twenty.[13]

15 AUGUST
SATURDAY

Overnight in Badajoz, Yagüe's troops brought a further 1200 people into the bullring. No names were taken. There were to be no records. At 7:30 am the machine guns struck up their murderous task again.

This was not spontaneous killing derived from long-standing grievances, as was so often—if inexcusably—the case in the extra-judicial executions that had prevailed in Barcelona and Madrid (and elsewhere) in the first days of the uprising. No, this was a centrally-organised and sanctioned action that formed an essential part of Franco's policy. In Badajoz it would last for not weeks but months. The instructions had been to "leave no left-wing leader alive."[1] Many who had fled to Portugal were induced to come back; most were then eliminated. In the wash up, Yagüe lost 44 men and suffered 141 wounded in the Battle of Badajoz. On the other side at least 4,000 people were executed—about 10% of the population—and estimates go as high as 9,000.[2]

Franco's people denied the massacre. They asserted it was just part of the normal course of war. There was nothing special at Badajoz. But then, an interview with a sympathetic journalist from the *New York Herald Tribune*, however, Yagüe confessed:

> *Of course we shot them. What do you expect? Was I supposed to take 4,000 reds with me as my column advanced, racing against time? Was I supposed to turn them loose in my rear and let them take Badajoz again?* [3]

From this time onward the wild-looking Yagüe came to be

known as the "Butcher of Badajoz". It is said that he was proud of the sobriquet.

At 9:00 am the *Nahlin* sailed the 14 miles from Trogir to Split.[4] Duff and Diana Cooper had by this time arrived in Split from Venice. Soon after 10:00 am they were met by one of the guests from the King's party, most likely Humphrey Butler. Lady Diana wrote:[5]

> [He wore] *very shabby sloppy trousers, blue grubby little short-sleeved jersey, yachting cap minus badge. He told us that the only disappointments were no sandy coves for bathing (and indeed the sand is like the pumice you scrub your feet with) and the impossibility of landing because of the yelling, jostling crowd that does not leave the King space to breathe. If he walks to the sights (the churches and old streets) they follow shouting "Cheerio!" and surround him so that he can see nothing.*
>
> *We went aboard and there were greeted by the young King radiant in health, wearing spick-and-span little shorts, straw sandals and two crucifixes on a chain round his neck. Our fellow-guests are Helen Fitzgerald, Pootz and Humphrey Butler, Jack Aird and Wallis.*

The Nahlin did not stay long in Spit, setting off at 2:30 pm for the pretty resort of Starigrad ("Old Town"), on the northern side of the island of Hvar, 21 miles distant.

> *We did not see Split. The others could not face another forced landing, so we set steam for a near island through the magic light that makes a background of ethereal mountains, the same colour and consistency as the benign little clouds floating round them …*
>
> *No sooner was the yacht sighted than the whole village turned out a million children and gay folk smiling and cheering. Half of them didn't know which the King was and must have been surprised when they were told. He had no hat (the child's hair gleaming), espadrilles, the same little shorts and a tiny blue-and-white singlet bought in one of their own villages. The other girls were rather seriously fixed, but Duff and I followed our Sovereign's lead …*

> *The crowds were handled fairly cleverly by the detectives with the help of a local policeman and the equerries, who held hands across until we were far away on a stony path up a hill. It was not very pretty, but at least we were free of the mob, and the detective was told to pick wild rosemary for the ship.*
>
> *Following the road over the hill took us back into the little town a lovely church and campanile, Italian-but-not-quite, and all the bells ringing. The staff were sure that they were ringing for the King, but I was not so certain, and sure enough by great luck it was a feast day, and there passed a procession of clerics in their best, the Virgin and Child beneath a silver canopy, and a long procession of townsfolk which relieved the density of the "send-off" mob. Still there were hundreds left throwing flowers. One woman had a huge magnolia grandiflora, but by gesture she made clear that it was not for me and that I must get it to the King. I made a gallant effort and forced it into his hand when he was talking to someone else.*
>
> *At last we were on board again, and it was considered to have been a great success.*
>
> The King and Wallis had been walking hand-in-hand in Hvar.[6] Apart from the good wishes of the church-goers, they had also attracted the attention of a hundreds of students "who materialised out of nowhere" and, seeing them as lovers, they wished them happiness and a long life: "Zavila ljubav!" they cried out, the Serbo-Croatian equivalent of "Vive l'amour!"

The religious celebration that Lady Diana and her fellow Protestants had just witnessed in Hvar was The Feast of the Assumption, the celebration of the day the Virgin Mary was received in Heaven. It was a big thing in Spain too.

Today, in Seville, Franco used the excitement and pageantry of the religious holiday to stake his claim for the leadership of the junta. He dreamt up a brilliant manoeuvre. One of Franco's problems was that no none really knew what he stood for. He was against the Popular Front government, of course; they all were. He was against chaos and in favour of order; all the junta agreed with that. He was against socialists, communists, anarchists and anyone on the Left; so too, they were all against them. And of course he was on the side of the Church. But where did he stand on the monarchy? Some senior members of the junta were republicans, at least in theory; Mola and Quiepo, for example.

Franco chose the flag as his vehicle. The Spanish National Flag was three equal horizontal stripes—red and yellow/gold, the traditional Spanish colours, and *morado* (the purple/red colour of the mulberry.) Today, in a grand ceremony in Seville's Plaza de San Fernando, Franco proclaimed the old monarchist flag—three unequal horizontal stripes, thinner red stripes at top and bottom and a yellow/gold one in between—the true national flag.

Mola in the north and Queipo in the south had both been flying the Spanish National Flag. But the whole point of having a flag is to distinguish oneself from the other lot, and the Republican forces were naturally flying the National Flag. Mola and Quiepo could therefore hardly object to Franco's proclamation. The two competing royalist factions, for their parts, were thrilled to be acknowledged. (Alfonso XIII had fled in 1931, without formally abdicating; his heir Don Juan had returned to Spain in the first days of the uprising, notwithstanding the imminent birth of a child, to sign up with Mola—but Mola had sent him packing, back to Italy. The Carlists, promoters of the alternate monarch, 86-year-old Alfonso Carlos, who would expire within the month, possessed a particularly savage 30,000 private military army known as the Requeté.) The Falange too, afraid that they were becoming a marginal player, was happy to have a unifying symbol to which they could subscribe. But there was more to the proclamation: it allowed Franco to promote a monarchy without a king.

With the military success of the rebels, crowds at religious events grew in the conquered zone. People started to attend church for the first time. Today's Feast of the Assumption provided an opportunity for all the residents of Seville to show their conformity. First up, there was the traditional mass in the cathedral, overseen by the reactionary Cardinal Ilundain. Next, there was an enhanced and over-the-top procession of graven images of Our Lady—and, in the way of the new order, special military parades meshed with the religious celebrations.

Franco arrived at Seville's Plaza de San Fernando with a large contingent of supporters including the mad and grotesque General Millán Astray. The local worthies received Franco as the prospective Caudillo. Quiepo, who had at first said he would not attend the ceremony—"he knows where I am"—turned up and made a long rambling speech from the balcony of the town hall supporting "our flag, the authentic one, the one to which we have sworn loyalty, and for which our forefathers died, a hundred times covered in glory."[7] He quoted poetry and couldn't be shut up. Eventually he embraced and kissed the new flag. Cardinal Ilundáin, providing yet another imprimatur of the Church to the uprising, did the same. Franco spoke briefly in his strange high-pitched voice and, ignoring the irony of the Muslim troops that would help achieve it, referred to the new flag as the banner of the "new Reconquista."

A small plane then flew over the square dropping rebel propaganda leaflets.

The traditional British Empire v USA athletics contest was a peculiar event. The 1932 contest had taken place on 14 August that year in San Francisco following the LA Games and, with some exaggeration, it was promoted as the "Fifth Renewal" of a British/US contest post Olympics; to achieve that number of renewals the promoters were counting a minor British/US athletics carnival that had followed the 1908 London Games. Nevertheless, since 1920 there had been a British Empire

v USA contest immediately following the Games in each Olympic year. Queens Club, a fancy tennis establishment, had been the venue in 1920; Stamford Bridge, the home of Chelsea soccer club, had been the venue in 1924 and 1928. Today it was the great sports field at White City in west London.

The contest was peculiar because it was based on relays. Traditional relays in which the baton is passed from one runner to another, to be sure, but also "relays" where a team's individual efforts were added together to reach a score. Thus, in the long jump for example, each distance achieved by three competitors on one side was added together to make a total distance and compared to the three on the other side.

The Empire had yet to win against the USA although, as *The Times* enthusiastically reported, it had been a tie when "each side scored five wins" in 1920.[8] A big crowd was anticipated for the "International Relay & Team Match". Everyone knew that Jesse Owens would be there; but so too Jack Lovelock for the Empire and members of the victorious British 4 x 400 m Relay team, and Ralph Metcalfe, Glenn Cunningham, Cornelius Johnson and Dave Albritton, Earle Meadows, Archie Williams, Jimmy Luvalle, and John Woodruff (the Berlin 800 m champion) for the USA.

It was a bright and warm sunny day in London. A parade of athletes at 2:30 pm was a feature. Jesse Owens, as usual, was the crowd's favourite. By 2:45 pm the first event—the Two Miles Relay—was underway. Everything was in Imperial measures, so this was 880 yards for each of four runners. The Americans won by three yards.

At 3:05 pm, Jesse Owens appeared in the feature event, a 400 yards relay. Two Brits, a Canadian and a South African ran for the Empire. The US team comprised Marty Glickman's optimal choice: Frank Wykoff, Glickman, Owens and Metcalfe. Winning by 9½ yards, the US team waltzed through. It was a new world record of 37.4s for an event that was rarely contested at international level; unfortunately, when translated to 400 m it was only 40.9s—a good second slower than the world record the US team had run in Berlin.

> The gates were closed at 3:45 pm when the White City's capacity of 90,000 had been reached. It was an incredible crowd; the organisers were expecting perhaps 50,000. Jesse gave an exhibition of long jumping in addition to his relay appearance and, throughout the afternoon he was swamped with autograph-seeking crowds. It was all over by 6:00 pm. The US won almost every event, the Three Miles Team Race (with Jack Lovelock for the Empire) and the Mile Relay (with three of the four Brits who had won the equivalent 4 x 400 m in Berlin) being the exceptions. Everyone enjoyed themselves. It was, as *The Times* reported, "provocative of nothing but amity."[9]
>
> It was the last time Jesse Owens would represent his country.

In Berlin, the Games had just one day to go.

This evening everyone who was anyone was invited by Reich Propaganda Minister Joseph Göbbels to a "Sommerfest". For the evening he had taken over the Pfaueninsel ("Peacock Island"), old Imperial possession but now a nature reserve. A good 30 km south west of Berlin, Peacock Island was located in the Havel river at Wannsee, near Potsdam. It was a convenient venue for Göbbels, as his summer house was a short boat ride across the Wannsee on the exclusive Schwanenwerder island; it was less convenient for the thousands of guests who were driven out from Berlin in a convoy of cars. That said, the 2000 guests were most efficiently transported with the police controlling the huge logistical exercise expertly.

The Wehrmacht had built a pontoon bridge to enable easy access to the island, and soldiers lined the bridge forming an honour guard, presenting oars as the guests arrived.[10] For Göbbels the Olympics had been a great success, and this event was important to him. Fortunately the weather was kind. The island was lit up with "huge butterfly lanterns glowing in the trees."[11] Guests were taken to their assigned places under coloured marquees scattered

15 August

about the grass where they found tables groaning with food and wine. Vintage champagne flowed. Magda Göbbels was dressed in white organdie, Göbbels in white double-breasted gabardine; together they moved among the guests in a disarmingly gracious manner.[12]

There was a definite louche atmosphere with a number of movie starlets among the guests and the girl pages dressed in "theatrical" uniforms.[13] Some athletes were also invited to party, albeit only females.

Göring was there, of course, and according to triple gold medallist Helen Stephens, she was invited to meet him in "Göbbels' house"—where, the gross Reichsmarshall allegedly greeted her dressed in a black bathrobe with his legs akimbo. Scantily clad women apparently crawled out from under a long table where Göring sat and, no sooner had she been offered a goblet of red wine from the voluptuary than he asked her to join him in another room for "a little talk". None of this would have fitted Helen Stephens' own preferences; in any event, she was saved by an attendant who interrupted the Prime Minister telling him that he had a telephone call. It all sounds rather sensational, but that is Stephens' account.[14]

After dinner, at about 10:00 pm, there was a huge fireworks display. The display was splendid but the noise and shooting sounds were so loud the US Ambassador compared it to the sound of warfare.[15] The skies stayed lit for some time, coloured by the now-extinguished fireworks, and a newfound quiet allowed Göbbels' Summer Festival to draw to its close. Very late, after most of the guests had retired, some of the "rougher Nazi types" allegedly became over familiar with the girl pages, the starlets and other female guests.[16]

The official Report read:[17]

Dr Goebbels on behalf of the German Government arranged a

garden party on Peacock Island on the last evening before the Games ended. This turned out to be an extremely attractive setting under a starlit summer sky, with no breeze stirring. About 2,000 guests were present. The natural charm of the dreamy island was enhanced by artificial lighting. Governed by the spirit of good fellowship and comradeship as well as happiness, the party went on until the small hours of the morning.

Göbbels had shown that he could put on a great party, undoubtedly the most expensive of the Games. The fantastic Olympic entertainments were now over. Von Ribbentrop had set the standard for partygoers. Göring then took their indulgence to a new level.

The consensus was that Göbbels' evening, grand as it was, "lacked the elegance and chic of Ribbentrop's and lacked the extravagance of Göring's";[18] Göbbels' event was too big and had admitted newcomers, some of whom had let the side down. On balance, therefore, Herman and Emmy Göring had won the battle of the receptions.

16 AUGUST
SUNDAY

When the US athletic troupe set off at dawn this morning for the airport, Jesse Owens and Larry Snyder stayed in their London hotel rooms. Together with all the athletes they had dutifully attended the gala dinner last night at the Hotel Victoria ("at 7.30 o'clock prompt"). Jesse was quiet[1] and kept his counsel, but he had already sent a telegram to the AAU:

> SICK AND UNDERWEIGHT. CANNOT COMPETE IN STOCKHOLM. FAMILY WAITING FOR ME. GOING HOME. JESSE OWENS

In no time Snyder's phone rang.[2] Daniel Ferris was calling on a crackling line from Berlin, demanding to know why the two were not on their way to Stockholm.

Snyder was forty-two and Caucasian. He was a graduate of Ohio State and had been their head coach since 1932; two members of his Ohio State squad were on the 1936 US Olympic team—Jesse Owens and Dave Albritton, both black. Although Snyder came from a traditional conservative Midwest background, he had genuine empathy for and rapport with his black charges; he knew the challenges they faced in 1930s America. Snyder told Ferris:

> *Jesse's got a big chance back home. He's got a break that comes once in a lifetime and never comes at all to a lot of people. It's tough for a coloured boy to make any money. What kind of a friend would I be to stand in his way?*

Unmoved, Ferris replied: *"You know I'll have to suspend him."*

Furious, Snyder then let go at Ferris. He told Ferris that he and Brundage did not control the Big Ten (the group of mid-West universities that competed amongst themselves, of which Ohio State was a member). Before slamming down the phone he gave Ferris a piece of his mind:

Listen, you're spending money on a call that could be spent making up those Olympic deficits of yours!

Federico García Lorca, Spain's most famous poet, had spent the last four weeks in his hometown of Granada. He was a moderate left supporter of the Popular Front and a notable member of the avant-garde. At 38, he was already a celebrated international intellectual. And his travelling theatre had been in the forefront of the Second Republic's goal of freeing the rural masses from the "vulnerability of ignorance"[3]. It was these things that made him a target for the Right.

Lorca, as he was colloquially known, had taken the overnight train on 16/17 July from Madrid to Granada. One purpose was to escape the civil unrest of Madrid. On arrival in Granada he moved into his fine summer house in the suburb of Herta de San Vicente. The Army rebellion started the next day.

With the assistance of the local Guardia Civil, Army rebels took Granada on 20 July. Lorca's brother-in-law, Granada's left wing mayor Manuel Fernandez-Mantesinos, had been arrested by the rebels that very evening—nearly four weeks ago—in the City Hall. Thousands of supporters of the Government—socialists, communists, left republicans, workers and intellectuals—were rounded up over the coming days. About 4000 people were liquidated in Granada and its immediate surroundings during the next two years, with 572 taken out in this month of August 1936 alone.[4] Fernandez-Mantesinos himself was executed early this morning in the Granada cemetery.

Intellectuals were in particular danger. In the immediate aftermath of the uprising the rector of the university, the top professors of paediatrics, law, pharmacy and history, engineers and physicians—all these were exterminated. Lorca had literary connections with the Right, and he sought shelter in the home of a Falangist poet, Luis Rosales.

This morning, a few hours after the execution of his brother-in-law, a squad comprising Guardia Civil police, a local Rightist politician and two other goons discovered Lorca at the Rosales home and took him in. Lorca was famous, openly gay and a Republican. Which of these qualities most offended the new rulers of Granada is unknown, although one of his captors later said that he "did more damage with his pen than others with their guns."[5]

The local rebel commander sent a message to the hateful Quiepo in Seville for instructions.[6] "Give him cafe, much cafe," came the reply—which was slang for "kill him".[7] There was no trial. There were no charges. At 4:45 pm on 18 August 1936, this coming Tuesday, Lorca and three others—a disabled primary school teacher and two political activists—were hustled into a smart Buick automobile.[8] They were then "taken for a ride" and shot dead in the countryside north east of Granada. The next day one of his executioners boasted: "We just killed Frederico García Lorca. I put two bullets in his arse for being queer."

While Jesse Owens and Larry Snyder were taking telephone calls in London and Lorca was being taken into custody in Granada, the *Nahlin* was weighing anchor. From 7:00 am it sailed the 58 miles from Starigrad to Privizal Bay on the island of Korcula, taking a little over 4½ hours and arriving just before noon.[9] Lady Diana Cooper had come down with a fever, but she happily reported the bucolic scene:[10]

> *I think it is off the island of Lissa, but one can't tell. One never sees the Captain and there are so many thousands of these little islands. One always feels oneself to be in a kind of Garda, only without vegetation or habitation.*

All the others off to see an old town and it has been a wild success ... Crowds had been well controlled ... I can't be well enough tomorrow to visit Ragusa [Dubrovnik], *so they'll do it without me, and tonight there is to be folk-dancing.*

In the coming days, Lady Diana, so happy to be here at the fabled island of Korcula with the King and his friends, would start to criticise the scene—and Wallis.

Edward was given to walking the streets of the towns they visited in shorts and shirtless; or as Lady Diana would have it: "spick-and-span little shorts, straw sandals and two crucifixes around his neck ..."[11] She noted, perhaps reproachfully, that Wallis "has duplicates on her wrist [of the crosses that Edward wore as a chain]."[12] What's more, she didn't like Wallis' advanced dress sense: "She looked a figure of fun in a child's piquet [*sic*] dress and a ridiculous silly bonnet ..."[13]. Nor did she like Wallis' voice, "rasping out wisecracks". And she didn't like the way Wallis bossed Edward about.

Nahlin steward Jim Richardson was equally critical: "[He] didn't seem like a King," he wrote to his mother, "The King is much like an Oxford University student that has never grown up ...",[14] drinking too much and playing jigsaw puzzles that he never finished. Richardson noted Wallis' "high pitched metallic American voice" and reported the "strong hold" she had over Edward.

Edward was suffering from monomania. Wallis could do no wrong. To him she was the perfect woman. She may not have been a classic beauty, but she was chic, modern and amusing. They were on holiday and he wanted to indulge her. In doing so, he indulged himself. When the staff or guests asked about the agenda for the day, he would invariably turn to Wallis:

Wallis, what are the plans for the day?

The happy couple knew that the Royal family and Prime

Minister Baldwin were deeply concerned about their affair but they carried on as if there was nothing unusual or potentially controversial about the cruise or their behaviour. That was not the view of the American press which followed the flotilla's progress avidly, publishing photographs of Edward and Wallis together and speculating on the King's relationship with "Mrs Ernest Simpson of Baltimore". Yet the British press remained silent. For example, today's events were blandly reported thus by a 17 August dateline in *The Times*:

> *Last night after dinner, the King went ashore on Korcula (Curzola) to fish, according to the Dalmatian custom, by the light of Chinese lanterns … His Majesty spent yesterday afternoon visiting the sights of Korcula, attended by the Secretary for War, Mr Duff Cooper… and inspected the cathedral of St Vitus, which was built on the island during the occupation in 1813.*[15]

There was no mention of Mrs Simpson. Ever. Only one unimportant small-circulation London magazine broke the British press' code of silence—*Cavalcade,* in its 22 August edition—when it published some photos including the one with Wallis touching Edward's wrist. With every major daily in Britain, though, it was all the correct agreed form: no mention of Wallis, just the occasional reference to the King on his private holiday. Newspapers throughout the Empire simply carried the London dailies' reports. US citizens could read the true nature of King Edward VIII's private life in their print media, but the King's subjects—save for a few privileged insiders—were kept in ignorance.

As Hitler made his triumphal final approach to the Olympic Stadium for the Games' closing ceremony, Avery Brundage called a press conference with his side-kick Daniel Ferris. Self-important and self righteous as always, all that was missing from the mandarin who ran US athletics was the black skullcap of a hanging judge. Brundage, perhaps still recovering from the joys of Göbbels' hospitality last night, allowed Ferris to pronounce Jesse Owens' death sentence as an amateur athlete:

We had no alternative under the circumstances but to disbar Owens,

said Ferris.

It is an open and shut case of violating an agreement ... Owens has failed to fulfil his contractual obligations. And so the suspension is automatic. He is barred from this moment onwards.

It was raining in London. And some hours later in his London hotel lobby, Jesse Owens delivered his own sad obituary as an amateur athlete:

This suspension is very unfair to me. There is nothing I can get out of this [Scandinavian] *trip. All we athletes get out of this Olympics business is a view of a train or an airplane window. This track business is becoming one of the biggest rackets in the world. It doesn't mean a damn thing to us athletes ...*

This was the most famous athlete in the world. He had spent the last week travelling through Europe as a performing seal, fundraising for the Amateur Athletics Union and the American Olympic Association. A week ago he had won a fourth gold medal representing the United States. Today the AAU and Avery Brundage chewed him up and spat him out.

Today was the last day of the Olympics. The gates of the Stadium were opened at 8:30 am. A full house had been anticipated and by 10:00 am, when the jumping section for the three-day equestrian competition was to start, the arena was full.

To some observers the military presence in Berlin looked greater today than had been the case throughout the Olympic fortnight. SA and SS units seemed to be everywhere.[16] Perhaps it was just visitors reflecting on the scene they would soon be

16 August

leaving. Hitler's final promenade from the Wilhelmstrasse to the Olympic Stadium certainly saw the military out in great numbers. He arrived at the Stadium in time for the 3:00 pm start of the "Prix des Nations", the Olympic show jumping—confusingly a separate event from the three-day jumping which had taken place in the morning. It was to take up much of the afternoon.

Each horseman saluted the Führer. In the case of the Germans, Italians and like-minded South Americans, they used the Nazi salute; Hitler acknowledged them with his "Old Guard" sloppy bent arm version of the Nazi greeting. Interspersed with medal presentations for recent events such as the rowing, the show jumping "was very exciting, even breathless," according to Chips Channon.[17] Their was high drama, for example, when a German cavalry lieutenant, competing with his dislocated arm in a sling from an earlier fall and needing to complete the course for his team, fell again. He remounted in obvious great pain and finished the course to the frenzied cheers of his countrymen.[18]

Importantly for the hosts, Germany won both the final two events—the individual and the teams show jumping. Indeed they had "won" the Games; of 89 medals won by Germans, 33 were gold; the USA won 56 medals, 24 of which were gold. It was not lost on the Nazis that Italy and Japan too had done well, and that Britain and France had not.

The Prix des Nations show jumping was designed to morph into the Closing Ceremony at precisely 7:37 pm—with the Olympic Flame expiring as the sun sank over the horizon.[19] This plan allowed for the introduction of the same "cathedral of light" effects that were last seen at the Opening Ceremony (and first seen at the Nuremberg rallies).

As the dark came upon the Stadium trumpets sounded out the Olympic fanfares, the Olympic Orchestra played a parade march and the floodlights flamed up. Flags of the fifty nations were marched into the Stadium. Count Baillet-Latour stepped into the arena and mounted a rostrum—where he made a brief speech in French, translated in English on the scoreboard, which invoked the inevitable (if unfulfilled) "call upon the youth of every country to assemble in four years time in Tokyo there to celebrate with us the Games of the XIIth Olympiad."

The fifty national flags were lowered. A rocket was sent up and its red hue lit up the Stadium as the searchlights were blinked off, one by one.[20] A sole searchlight stayed on the Olympic Flag; it was slowly lowered. Eight men picked the flag up and carried it by its corners to the rostrum. The Olympic Fire slowly lowered its flame over the Marathon Gate, flickered and then expired—and there was silence. It was the false ending all melodramatic movies must have, and this Closing Ceremony followed the same script.

The Olympic Bell slowly broke the silence, gently rising in sound. The searchlights ramped up again. A trumpet fanfare welcomed Baillet-Latour and the Mayor of Berlin to the rostrum where they solemnly received the Olympic Flag for safekeeping—and withdrew. The Olympic Orchestra played the "Olympic Farewell" and, from the ether, a ghostly Big Brother-like voice breathed "I summon the youth of the world to Tokyo" as the circling searchlights met. Then the huge choir started up an old German folk song, a sort of German *Auld Land Syne*. Seemingly the whole stadium joined in:

Play is at an end! Play is at an end!

Joyful, all joyful together. Strong are we now for all weather!

Homeward we wend! Homeward we wend!

Happy to know! Happy to know!

Peace in our friendship and gladness. Smiling and banishing sadness.

Homeward we go! Homeward we go!

First let us tell. First let us tell.

16 August

Sunsets that bid us their greeting. Rise up again for a meeting!

Till then, farewell! Friends all, farewell!

But the crowd was not ready to leave. Perhaps they were expecting something from Hitler, who sat quietly in the Honour Loge in the darkness.

Members of the crowd started to cry out "Sieg Heil!" and "Heil Hitler!" Perhaps it was spontaneous. Perhaps not. One by one they rose to their feet, and with their right arms raised in salute they sang the National Anthem—and then, the sinister Horst Wessel Song.

Four weeks ago in Barcelona the promise of the People's Olympiad had been celebrated with Beethoven's immortal "Ode to Joy", a hymn to man's humanity towards man. And here in Berlin, perhaps appropriately, the last words heard at these Berlin Olympics were the hate and bile of the Nazi's torch song:

Bald flattern Hitlerfahnen uber allen Strassen, die Knechtschaft dauert nur noch kurze Zeit.

(Soon Hitler flags will wave over all streets; our subjugation will last only a little longer.)

EPILOGUE

When Edward returned to London from his holiday on 14 September—he flew from Zurich—he went straight to Fort Belvedere. He changed quickly into white tie, and rushed off to dinner with his mother at Buckingham Palace.[1] (Eight months after the death of her husband, Queen Mary had yet to move out to Marlborough House, her designated new home.) It was a tense meal, and the dowager queen and her son discussed the weather and the sightseeing he had enjoyed in the Adriatic and Greece through to Istanbul. There was no mention of Mrs Simpson.

The divorce proceedings between Wallis and Ernest Simpson were heard on 27 October 1936. Good ex-Guards officer that he was, Ernest admitted his adultery with "Buttercup Kennedy" at the Hotel de Paris, Bray; his evidence was supported by that of two waiters and a porter. The divorce was granted. It would become "absolute" after six months, that is in March 1937.

On 1 August Prime Minister Baldwin had been advised to take a complete rest for three months. He asked Eden not to "trouble me too much with foreign affairs just now"[2], and this Eden did—his diplomacy culminating in the Non-Intervention Treaty. By the time Baldwin came back to work the King's romance with Wallis demanded his attention. He discussed it with Edward at Fort Belvedere on 20 October. Not only were the American papers full of the story; even the lower classes were becoming aware of it.[3]

On 16 November the King summoned Baldwin to Buckingham Palace and told him that he was determined to marry the lady.

No remonstrations worked; the King's determination to marry Wallis was not negotiable. Baldwin even suggested the somewhat racy solution of Edward keeping Wallis as his mistress—"certain things are sometimes permitted to Royalty which are not allowed to the ordinary man"[4]—a proposal the King found "the height of hypocrisy"[5]. The Dominion leaders were canvassed and they did not support the marriage of their sovereign with a divorced woman. Finally, a morganatic marriage—that strange arrangement whereby the titles and privilege of a parent do not devolve to any children—was canvassed, but it too did not find favour.[6]

The problem was Wallis' divorce. Indeed two divorces. Times were changing, but not for the British Monarch—who is, after all, however ceremonial the post, the Supreme Governor of the Church of England; what's more, his royal style and title asserts he is Defender of the Faith.

In the end it was all too much. George V had said that Edward would not last a year "after I am dead"[7], and he was right.

The story of the King's romance broke on 3 December 1936—to a largely unknowing, surprised and deeply shocked Empire. Wallis had been secreted off to the Continent the night before the news broke.

Edward's abdication took effect on 11 December. That evening he made a brilliant radio broadcast from Windsor Castle. He had wanted to argue his case for keeping the throne but Baldwin would not allow it; Churchill helped him craft the final version.

Speaking in that distinctive mid-Atlantic tenor, Prince Edward, for that he is how he was introduced, reported to the Empire—and bid his former subjects farewell:

At long last I am able to say a few words of my own. I have never wanted to withhold anything, but until now it has not been constitutionally possible for me to speak.

A few hours ago I discharged my last duty as King and Emperor, and now that I have been succeeded by my brother, the

Duke of York, my first words must be to declare my allegiance to him. This I do with all my heart.

You all know the reasons which have impelled me to renounce the throne. But I want you to understand that in making up my mind I did not forget the country or the empire, which, as Prince of Wales and lately as King, I have for twenty-five years tried to serve.

But you must believe me when I tell you that I have found it impossible to carry the heavy burden of responsibility and to discharge my duties as King as I would wish to do without the help and support of the woman I love.

And I want you to know that the decision I have made has been mine and mine alone. This was a thing I had to judge entirely for myself. The other person most nearly concerned has tried up to the last to persuade me to take a different course.

I have made this, the most serious decision of my life, only upon the single thought of what would, in the end, be best for all.

This decision has been made less difficult to me by the sure knowledge that my brother, with his long training in the public affairs of this country and with his fine qualities, will be able to take my place forthwith without interruption or injury to the life and progress of the empire. And he has one matchless blessing, enjoyed by so many of you, and not bestowed on me—a happy home with his wife and children.

During these hard days I have been comforted by her majesty my mother and by my family. The ministers of the crown, and in particular, Mr. Baldwin, the Prime Minister, have always treated me with full consideration. There has never been any constitutional difference between me and them, and between me and Parliament. Bred in the constitutional tradition by my father, I should never have allowed any such issue to arise.

Epilogue

Ever since I was Prince of Wales, and later on when I occupied the throne, I have been treated with the greatest kindness by all classes of the people wherever I have lived or journeyed throughout the empire. For that I am very grateful.

I now quit altogether public affairs and I lay down my burden. It may be some time before I return to my native land, but I shall always follow the fortunes of the British race and empire with profound interest, and if at any time in the future I can be found of service to his majesty in a private station, I shall not fail.

And now, we all have a new King. I wish him and you, his people, happiness and prosperity with all my heart. God bless you all! God save the King!

His dilemma aroused widespread support among free thinkers, but the hurdle of Wallis' marriages was too much for most—and, by and large, the former King's former subjects understood that he had to go. For many Wallis would always be "that woman".

Edward's younger brother Bertie—Albert Frederick Arthur George—took the throne as George VI. A nervous and uncomplicated man he had never expected to be king. ("This is absolutely terrible, I'm quite unprepared for it … I am only a naval officer, it's the only thing I know about.") With good advice and a strong wife and family unit, Bertie proved to be a safe choice. The Second World War helped the British monarchy settle into a new public posture. It enabled George VI and his small family—"we four"—to show their spirit and concern. A lifetime smoker, he died in 1952, aged 56, not directly of cancer as was expected but of a coronary thrombosis. His daughter Elizabeth has proved to be the model constitutional monarch by taking a genuine interest in the affairs of state and providing increasingly knowledgeable and experienced advice to her prime ministers; she has adopted the maxim that public appearances are paramount (something

Edward understood) and private foibles, follies and indulgences should be kept private (where he demonstrably and utterly failed).

There was now an uncomfortable separation for Wallis and Edward, necessitated by Wallis' incomplete divorce proceedings. Wallis took refuge at her friends Herman and Katherine Rogers' villa, Lou Viei, a converted monastery above Cannes in the South of France. Edward had been offered accommodation at a Rothschild palace outside Vienna, Schloss Enzesfeld; from there he showered his brother, the new King, with increasingly unwanted letters of advice and also ran up enormous telephone bills (calling Wallis in Cannes) which he left for his hosts to pay. As soon as they could reunite they did so, at the Chateau de Candé, a fine country house near Tours owned and recently refurbished at great expense by controversial industrialist, Charles Bedaux. Edward and Wallis hardly knew their host but were happy to accept his largesse, a syndrome that became central to their on-going joint lifestyle.

Edward and Wallis were married on 3 June 1937 at the Chateau de Candé. No member of the Royal Family attended. Edward had taken the title Duke of Windsor, so Wallis became the Duchess of Windsor. By all rights and precedence, as the wife of a duke of the royal blood, she was also entitled to be known by the style or title "Her Royal Highness". This was, however, in the gift of the new king and, as a result of dubious advice, George VI denied it to her. Edward never forgave his brother for this and insisted that, in their household at least, Wallis was to be addressed as Her Royal Highness.

Edward and Wallis made an ill-advised visit to Germany in October 1937. It had been arranged by their new friend Bedaux. To this day photos of their meeting with Adolf Hitler provide "proof" of their Nazi sympathies.

With the advent of the Second World War it was found convenient to ship the Duke and Duchess off to the Bahamas,

Epilogue

where Edward served as Governor. He was far away from the action and that suited his brother and the British authorities. The role bored him and he was not a success in it. After the war Britain never offered him another job and, as a former sovereign, it was inappropriate for him to take up any commercial activity.

A request to return to his beloved Fort Belvedere was denied Edward. Again he blamed his brother. In 1938 the Duke and Duchess had leased an elegant stand-alone townhouse in Paris, 24 boulevard Suchet, and also a grand villa at Cap d'Antibes in the South of France, Chateau de la Cröe; to these they returned after the war. In 1952 the City of Paris provided the Windsors with permanent accommodation at a peppercorn rent—a mansion in the Bois de Boulogne, near Neuilly, now known as Villa Windsor, and for the rest of their lives this was their principal abode. To supplement their Paris abode, they bought a mill in the country, Le Moulin de la Tuilerie, at Gif-sur-Yvette, south of Paris, where the Duke could potter in the garden on country weekends and in the summer. In New York, Suite 28A in the Waldorf Towers was always available for them; the Windsors stored their own furniture there and it was moved in for their annual visit.

The Duke and Duchess of Windsor lived a shallow life of leisure and comfort: Palm Beach, Florida and other resorts in the winter and Paris, the French countryside and fashionable watering holes in the summer. They were the toast (and talk) of fashionable society; to old money in the US "the Dook" and Wallis were famous free-loaders.

Wallis was indulged totally by Edward; she was the world's best dressed woman and one of the most bejewelled. Wallis' most famous quote—"You can never be too rich or too thin"—may have been apocryphal; it didn't matter, everyone believed it to be hers. She became a most famous and accomplished hostess; Wallis' guidelines for household management are the rule book for the rich and status-conscious to this day.

Edward's question—"What are the plans for the day, Wallis?"—had migrated from Fort Belvedere and the Adriatic to the Bois de Boulogne, the Mill and to wherever the Duke and Duchess were residing at the time. She ran the show.

Edward's father, King George V, was described by his biographer thus:

As his official biographer I felt compelled to admit, King George V was distinguished by no exercise of social gifts, by no personal magnetism, by no intellectual powers.

It would not be fair to ascribe the lack of all these qualities to Edward. He was in fact very good with people—if that were his want—and, at least as a young man, he had film-star magnetism. There was one skill that the father did teach his son, however, and it is worth noting because it meant much to his interlocutors: the skill to remember names and faces. Like his father, Edward was capable of remembering names and faces not just to the end of an evening but for years to come.

George V's biographer concluded his description of the monarch with a list of further qualities that were shared by father and son:

He was neither a wit nor a brilliant raconteur, neither well-read, nor well-educated, and he made no great contribution to enlightened social converse. He lacked intellectual curiosity ...

Edward died on 28 May 1972. He was 78. Wallis inherited his entire estate. For the funeral, one of the few times Wallis visited England after 1936, she was the guest of Queen Elizabeth at Buckingham Palace. At the funeral itself, in St George's Chapel, Windsor Castle, she was—even in her widow's weeds—the chicest person in attendance. Wallis died in 1986, aged nearly 90. For her last years she was incommunicado, a bedridden recluse, dependent upon and exploited by her formidable lawyer Maître

Epilogue

Suzanne Blum. Wallis' tomb is adjacent to Edward's at Frogmore, the royal burial ground at Windsor, and reads simply "Wallis, Duchess of Windsor".

The divorce of Wallis and Ernest Simpson not only freed Wallis to marry Edward, it also freed Ernest to remarry. On 19 November 1937, three weeks after Mary Raffray's own divorce was finalised, they married. Ernest and the third Mrs Simpson had one child, a son, Ernest Henry Child Simpson, who was born in 1939. Mary died young, of breast cancer in 1941, aged just 45.

Young Ernest Simpson was cared for by relatives in north America during the Second World War and returned to England in 1946. Brought up as a privileged English middle-class boy, he attended Harrow and the toney Swiss school, Le Rosey; in due course he joined the Coldstream Guards, his father's old regiment. Soon after his father's death in 1958, he was informed of the family's Jewish heritage by his aunt, Maud Kerr-Smiley. He promptly changed his name to Aharon Solomons.[8] Solomons moved to Israel in 1962 and served in the Israel Defence Force. His two marriages have produced three sons.

From mid-August 1936 it took Franco another two and a half years to conquer Spain.

After capturing Badajoz and Mérida, most argue that it was a tactical mistake for him to have General Varela's troops branch off to "liberate" Toledo and the Alcázar citadel. In a bloodbath of Badajoz proportions, Franco's men finally took Toledo and the Alcázar on 27 September 1936; their victory included the now ritual beheading of captured enemies.[9] While this diversion delayed the Army of Africa's advance on Madrid, and may therefore have been a mistake in the actual prosecution of the war, it was an enormous rebel propaganda victory. It promoted Franco's hero status among his supporters, and helped secure him leadership of the rebel junta.

On 1 October 1936 Excelentísimo Sr. General Don Francisco Franco Bahamonde—that is, General Francisco Franco—was invested by the junta as Head of State. The elaborate ceremony held in the new rebel seat of Burgos was attended by diplomats from Germany, Italy and Portugal. The new "government" styled itself Nationalist, a term that was picked up and adopted by the media; in contrast, the elected government of Spain became "the Republican government".

The Nationalists soon promoted a personality cult with Franco, their undisputed leader, the centre of the ubiquitous slogan "Una Patria, Un Estado, Un Caudillo". It echoed Hitler's "Ein Volk, ein Reich, ein Führer".

The prospect of Franco's Nationalists winning in Spain shocked people all around the world—not just in Europe, but in America and the Antipodes. For many, the decisions of their leaders not to intervene was too much. As a result, more than 40,000 men (and women) came from all corners of the world to join the militias, establish the so-called International Brigades or serve as non-combatants in support of the Republic.[10] Why did they come?[11]

Sam Wild, an ex merchant seaman from Manchester, gave a common answer:

> *Well, to me it was elementary. Here was fascism spreading all over the world, the rape of Abyssinia, the rise of fascism in Germany and the persecution of the Jews there, and the rise of the Blackshirts in Britain with their anti-Semitism ... I felt that somebody had to do something to try and stop it.*

The future head of British trade unions, Jack Jones had a similar story:

> *The awful realisation that black fascism was on the march right across Europe created a strong desire to act. The march had started with Mussolini and had gained terrible momentum with Hitler and was being carried forward by Franco. For most young people there was a feeling of frustration, but some determined to do anything that seemed possible, even if it meant death, to try to stop the spread of fascism ... This was Fascist progression. It was real and it had to be stopped.*

The success of the Army of Africa and Mola seemed inevitable. By October 1936, everyone had expected Madrid to fall to the pincers movement of Mola's rebels from the east and Yagüe's from the south and west. When Mola was criticised for having only four columns under his command, he unwisely boasted of a "fifth column" among the city's citizens; it caused many residents to be suspected of disloyalty to the Republic. This brought on the inevitable repercussions—public order having largely broken down—including non-judicial incarceration and executions.

Not least among those expecting the capital to fall were the members of the Popular Front government. Giral had been replaced as PM by Largo Caballero ("the Spanish Lenin") in early September. The Government scampered off to Valencia on 6 November, and it was headquartered there for the rest of the war.

But Madrid was saved by the incredible bravery and persistence of about 40,000 Republican supporters. There is no doubt that the International Brigades were part of this success, and they have been widely applauded for their participation. Even so, they only represented about 3,000 troops. It was, therefore, the loyal Army, the militias, the Guardia Civil and the Assault Guards as well as the International Brigades that should share the accolades—and the arrival of new Soviet aeroplanes and war matériel.

In Barcelona, the counter-revolution was working. The barricades had come down in October. By the time George Orwell first arrived in Barcelona in December 1936 he found a worker's paradise:

It was the first time that I had ever been in a town where the working class was in the saddle ... Every shop and café had an inscription saying that it had ben collectivized ... Waiters and shop-walkers looked you in the face and treated you as an equal. Servile and even ceremonial forms of speech had temporarily disappeared ... Almost my first experience was receiving a lecture from an hotel manager for trying to tip a lift boy ... There was much in it that I did not understand, in some ways I did not even like, but I recognized it immedi-

> *ately as a state of affairs worth fighting for.*
>
> *... with all this there was something of the evil atmosphere of war. The town had a gaunt untidy look, roads and buildings were in poor repair, the streets at night were dimly lit for fear of air-raids, the shops were mostly shabby and half-empty. Meat was scarce and milk practically unobtainable, there was a shortage of coal, sugar, and petrol, and really serious shortage of bread ... Yet so far as one could judge the people were contented and hopeful.*[12]

Diplomacy was doing its bit. The Non-Intervention Committee. which was to administer the Non-Intervention Treaty, met for the first time in early September. It was a joke.

Twenty-four nations had signed up to the Non-intervention Treaty—France, Britain, Germany, Italy, the Soviet Union, Portugal and so on. The Committee was chaired by an Englishman, Ivor Windsor-Clive, the 47-year-old 2nd Earl of Plymouth. The Soviet Ambassador to the Court of St James, Ivan Maisky, was not impressed:[13]

> *In this large, imposing and well-groomed body dwelt a small, slow-moving and timid mind. Nature and education had made Plymouth a practically ideal personification of English political mediocrity, nourished by the traditions of the past and by well-worn sentiments. As chairman of the Committee, Plymouth presented an entirely helpless and often comic figure.*

The Committee's job was to stop the flow of armaments (and subsequently personnel) from the signatories to the combatants. In between meetings, which were charades of insincerity, border posts were set up and observers installed (although not on the leaky Portuguese/Spanish border); there were naval patrols and blockades.[14] None of it worked, and most of the signatories didn't care.

Over the course of the next two and half years Italy sent about 75,000 servicemen to aid the Nationalists, the maximum at any one time being perhaps 40,000 to 50,000.[15] Mussolini also supplied about 660 aircraft, 150 tanks and perhaps 1000 artillery pieces. Germany sent fewer men, perhaps 16,000 in total and 10,000 at its maximum—but within this complement were a total of 5,000 in the crack Condor Legion. In addition, Hitler supplied about 600 planes, 200 tanks and 1,000 artillery pieces. Much of this was provided on credit.

For the Republicans, the Soviet Union sent perhaps 3,000 men (albeit that they came to occupy key positions in the Republican forces), about 1,000 aircraft, 900 tanks and 1550 pieces of artillery. All this was paid for by the Republican Government; they had shipped three-quarters of the nation's gold to the Soviet Union for this purpose.

The effect of the Non-Intervention Treaty was to deny the Republicans legitimate supplies of military matériel and to force them into the Soviet's hands. The British goal had always been to "localise the disturbance … [and] prevent outside assistance from prolonging the war."[16] British Labour peer, Lord Strabolgi, called it "malevolent neutrality."[17] Anthony Eden, opined "better a leaky dam than no dam at all."[18] Churchill, who had initially supported the treaty, called it "an elaborate policy of humbug." Pandit Nehru thought it "the supreme farce of our time."[19]

The Spanish President, Manuel Azaña prophetically summarized the situation in his diary entry of 31 May 1937:[20]

Our greatest enemy until now has been the British government. All schemes devised for non-intervention and their consequences have damaged the government and favoured the rebels. Their hypocrisy has become so obvious that it seemed infantile cynicism. It is a great thing to say that this is done to preserve the peace in Europe. But to think that Germany or Italy would declare war on Britain or France if the Spanish Government bought arms in these two countries is sheer stupidity. The best way to avoid a general war is not to permit Germany and Italy do what they like in Spain. How can the triumph of the rebels, the protégées of Germany and Italy, be in the interests of the British?

When Orwell returned to Barcelona from the Aragon Front in April 1937 he came back to a city that had changed:

Now the tide had rolled back. Once again it was an ordinary city, a little pinched and chipped by war, but with no outward sign of work-

ing-class predominance ...

There were two facts that were the keynote of all else. One was that the people—the civil population—had lost much of their interest in the war; the other was that the normal division of society into rich and poor, upper class and lower class, was reasserting itself.[21]

A few weeks earlier, in March 1937, Franco had temporarily halted the Madrid offensive so as to concentrate on the North. San Sebastian had fallen in September 1936. Over the summer Franco's troops captured the rest of the Basque country, notably the industrial cities of Bilbao (mid-June) and Santander (late August). In achieving this the Nationalists lost the support of much international public opinion when they bombed and largely destroyed the historic Basque city of Guernica on 26 April 1937. The Condor Legion was responsible for this—the deliberate bombing of a civilian population, the first such atrocity in modern times. Franco's PR people put about the incredible story that the Republicans had bombed and strafed their own people—but at last no-one believed them.

For most of the next year there was something of a stalemate. Constant battles took place in and around Madrid and in the hinterlands, all to little avail. Meretricious players like Ernest Hemingway and André Malraux had come on the scene and hung around. The borders of the Republican and the Nationalist Zones stayed largely unchanged until May 1938.

While the Republic was holding the fort in Madrid and fighting amongst themselves in Barcelona, Franco was consolidating his control of the Nationalist Zone. His leadership was now unquestioned.[22] He refused all offers of mediation; the ideas that the Papacy or the United States might play such a role were rebuffed by him out of hand. Franco was maintaining the posture he had articulated to Jay Allen on 27 July 1936: he would do whatever it takes and would eliminate anyone in his way.

At times there was another worldliness to it all. Take adventurer Juan Antonio Ansaldo, for example. This is the man who crashed the plane carrying Sanjurjo in Estoril, Portugal on 20 July 1936. An insouciant extract from his 1937 diary reads:[23]

8:30 am Breakfast with the family (at San Sebastián).

9:30 am Departure for the front. Bombardment of enemy batteries. Machine-gunning of trenches and convoys.

11:00 am A little golf at Lasarte…

12:30 pm Sun-bath on Onderreta beach and short swim in the calm sea.

1:30 pm Beer, shrimps, and conversation in a café.

2:00 pm Luncheon at home.

3:00 pm Short siesta.

4:00 pm Second war mission, similar to that of the morning.

6:30 pm Cinema. Old but fine film of Katherine Hepburn.

9:00 pm Aperitif at the Bar Basque (San Sebastián). A good "Scotch". Animated scene.

10:15 pm Dinner at Nicolasa's, war songs, company, enthusiasm…

For his part, Franco callously took to the killing fields. From March 1937 executions in the new Nationalist Zone required his approval.[24] He gave it freely. Strangulation by the garrotte[25] was his preferred method; it was effective, painful and—importantly—it could be as slow as the executioner wished. Franco was given to reviewing the condemned list after lunch or over morning coffee. He ran through the list with alacrity. Where he was moved to be particularly savage or wished to make a public point, he would mark the approval garrote y prensa (garrotte with press report): that way the victim's family and acquaintances would know that he or she had suffered greatly.

In March 1938 the Nationalists gained control of Lleida and the hydroelectric dams that produced Catalonia's electricity. By mid April, they had split Catalonia from the rest of the Republican Zone by driving from Lleida to the sea at Vinaròs.

In July, the Republic made a last ditch—and foolhardy—drive across the Ebro River. Its failure, by November, was the beginning of the end.

The Republic was desperate. In the hope that the decision might get some support from their erstwhile friends, the Republican Government disbanded the International Brigades. There would be, they announced, no more foreign troops on the Republican side.

On 1 November 1938, a complement of 13,000 International Brigadists made their final appearance. They marched along the Diagonal in Barcelona behind rolling tanks and artillery, cheered and heralded by enthusiastic crowds. Children were held up to be kissed, flowers rained on the soldiers, girls broke into the parade to embrace their heroes; planes swooped low in celebration, diving almost to street level.

Many of the Brigadists would join the People's Army. Most were off home; others to oblivion. Yet again La Pasionara found the words:

It is very difficult to say a few words in farewell to the heroes of the International Brigades, because of what they are and what they represent. A feeling of sorrow, an infinite grief catches our throat—sorrow for those who are going away, for the soldiers of the highest ideal of human redemption, exiles from their countries, persecuted by the tyrants of all peoples—grief for those who will stay here forever mingled with the Spanish soil, in the very depth of our heart, hallowed by our feeling of eternal gratitude.

From all peoples, from all races, you came to us like brothers, like sons of immortal Spain; and in the hardest days of the war, when the capital of the Spanish Republic was threatened, it was you, gallant comrades of the International Brigades, who helped save the city with your fighting enthusiasm, your heroism and your spirit of sacrifice.—And Jarama and Guadalajara, Brunete and Belchite, Levante and the Ebro, in immortal verses sing of the courage, the victim, the daring, the discipline of the men of the International Brigades.

For the first time in the history of the peoples' struggles, there was the spectacle, breathtaking in its grandeur, of the formation of International Brigades to help save a threatened country's freedom and independence—the freedom and independence of our Spanish land.

Communists, Socialists, Anarchists, Republicans—men of different colours, differing ideology, antagonistic religions—yet all profoundly loving liberty and justice, they came and offered themselves to us unconditionally.

They gave us everything—their youth or their maturity; their science or their experience; their blood and their lives; their hopes and aspirations—and they asked us for nothing. But yes, it must be said, they did want a post in battle, they aspired to the honour of dying for us.

Banners of Spain! Salute these many heroes! Be lowered to honour so many martyrs!

Mothers! Women! When the years pass by and the wounds of war are stanched; when the memory of the sad and bloody days dissipates in a present of liberty, of peace and of wellbeing; when the rancour has died out and pride in a free country is felt equally by all Spaniards, speak to your children. Tell them of these men of the International Brigades.

Recount for them how, coming over seas and mountains, crossing frontiers bristling with bayonets, sought by raving dogs thirsting to tear their flesh, these men reached our country as crusaders for freedom, to fight and die for Spain's liberty and independence threatened by German and Italian fascism. They gave up everything—their loves, their countries, home and fortune, fathers, mothers, wives, brothers, sisters and children—and they came and said to us: "We are here. Your cause, Spain's cause, is ours. It is the cause of all advanced and progressive mankind."

Today many are departing. Thousands remain, shrouded in Spanish earth, profoundly remembered by all Spaniards. Comrades of the International Brigades: Political reasons, reasons of state, the welfare of that very cause for which you offered your blood with boundless generosity, are sending you back, some to your own countries and others to forced exile. You can go proudly. You are history. You are legend. You are the heroic example of democracy's solidarity and universality in the face of the vile and accommodating spirit of those who interpret democratic principles with their eyes on hoards of wealth or corporate shares which they want to safeguard from all risk.

We shall not forget you; and, when the olive tree of peace is in flower, entwined with the victory laurels of the Republic of Spain—return!

Return to our side for here you will find a homeland—those who have no country or friends, who must live deprived of friendship—all, all will have the affection and gratitude of the Spanish people who today and tomorrow will shout with enthusiasm—

Long live the heroes of the International Brigades!

The 13,000 Brigadists were the last of the perhaps 35,000 who had made up the International Brigades. Of these, the maximum number in Spain at any one time was probably no more than 18,000.[26] Perhaps as many as 8,000 died, while an additional 3,500 were seriously wounded. Fully 25% were Jewish.[27]

Barcelona itself fell to the Nationalists on 26 January 1939. Exactly fifty-seven years later, on 26 January 1996, Spain's democratic government honoured La Pasionara's pledge. All living Brigadists (and other Republican volunteers such as militia members and non-combatants) were granted the right to Spanish citizenship. There were perhaps 600 still alive.

Panic broke out when the Nationalists captured Barcelona. Yagüe's troops were granted their now traditional few days of looting as a "war tax". About 450,000 Republican supporters clogged the roads to France to seek refuge there. As the refugees moved, raggle taggle towards the border, they were strafed by Condor Legion planes. Desperate people committed suicide; the photograph of a man who hanged himself from a tree is one vivid memorial to their plight.

Daladier's French government opened and closed the border to the refugees, and finally opened it again. As part of a most shameful chapter in French history, the women and children and the old were put into transit camps; the defeated soldiers were dumped into unsanitary new temporary camps, several located among the sand dunes around Perpignan. Senegalese conscripts disarmed the Republican fighters and

Epilogue

> treated them with disdain; their camps were enclosed within barbed wire, the latrines were open pits and—more often than not—the men were compelled to sleep in the open through the cold winter. Those with money or connections could move on to Paris or Mexico or other safe havens; those who undertook not to make any claim on French social security could move out; about 25,000 found their way to join up with the Free French in the Second World War.
>
> Franco's forces marched into Madrid on 28 March 1939. An effusive message arrived from the new Pope Pius XII: "Lifting our hearts to God, we give sincere thanks with your Excellency for the victory of Catholic Spain."[28]
>
> Mola was right, there was a Fifth Column in Madrid: most of the bourgeoisie, exhausted by the years of war and whatever their original alliances, cheered the success of the Caudillo. The Nationalists' victory had cost more than half a million lives.

Jesse Owens was a party to one more world record. On 24 August 1936 he arrived back in New York on board the *Queen Mary*; the British vessel set a new record for the westward passage to America of a little more than four days. Jesse enjoyed ticker-tape parades in New York and Cleveland: "For a time, at least, I was the most famous person in the entire world," he later reminisced.

Jesse deferred his last academic year at Ohio State in order to cash in on his fame and provide for his wife and child and his parents. The promised contracts did not materialise. He was hired to get out the black vote for Republican presidential candidate Alf Landon; this gave him the opportunity to put on the record that "Hitler didn't snub me—it was our President who snubbed me. He didn't even send me a telegram."[29]

There was money coming in, but not of the order anticipated and promised. By Christmas 1936 he was running against a race horse in Havana. (He won.) Various business ventures came and went. In the 1950s the Eisenhower administration found some quasi-diplomatic work for the lifetime Republican. He kept in great shape: on a goodwill tour of India in 1956, at the age of 43, he ran 9.8s for 100 yards.[30] In due course corporate America found it advantageous to employ the self-effacing, uncomplicated and charming champion as a representative. At first he criticized the black power salutes given by two of his sprint successors at the 1968 Mexico Olympics; four years later he recanted, accepting that blacks were still given a bum deal in the USA and that peaceful protest was entirely legitimate. A heavy smoker, he died of lung cancer in 1980, aged just 66.

Ralph Metcalfe, always the runner-up, had a most distinguished post-athletics career. After his first degree he did a masters; he coached track and lectured in political science. A first lieutenant in the US Army, he was awarded the Legion of Merit medal in the Second World War. After serving as an alderman for the South Side of Chicago from 1955, he was elected to the US Congress in 1970. A Democrat, Metcalfe co-founded the Congressional Black Caucus. He died in office in 1978, aged 68.

Speculation that Stella Walsh was not all girl was confirmed in 1980. Walsh was a fatal innocent victim of the cross-fire in a supermarket holdup in Cleveland, Ohio; an autopsy disclosed partially-developed male genitalia and chromosome tests showed that she was intersex. She continued to compete after the Berlin Olympics, winning countless US titles in track, discus and long jump—the last in 1951. In 1947 she married a boxer, Neil Olsen, and although the marriage didn't last she carried his name for the rest of her life.

Ironically, it was Helen Stephens, suffering from similar innuendo to Walsh, who was subjected to the humiliation of a physical inspection by Olympic authorities; it cleared her of the unfounded assertions. Stephens was a great all-rounder. In Berlin she not only won the sprints and the relay, she competed in the

Epilogue

shot put. Post Olympics, until 1952, she played professional softball and basketball, and she owned and managed a basketball team. She became a civil servant, serving as an aeronautical research officer in the US Defense Department, and died in 1975. She never married.

Glenn Morris *did* go to Stockholm for Brundage and the AAU that week in August 1936, immediately after the Olympics. An "injury" truncated the tour for him, however, and he returned to Leni Riefenstahl's arms for a few days from 19 August. Among other things, this enabled her to reshoot some of the sequences that are featured in *Olympia*.

There were mountains of film to be cut and edited. It took Leni another eighteen months for her to be happy with her work. The two part four-hour movie had its official opening night on 20 April 1938. It was Hitler's 49th birthday, and the Führer was in attendance. No matter how much Leni denied her Nazi connections, there is little doubt *Olympia* and Leni had the full backing of the Reich and of Hitler himself. That said, the movie is a masterpiece.

It was the first full length feature film of an Olympic Games; every Olympics since 1936 has felt obliged to produce one. The film developed cinematic techniques that have become industry standard. Widely applauded on its release, with multiple versions in German, French and English, *Olympia* won the Coppa Mussolini for best foreign film at the 1938 Venice Film Festival. It was not a promotion of Nazism, as some would have it; it is a dazzling paean to Olympism and athleticism. Hitler and his cronies are scarcely featured; the equal heroes and objects of her (sometimes erotic) attention are Jesse Owens, whose black heritage Nazis deplored, and Glenn Morris.

The AAU awarded Glenn Morris the 1936 Sullivan Award for "the outstanding amateur athlete in the United States". Given Jesse Owen's falling out with the AAU, he was never a serious candidate for the award, but everyone—Glenn Morris included—thought it should be Jesse's.

Glenn married his college sweetheart and made a 70-minute B grade movie "Tarzan's Revenge" with Eleanor Holm. The movie was released in January 1938. There is no "Jane"; Tarzan's romantic interest is "Eleanor". Director Ross Lederman takes every opportunity to feature Eleanor in an incongruous, if fetching, white swimsuit. Glenn's Tarzan barely utters a word. Always in a loincloth, our square-jawed, jet-black haired hero, shows that his athletic excellence extended to being a fine swimmer. Together Glenn and Eleanor do a deepest jungle synchronized swim, and Eleanor shows off her prize-winning backstroke. It has become fashionable to bag the movie, although it is no better or worse than most Hollywood efforts of the era; gossip columnist Hedda Hopper appears as Eleanor's mother.

Leni Riefenstahl arrived in New York to promote *Olympia* on 4 November 1938. Five days later Hitler's notorious Kristallnacht—the orchestrated violence in Germany and Austria against Jews, their synagogues and property—started. The reaction to this pogrom was widespread, not least in America; it meant that the film's US release was cancelled.[31] Who knows? Had *Olympia* been shown in the US at this time, featuring Glenn Morris in all his glory as it did, the champion's life story may well have turned out for the better.

Morris' marriage did not survive the notoriety that came with his Olympic victory. He played some professional football and sold life insurance. The war in the Pacific traumatised him, and he cracked up. A heavy drinker and smoker, after the war he drifted from job to job in northern California. In 1974, on his deathbed, his sad conclusion was that "I should have stayed in Germany with Leni."[32] He was just 61.

Eleanor Holm joined Billy Rose's *Aquacade*, a water-based spectacular that toured the country in the style of the Ziegfeld Follies. Rose, originally a songwriter, was perhaps the major impresario of the time. Eleanor was divorced by Art Jarrett in 1937, he alleging adultery with Rose. Rose in turn divorced his wife, "Funny Girl" Fanny Brice, and Eleanor and Billy married in 1939. Together with Johnny Weissmüller, Buster Crabbe and new girl Esther Williams, Eleanor starred in *Aquacade* at the 1939 World's Fair; it was the fair's top attraction. The marriage lasted thirteen years, during which time Eleanor had the swastika brooch Göring had given her transformed into a Star of David; it ended with a spectacular financial settlement. For her third marriage, Eleanor Holm settled on an oil executive, Thomas Whalen. It was a great success. Before she died in 1984 Eleanor gave thanks to Avery Brundage: "without Brundage I would have been just another backstroke swimmer."

Gotthard Handrick, the pentathlon champion, joined the Condor Legion in May 1937: "Bilbao had just fallen when I arrived. I had believed I would be coming into a war-torn region, especially as the Santander offensive was imminent, but it was not so. In Vitoria, Spanish life pulsated just the way it had presumably done even before the war was started."[33]

Handrick took over command of the Legion's Jagdgruppe 88 in July 1937. The nose of his own fighter plane, a Messerschmitt 109, featured the Olympic rings, the notation "1936", and a laurel wreath surround. After more than a year's service, for which he was awarded the Nationalists' Spanish Cross, he returned to Germany in September 1938.

Handrick served with distinction in the 1939–45 War and won a gold German Cross. He was an example of a 1936 German Olympic champion who was able to get on with his life. "By and large," Handrick said in reference to the many cases of maladjustment, "I'm afraid for most German participants the Olympics were an experience which, if they didn't possess an excellent bundle of nerves, later on gave them a lot of difficulty to adjust to."[34] After the war he ran a successful Mercedes-Benz franchise in Hamburg. He died in 1978 aged 69.

Charles Leonard, the American who came second in the pentathlon, retired a Major General. He had seen active service in the Second World War, in the Korean and Vietnam wars, lived to 92, and is buried in Arlington Cemetery. The Italian bronze medalist, Silvano Abbà, died on 24 August 1942 while leading the Savoy Cavalry in the (successful) last cavalry charge in military history—at Isbuscenskij, near Stalingrad. He was 31.

Of the participants in the Peoples' Olympiad we know that perhaps 200 did not go home; they joined the militias to fight for the Republic. Others came back to fight, like Chick Chakin, the CCNY PE instructor. On returning to New York he became a frequent speaker at fund raising events for the American Medical Bureau to Aid Spanish Democracy. He felt compelled to return, however, and joined the largely Canadian Mackenzie-Papineau Brigade in July 1937; captured by the Nationalists in March 1938 he was summarily executed, aged just 33. (Boxer Irving Jenkins was dissuaded by his father from his desire to return; Jenkins died in 2010 aged 94.) Chakin's wife had ultimately supported his decision, and—as his widow—she became an important advocate of the Republican cause.

Charley Burley turned pro on his return to the US and had

Epilogue

his first professional fight in late September 1936. For the next fourteen years until his retirement at 33 he was an exemplar of the sweet science. Quite simply, Burley was one of the best boxers never to become a world champion; with the connivance of the Mob, which controlled boxing at the time, the title holders never had to face Charley. Even so, Eddie Futch—the coach of Joe Frazier, Larry Holmes and Ken Norton—came to describe Charley Burley as "the finest all-around fighter I ever saw."

Sohn Kee-chung, the "Kitei Son" of the 1936 Marathon, returned to Japanese-occupied Korea a national hero and a symbol for the nationalist cause. He carried the flag for the newly independent Korea at the 1948 London Olympics. And when Seoul hosted the 1988 Olympics, the nation's hero carried the Olympic Torch on its final leg into the stadium: "He came through the tunnel with the torch, and everyone knew who he was. They didn't have to be told. There was this huge roar. He jumped up into the air and seemed to bound around the track."[35] Sohn died in 2002.

Jack Lovelock completed his medical studies in Britain and served in the Royal Army Medical Corps during the Second World War. He was working in New York in 1949 when, feeling dizzy, he telephoned his wife to inform her that he was not feeling well and was coming home; on the way home he fell under a subway train and was killed. Lovelock was only 39.

In reviewing the year 1936, The *New York Times*' distinguished sports journalist, Arthur J Daley, said of the Berlin Olympics:[36]

> *Perfect in setting, brilliant in presentation and unparalleled in performance, the Olympic Games of 1936 stand apart in history as the greatest sporting event of all time. With the fanatical support of the entire German nation backing it, with 5,000 athletes from fifty nations competing and with the most incredible number of 4,500,000 spectators witnessing the show, the Berlin Festival set a standard of such superlative excellence*

that it may never be matched again.

The brains behind the triumph was of course Carl Diem. In the years leading to the 1939–45 War he became closely involved with the Nazi regime. Largely through him, Germany sought to control the Olympic Movement. De Coubertin's papers were acquired by a new International Olympic Institute in Berlin with Diem at its helm. The Institute took over editorial of the IOC's official publication. He wrote articles and made speeches linking the glory of sport, and the discipline of sports training with militarism. Sparta was an inspiration for these thoughts. The final manifestation of this madness was a wild speech he gave at the Reichssportsfeld to teenage Hitler Youth on 18 March 1945; he urged them to fight a "hero's death" in these last days of the Third Reich.[37] Despite this record, Diem was largely resuscitated after the war. He renewed his career in sports administration and was a welcome guest in the Olympic movement. He died in 1962, aged 80, widely recognised as "Mr Olympia".

Lewald resigned from the IOC, as required, in 1938. He died in somewhat reduced circumstances, aged 86, in 1947. Baillet-Latour died in Nazi-occupied Belgium in 1942; Hitler sent flowers and Carl Diem to the funeral.

Avery Brundage came to dominate the IOC. He was elected President in 1952 and served in that capacity for twenty years. Authoritarian and intolerant, an over-zealous enforcer of amateurism in the era of shamateurism, many athletes came to hate him. His first wife died in 1971. At 85 he remarried; his bride, a German aristocrat, was 48 years his junior. There were no children from either marriage; as evidence of his long-standing "zipper problem", however, he fathered two children to a Finnish mistress in 1951 and 1952. He died in 1975 aged 87.

Juan Antonio Samaranch was Brundage's protégé. He was the sixteen-year-old boy we met back in Barcelona the weekend that the Peoples' Olympiad had been scheduled to start. Thirty

Epilogue

years later, in 1966, Samaranch was elected to the IOC.

As a sixteen-year-old Samaranch was already a member of the JAP—*Juventudes de Acción Popular*—the neo-fascist youth group associated with the right-wing CEDA party.[38] Two years later, when he turned eighteen on 17 July 1938, he was conscripted into the Republican Army. The Civil War was going the Nationalists way. Samaranch soon deserted, and he then defected to the Nationalists.

In Franco's Spain Juan Antonio Samaranch became an active and important member of the *Movimento Nacional* ("Nationalist Movement"); he served in the Cortes from 1964 to 1977 and was Franco's Sports Minister 1973–77. As President of the IOC from 1980 to 2001, Samaranch was largely responsible for bringing the 1992 Games to Barcelona. The circle was thus complete, as the principal venue for the Barcelona Olympics was the refurbished Olympic Stadium—the very arena that was to have hosted the 1936 Peoples' Olympiad.

Within days of the Berlin Games' Closing Ceremony Hitler delivered his infamous "autarky" manifesto: Germany should prepare itself to be totally independent of other powers, thereby making itself ready for war.

Hitler and his successor-for-a-day Göbbels avoided the Nuremberg War Trials by their suicides on 30 April and 1 May 1945. As part of his evidence on 14 March 1946, however, Göring confirmed the long-suspected use of Spain as a testing ground for the future war:[39]

> *When the Civil War broke out in Spain, Franco sent a call for help to Germany and asked for support, particularly in the air. One should not forget that Franco with his troops was stationed in Africa and that he could not get the troops across, as the fleet was in the hands of the communists, or, as they called themselves at the time, the competent revolutionary government in Spain. The decisive factor was, first*

of all, to get his troops over to Spain.

The Führer thought the matter over. I urged him to give support under all circumstances, firstly, in order to prevent the further spread of communism in that theater and, secondly, to test my young Luftwaffe at this opportunity in this or that technical respect.

With the permission of the Führer, I sent a large part of my transport fleet and a number of experimental fighter units, bombers, and antiaircraft guns; and in that way I had an opportunity to ascertain, under combat conditions, whether the material was equal to the task. In order that the personnel, too, might gather a certain amount of experience, I saw to it that there was a continuous flow, that is, that new people were constantly being sent and others recalled.

Berlin was largely flattened by Allied bombing in 1944–1945 and most of the buildings of the Third Reich were destroyed; others have since been torn down so as to eliminate references to the Nazi past and to forestall nostalgia for Hitler's Germany. One great building has survived, however: the Reich Aviation Ministry, the scene of Göring's great party on 13 August 1936. It has had a fascinating story. After the war it fell into the Soviet zone and housed the Soviet military administration; in 1949 it hosted the enactment of a new constitution for the German Democratic Republic, by which Germany was definitively divided into East and West; it then became the "House of Ministries" of the GDR and as such was the scene of a major uprising against the Communist regime in 1953. Today it is the Ministry of Finance.

The Reichssportfeld is now known as Olympiapark. It is still one of the world's great sporting complexes. The stadium itself, although substantially refurbished, looks almost as it did in 1936. The Berlin first division soccer team Hertha has its administrative headquarters in the old Friesenhaus, the female "village" for the Games, and plays its home games in what is now designated the Olympiastadion. The Olympic Village is in some disarray but is slowly being restored. Used as Soviet military barracks until 1992, crumbling pre-fabricated housing blocks cover part of one hillside that had been athletes' cottages; the lake has

> been drained and the Finnish sauna has disappeared. Most everything else is there and recognisable, though: the running track, the gymnasium, the swimming pool, the entertainment building and the great dining halls. Some of the athletes' cottages have been restored, notably that which housed Jesse Owens.

Lluís Companys, the former President of Catalonia, was executed on 15 October 1940 at Montjuïc—for "military rebellion". When France fell to the Nazi invasion in June 1940, the Spanish Nationalist Government requested the extradition of those Republican figures still in France. Companys was arrested and transferred to Madrid in early September; there he was held in solitary confinement, tortured and beaten until 3 October, when he was removed to the Castillo de Montjuïc.[40]

Companys death was but one in what had become a holocaust of retribution. Logic had been turned in its head. Those who had defended the Republic were held responsible for the war. At least in this respect Franco was consistent; as early as 18 Jul 1937 Franco had decreed: "The National Movement was never an uprising. The reds were and are the rebels."[41]

With Franco there was never any prospect of reconciliation. This was as true during the war as it was after his victory. Of the approximately 500,000 deaths in the Civil War itself, independent experts estimate that as many as 200,000 were the result of extra-judicial executions in the Nationalist Zone.[42] (The same analysis shows Republican supporters killed about 50,000 without any proper trial.) Tens of thousands were executed by the Nationalists post-victory, albeit as a result of a quasi-judicial process.

Refugees were encouraged to come back from France, and as many as 180,000 may have done so. They were immediately incarcerated in more than two hundred concentration camps located throughout the country. Count Ciano, Mussolini's foreign minister, reported that "They are not prisoners of war, they are slaves of war."[44] The last such camp did not close until 1947, after more than 400,000 prisoners had passed through them.[43] As a part of a complex system of "rehabilitation", "restitution" and repression, prisoners were put to work in mines, on railway construction and even the Caudillo's mausoleum. Thousands died. And thousands of political prisoners continued to be incarcerated well into the 1950s.

Franco played a deft hand in World War II. When Germany invaded Poland on 1 September 1939, he declared the "strictest neutrality". This moved to "non-belligerence" once France fell in June 1940. He offered Spanish troops if Germany would support a take-over of Gibraltar and various French possessions in Africa, including French Morocco—an ask too great for Hitler's agreement. An infamous meeting with Hitler on 23 October 1940—in Hendaye, just across the border in France—resulted in an agreed protocol whereby Spain would enter the war when requested. Eighteen thousand Spanish volunteers joined Germany's attack on the Soviet Union after September 1941, and Franco provided sanctuary for the German navy in Spanish ports. By November 1943, however, as German prospects faded, Spain's "non-belligerence" returned to "neutrality". By 4 November 1944, Franco asserted that the Nationalist Government had never been fascist or national socialist and had never been allied to the Axis Powers.[45]

Many hoped that the end of the Second World War might bring pressure on Franco to return Spain to democracy. To that end it was denied membership of the United Nations. Nor was it included in the Marshall Plan, or invited to join NATO.

In 1947 Spain theoretically became a monarchy. Franco—specifically he, as Caudillo—would have the right to nominate who the monarch might be, and such an accession would only take place on Franco's death or incapacity. (In 1969 Franco nominated a grandson of Alfonso XIII, Juan Carlos, as the future King of Spain.) One consequence was the ennoblement—by Franco—of the Caudillo's colleagues from the Civil War: Mola and two fascist leaders, Calvo Sotelo and José Antonio Primo de Rivera, were made dukes—albeit posthumously; Quiepo, Kindelàn and Yagüe were created marquises, again the last two having already gone to their maker. In the cases of the deceased new nobles, their descendants immediately inherited the titles. Monarchists were happy, even though there was still no "King" on the throne.

The Cold War gave Franco the opportunity to ingratiate himself with the United States, and he positioned himself as a bulwark against communism. The year 1953 proved to be a bumper one for the dictator: the USA provided extensive economic and military aid to Spain via the Pact of Madrid and, in return, Spain granted strategic air and naval bases to the United States; and then, Franco's pious wife and the Spanish Church would have been thrilled that Pius XII awarded him the Vatican's highest civil honour—Knight of the Supreme Order of Christ. By 1955 Spain was a member of the United Nations.

Léon Blum, who died in 1950, expressed only one profound

regret in his life: that he could not "save Spain". Pablo Casals never returned to Barcelona or anywhere in Spain. Nor did Picasso. Both died in 1973. Meanwhile, Franco, the failing old Fascist hung on to power. His penchant for cruelty never faltered, however: in March 1974 he readily acquiesced in the strangulations of two men by garrotte, the last such executions anywhere.

Franco died on 20 November 1975. After two generations of cultural and political oppression the tyrant was gone, and Spain would soon be free.

What can be learnt from those four weeks in the summer of nineteen thirty-six? When it all went wrong.

That you can never know everything about an event, even if you are at the centre of it. That events have consequences, sometimes far away. That the victory of good over evil often takes a long time. That tolerance is not a pejorative term; nor is its corollary, compromise. That success or glory at an early age is not a predictor of happiness. That there is no private life for those in public life. That power can corrupt and absolute power always does. That there is an honesty and purity in sporting endeavour which reflects the very best in humankind.

None of this is particularly profound. Much of it is self-evident. And, of course, a comprehension of these truths does not flow exclusively, or even principally, from those four weeks. It is the vividness of those extraordinary events in the summer of '36, however, that makes the lessons from them so much more obvious—and leads us to understand why it all went wrong.

In the end, as always, the philosophers get it right:

Eternal vigilance is the price of liberty.[46]

Tyranny is always better organized than freedom.[47]

Sports do not create character. They reveal it.[48]

Those who do not remember the past are condemned to repeat it.[49]

Only the dead have seen the end of the war.[50]

General Franco arrives in Tetuan, Spanish Morocco on 19 July 1936

Left
General Quiepo de Llano led the rebel uprising in Seville. His regular radio broadcasts were vulgar, incendiary, misogynous and threatening

Above
Frederico Garcia Lorca, Spain's greatest poet, was one of Quiepo's victims; he was executed on 18 August 1936

Left
15 August 1936, Seville: Franco, Quiepo and the Archbishop of Seville, Cardinal Ilundáin

Top
Republican soldiers and non-combatants alike rightly feared Franco's Moroccan troops from the Army of Africa

Middle
20 July 1936: the first Moroccan troops arrive in Seville

Bottom
Early August: German-supplied Junker 52s effected the airlift from Morocco to the mainland

Supporters of the Republic came from all over the world

Left
Australian nurses

Lower Left
Germans predominated in the Thaelmann Battalion

Below
US citizens formed the Abraham Lincoln Brigade

The POUM militia, pictured here at Barcelona's "Lenin Barracks", drew members from many countries - including George Orwell, the tall man at the rear

Posters supporting the Republic

'Nationalist' posters

Top
Franco enjoyed the active support of Nazi Germany

Middle
The Spanish Church sided with Franco and afforded him the trappings of a Spanish monarch

Bottom
VCA – Viva Cristo Rey ("Long live Christ the King") was invoked by the Nationalists at Franco's 1939 victory parade

Many hoped that the end of the Second World War might bring pressure on Franco to return Spain to democracy. To that end Spain was denied membership of the United Nations. It was not included in the Marshall Plan nor invited to join NATO.

By 1955 Spain was a member of the United Nations, and in December 1959 US President Eisenhower paid it a State Visit

Franco's preferred method of execution was the garrotte, which resulted in death by asphyxiation. He last authorised such an extermination in 1974

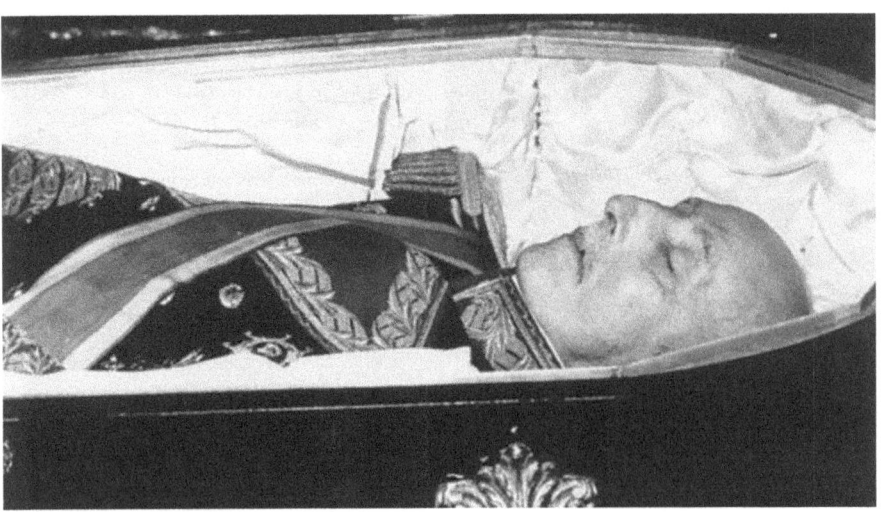

The Caudillo died of natural causes in 1975

NOTES

18 July

1 *Diary of Carmen Samaranch*. Carmen Samaranch, who died in 2014 at the age of 101, was Samaranch's half sister and seven years his senior. Their father, Francisco Samaranch, married twice. His first wife, mother to Carmen and a boy, died from influenza in 1918; Juan Antonio was the eldest of four children from the second marriage.

2 HTB 97, 105.

3 12 June 1936 letter to Sir Walter Citrine, General secretary of the Trades Union Congress.

4 CB 15.

5 HO 72.

6 The French Government granted FF 600,000 to support a team for the People's Olympiad and FF 1,100,000 to the French team for the official Berlin Olympiad; NG 151–2.

7 Riordan, J. (1984) "The Workers Olympics" in *Five Ring Circus: Money Power and Politics in the Olympic Games* (London)—Adam Tomlinson and Garry Whannel, 98–112.

8 Letter from the Organising Committee, Barcelona Peoples' Olympiad, 21 May 1936.

9 American Jewish Yearbook, *Review of the Year 5696* [sic], p. 187.

10 OA 30; HO 63.

11 BG 157.

12 The leaders of the Spanish church were insubordinate. In fact, ten days after the proclamation of the republic, the Papacy had asked the bishops to "recommend to the priests, religious and faithful of your diocese to respect the constitutional powers and obey them in the interests of public order and the common good"; TSCW (P) 45.

13 Dolores Ibárruri ("La Pasionara").

14 F 122; TSCW 157; the attendees included Franco, Varela, Fanjul and Orgaz.

15 NYT 30 December 1976; Pablo Casals Scrapbook, p. 27.

16 Eric Siblin, *The Cello Suites*, 105.

17 Kaldis, *Latin Music Through the Ages*, 73.

18 Paul Elie, *Reinventing Bach*.

19 TSCW (P) 96.

20 F 136.

21 F 139.
22 F 140.
23 FF 73–89.
24 It had been built for the International Exhibition (or World's Fair) of 1929.
25 BG 130, 147.
26 TBFS 74.
27 RFR 46.
28 HO 71.
29 Amateur Athletic Union.
30 HO 71.

19 July

1 TSCW 223.
2 HTB 106.
3 F 149; TBFS 69.
4 IAS 27–8.
5 TSCW (P) 111.
6 TSCW 223; RFR 47–8.
7 TOOTABL 5.
8 CB 20.
9 TOOTABL 5.
10 BG 148.
11 F 143–5.
12 BG 155.
13 OA 58; TBITB 305.
14 BG 156.
15 TBFS 78.
16 RFR 45.
17 TSPCW (P) 20.
18 RFR 46–68.
19 IAS 22.
20 *LA Times*, 25 July 1992.
21 *Fighting for an Ideal*; the City College Community and the Spanish Civil War; Chapter 1.
22 TOOTABL.

23 WssD 10.
24 IAS 24.
25 TSCW 224.
26 IAS 24.
27 TOOTABL.
28 TSCW 232.
29 TBFS 77.
30 It was twenty years since the Battle of Verdun, where Generals Robert Nivelle and Phillipe Pétain had first invoked "On ne passe pas!"
31 BG 148.
32 BG 158.
33 TSCW 324.

20 July

1 TSCW 237.
2 BG 148.
3 TSCW 233–4.
4 TSCW 234.
5 He was put on trial for treason on 15 August 1936, found guilty and executed on 17 August.
6 Report 515.
7 TNO 130.
8 Among others it featured Ernst Rohm, head of the SA. He was executed in 1934 and Hitler ordered all copies of the film to be destroyed; one copy survived, however, emerging intact in 1994.
9 NG 3–5; OA 54–5.
10 TSCW 243; F 151–2.
11 ALBA, Bernard N Danchik Papers 033.2.
12 BG 148.
13 CB 16.
14 TSCW 47.
15 PPP 14.
16 Speech 13 October 1931.
17 TSCW 54.
18 TSCW 237–8.
19 This is a reference to Companys having represented the CNT as a barrister.
20 TSCW 237.

21 July

1 Tom Wetzel www.libcom.org.

2 IAS 10.

3 IAS 72; www.thames.me.uk.

4 BG 149.

5 ALBA, Bernard N Danchik Papers 033:2.

6 TLD 224–5; Angela Lambert, *1939: The Last Season.*

7 TWS 174–5.

8 It was the scene of a high society scandal when the actress Tallulah Bankhead entertained a string of Eton boys there.

9 Ernest and Wallis Simpson were married at Chelsea Register Office, London on 21 July 1928.

10 The lady was almost certainly Mary "Buttercup" Raffray, who became his third wife on 19 November 1937.

11 TW 134.

12 TW 63–5.

13 She was the twin of Gloria Vanderbilt, mother to the famous fashion designer and artist.

14 TW 91.

15 TW 93; there is a bracelet dated 3/12/33 that may give some insight into the relationship.

16 TW 99.

17 The Duchess of Windsor, *The Heart Has Its Reasons* (David McKay Co, 1956).

18 17 Carnations 83.

19 KE8 278.

20 17 Carnations 88.

21 Obituary of Lord Dudley, *Telegraph*, 27 November 2013.

22 July

1 BG 150.

2 TBFS 124.

3 Guillem Carberell interview with Juan Antonio Samaranch, *La Vanguardia Sports*, 8 October 2010; *Diary of Carmen Samaranch.*

4 TBFS 124.

5 General Mola invented the term, meaning those sympathisers who keep their opinions to themselves or close allies. When he was leading only four columns on Madrid in October 1936 and his opponents argued that this

was too few to prevail, Mola asserted that their was a fifth column—underground—among sympathisers in the city.

6 RFR 72–3.

7 Eric Siblin, *The Cello Suites* (Vintage 2011) 107; Marshall C. St John, *Pablo Casals Scrapbook, A Portrait of Pablo Casals*, p. 27.

8 Guillem Carberell interview with Juan Antonio Samaranch, *La Vanguardia Sports*, 8 October 2010; *Diary of Carmen Samaranch*.

9 *Partido Obrero de Unificacion Marxista*, a neo-Trotskyist group of Catalan revolutionary (i.e. anti-Stalinist) communists. It is now a municipal library, the Andreu Nin, named after the POUM leader executed by Stalinists in 1937.

10 TBFS 147; TSCW 330.

11 Julian Jackson, *The Popular Front in France* (Cambridge University Press, 1988), p. 103.

12 BG 150.

13 ALBA, Bernard N. Danchik Papers.

23 July

1 BG 156–7, HO 80.

2 BG 158, NG 180, HO 79.

3 LB 5.

4 LB 195.

5 LB 476.

6 LB 239.

7 TSCW 331, LB 241.

8 CB 21.

9 IAS 31; HTC 43; BG 150.

10 On unification the party probably numbered 2,500; within nine months the membership was 50,000. Politics had become important: POUM had about 6,000 members at this time, and this number rapidly grew to perhaps 30,000 by the end of 1936; FP 194.

11. TSH 140.

12 TSH 141–2.

13 TSCW 274.

14 TSH 149.

15 TBITB 306.

16 BG 160.

17 TBFS 147.

18 TBFS 148.

24 July

1 BG 166.

2 OA 76.

3 When Berlin was divided the Lehrter Bahnhof fell into disuse. It was demolished in 1958. Today it is the site of the magnificent new Berlin Hauptbahnhof.

4 OA 77.

5 BG 167.

6 Swiss revolutionary Clara Thalmann, who had come to the Olympiad as a swimmer, was one; she signed up for the Durruti Column with her equally revolutionary husband, Pavel. Simone Weil, the French philosopher and mystic, was a subsequent recruit.

7 RFR 78.

8 TSCW 302–3.

9 NG 159.

10 Evelyn de Lacy, Sally Foster, *Born to Swim* (Wakefield Press, 2014) 33–4.

11 Report 174.

12 Report 186, 267.

13 BG 170.

14 Harry Gordon, *From Athens with Pride* (University of Queensland Press, 2014) 89.

15 Report 242.

16 OA 88.

17 CB 21; Muriel Rukeyser, *The Life of Poetry* ("Mediterranean") 135.

18 LB 237, 242.

19 TSCW 337.

20 LB 243.

21 British PM Baldwin recorded that he told Eden today "… that on no account, French or other, must he bring us into the fight on the side of the Russians." FF 91.

25 July

1 LB 243.

2 TSCW 338.

3 F 161.

4 LB 244.

5 LB 244.

6 Julian Jackson, *The Popular Front in France* (Cambridge University Press,

1988) 203; LB 245.
7 "Rather Hitler than Blum".
8 6, 10–11; TSCW 342.

26 July
1 TSCW 342.
2 ALC 11.
3 TSCW 343.
4 TWS 179.
5 TW 134.
6 TWS 176.
7 ALC 12.
8 TSH 149.

27 July
1 F 17.
2 F 16.
3 FF 28.
4 F 27.
5 TBFS 16.
6 F 30.
7 F 32.
8 TSCW 315.
9 TSCW 317.
10 TSCW 318; TBFS 131.
11 Alvarez-Buylla would in due course face an farcical show trial; charged with "treason", he was executed by the Franco forces in March 1937.
12 Franco was 1.63 m or 5' 4" tall.
13 *Chicago Daily Tribune*, 28 July 1936.
14 F 168.

28 July
1 Report 239–42.
2 HO 106.
3 Report 174.
4 Carol Levy, *The Olympic Pause* www.jewishmag.com; DG 147.
5 NG 182.

6 OA 65–6.

7 ALC 12–13.

8 TSCW 328.

9 Les Dropkin, *Cruising with the President*, prepared for the Potomac Association (2001) 7.

10 At his press conference today, when asked if he had received any report from Ambassador Bower in Spain in the previous 24 hours, he answered: "Nothing this morning".

29 July

1 NG 188; Report 506; Friedrich Wilhelm University was renamed Humboldt University in 1949.

2 Report of the Organizing Committee on its work for the XIIth Olympic Games of 1940 in Tokyo until the Relinquishment (1940).

3 Ibid, "Their efforts won Premier Mussolini's generous understanding".

4 NG 11.

5 NG 143–4; 10,000 Reich marks would today be worth in excess of $500,000.

6 Sherrill had been appointed a one-star general in charge of the New York State National Guard in 1917; more notably, he was a crack sprinter and is credited with inventing the crouch start in track events when a Yale sophomore.

7 BG 57.

8 BG 34.

9 BG 189; NG 188.

10 BG 23.

11 BG 56; NG 120.

12 HG 126.

13 TSCW 344; F 160–1.

14 TSCW 345.

30 July

1 F 157–8; TBFS 152; TSCW 350.

2 HG 138.

3 Thomas Wolfe, HG 138.

4 Report 420.

5 HG 139.

6 BTS 43.

7 Hart-Davis, *Hitler's Games* 45.

8 BG 22.
9 TSCW 348.
10 FDR 68.

31 July

1 TSCW 332.
2 TNO 62.
3 BG 244–5.
4 ALC 13.

1 August

1 Report 538.
2 Report 566–87; NG 190–201; BG 183–92.
3 HO 108.
4 Horst Wessel was a young Nazi thug who was shot dead at his front door, aged 22, allegedly by Communists. The Nazis promoted him and his memory as a martyr to their cause. The Horst Wessel Lied ("song") was developed by Wessel from a melody popular in the German Imperial Navy. The lyrics herald a paranoid fear of the Nazis' perceived enemies and call for attacks upon them in return. National versions of the song, with local lyrics, were adopted by the Falange in Spain and Vichy's Milice ("we shall smite the Jews and Marxists").
5 LB 247.
6 TSCW 350.
7 *Sydney Morning Herald*, 3 August 1936.
8 BG 245.
9 HO 2.
10 Thomas Wolfe, HG 155.
11 BG 185.
12 NG 194.
13 BTS 43.
14 HO 111.
15 DG 194.
16 BG 187.
17 HO 113.
18 DG 128.
19 DG 200.
20 According to page 546 of the Report, a Parisian journalist wrote: "At the

reception accorded the French team, one had the feeling that a great moment had arrived in the history of the world. Never was the War threat on the Rhine less than during these moments. Never were the French more popular in Germany than on this occasion. It was a demonstration, but one of comradeship and the will for peace".

21 FDR had encouraged the hand-over-heart gesture in the 1930s as a substitute for the "Bellamy Salute", which had an unfortunate similarity to the Nazi salute and was in widespread use throughout the USA in the 1920s and 1930s as part of a pledge of allegiance.

22 Report 577.

23 BTS 45.

2 August

1 In the ancient Olympics there was a pentathlon—a foot race, long jump, discus and javelin throwing and wrestling—and these are akin to today's decathlon.

2 F 161.

3 TBFS 109.

4 *Straits Times*, 1 August 1936.

5 Lady Diana Cooper, TT 456.

6 *Life*, 5 June 1950.

7 TWS 167.

8 KE8 232; TW 108.

9 TW 99.

10 Edward's long standing butler Mr Finch could not cop the new regime and resigned.

11 TWS 167.

3 August

1 BTS 43.

2 BTS 45.

3 NG 231; BG 199.

4 HG 173.

5 HG 176.

6 HG 177.

7 HG 178; Denis Smyth in Paul Preston and Ann L. Mackenzie (eds), *The Republic Besieged; Civil War in Spain 1936–39* (Edinburgh University Press, 1996) 88.

4 August

1 Shelly Baranowski, *Strength Through Joy* (Cambridge University Press, 2004) 65–6; NG 183, 204; BG 116.
2 HO 95.
3 TNO 213.
4 NG 234–5; BG 212–3.

5 August

1 F 161–2.
2 TSCW 325.
3 FF 91.
4 TLD 242.
5 F 162.

6 August

1 Report 830.
2 NG 284.
3 C 63.
4 C 105.
5 C 106.
6 NG 217.
7 BTS 47.
8 Report 633.
9 Report 507.
10 HG 206.
11 C 107.
12 C 106.

7 August

1 ALC 13–14.
2 BTS 47.
3 BG 227.
4 FDR 40.
5 TSCW 378.
6 TSCW 375.
7 TSCW(P) 145.

8 August
1 TSCW 351.
2 TBFS 366.
3 TBFS 149.
4 TBFS 130.
5 NG 240.
6 BG 263.
7 www.usham.org.
8 BG 228.
9 NG 255; OA 4, 312.
10 HG 203.
11 BG 251.
12 C 108.
13 BG 251.

9 August
1 BTS 48.
2 ALC 14.
3 TBFS132; TSCW 358.
4 TSH 311.
5 TSH 308.
6 HO 160.
7 HO 161.
8 He is the father of the actress Charlotte Rampling.
9 *US Olympics Association*, Summer Issue 2011, 5.
10 BG 231.
11 BG 232.
12 NG 259.
13 HO 163.
14 NG 259.
15 HO 162.
16 HG 202, TSCW 377, LB 249.
17 "Planes for Spain!"
18 *The Age*, 11 August 1936.
19 LB 234.
20 TSCW 377.

10 August

1 *The Times*, 11 August 1936, p. 12.
2 Dairy 3.
3 *Sunday Times*, 9 August 1936, p. 13.
4 AKS 306.
5 TWS 183.
6 KE8 282.
7 TLD 232.
8 Dairy 7.
9 Aird had recently acceded to a baronetcy, and was therefore Sir John Aird, Bt.
10 KE8 282.
11 Log, 10 August 1936.
12 In 2010 the bracelet sold at Sotheby's for £601,250.
12 FDR 47.
13 TSCW 378.
14 HO 160.
15 BTS 48.

11 August

1 TLCD 173.
2 TWS 180.
3 KE8 281.
4 *Life*, 5 June 1950.
5 ditto.
6 TWS 182.
7 Report 97, 508.
8 The Mitford sisters, six daughters of Lord Redesdale, all made their mark one way or another. *The Times* journalist Ben Macintyre caricatured them as: "Diana the Fascist, Jessica the Communist, Unity the Hitler-lover, Nancy the Novelist, Deborah the Duchess and Pamela the unobtrusive poultry connoisseur".
9 C 109.
10 TLD 247; BG 252.
11 NG 218.
12 BG 88.

12 August

1 Diary 8.

2 Diary 12, 13.

3 TWS 185.

4 TW 112.

5 On this tour there was a further recorded occasion of public nudity. By early September Edward and Wallis were in Vienna, staying at the Bristol; he went to the public Turkish baths—where one bathes naked—and his Scotland yard officer and six local detectives all followed the King's lead. (*The Age*, 3 October 1936.)

6 When serving on the Western Front, his equerries took him out to dinner in Amiens and handed him over to a prostitute known as Paulette; KE8 89.

7 *The Kings Counsellor*, edited Duff Hart Davis (Weidenfeld & Nicolson, 2006).

8 The particular technique that has gained most currency is that of *fang chung*. *Fang chung* is designed to relax the male by light and specific massage of the nipples, stomach, thighs and ultimately the genitals; it is said to be helpful in the prevention of premature ejaculation where a firm a specific touch between anus and urethra can delay climax.

9 C 108.

10 C 110.

11 NG 180.

12 BG 256.

13 TLD 250.

14 BG 250.

15 HG 210.

16 Report 166.

17 HO 109.

18 HG 227.

13 August

1 Donald McRae, *The Untold Story of Joe Louis and Jesse Owens* (Simon and Schuster, 2014).

2 TSH 303.

3 TSH 311–12.

4 FDR 13.

5 TSH 317.

6 HO 96, DG 141.

7 BTS 48.
8 TNO 247.
9 Report 508.
10 NG 218.
11 C 111.
12 DG 163.
13 HG 205.
14 BG 258.
15 C 111.
16 NG 219.
17 Joseph Howard Tyson, *The Surreal Third Reich* (iUniverse, 2010), 313.
18 DG 164.
19 ditto.

14 August

1 Dairy 16.
2 Diary 9.
3 TLD 234; J. Cooper *Diary* 10.
4 The Americans were housed in an excellent modern building built for German police cadets, who were presumably hardened by the cold water showers; TBITB 309.
5 Donald McRae, *The Untold Story of Joe Louis and Jesse Owens* (Simon and Schuster, 2014).
6 OA 231.
7 TSCW 361.
8 F 166.
9 TSH 318.
10 TSCW(P) 120.
11 TSH 318.
12 TSCW(P) 121; TSH 319.
13 F 166; TSH 318.

15 August

1 TSH 315.
2 TSH 321.
3 TSCW(P) 121.
4 Log 15 August 1936; Diary 17.

5 TLCD 174–5.

6 TWS 183.

7 TBFS 109.

8 *The Times*, 15 August 1936, p. 3.

9 *The Times*, 17 August 1936, p. 11.

10 HG 212.

11 BG 260.

12 TNO 157.

13 C 112.

14 Sharon Kinney Hanson, *The Life of Helen Stephens: The Fulton Flash* (Southern Illinois Press, 2004).

15 BG 162.

16 TNO 157.

17 Report 509.

18 C 112.

16 August

1 *Basil Dickinson's Diary*, Basil Dickinson Collection, State Library of New South Wales.

2 Donald McRae, *The Untold Story of Joe Louis and Jesse Owens* (Simon and Schuster, 2014).

3 TBFS 121.

4 TSCW 253.

5 TBFS 103.

6 TSH 174.

7 CAFE was the initiation cry for Falangists—"Camaradas! Arriba Falange Española!"; TSCW 195.

8 TSCW 911.

9 Log 16 August 1936.

10 TLCD 175.

11 TT 457; Lady Diana appears to have been innumerate: there were clearly three crosses on Edward's chain.

12 TW 136.

13 TW 135.

14 Jim Richardson, *Letter* to his mother in Devizes, 1936; auctioned at Mullock's, Ludlow, Shropshire, 2010; BBC Wiltshire 18 November 2010.

15 *The Times*, 18 August 1936, p. 10.

16 NG 294.

17 C 112.

18 TNO 183.

19 Report 1165.

20 NG 294; Report 1166–8.

Epilogue

1 TWS 194.

2 TBFS 150.

3 TLD 301.

4 TLD 316.

5 TLD 150.

6 Churchill suggested that Wallis, not being Edward's queen, might be known as the Duchess of Lancaster or indeed Cornwall—a solution found by Edward's great nephew, in not dissimilar circumstances, sixty years later; TLD 314, 349.

7 TLD 14; KEVIII 286.

8 The family name had in fact been Solomon.

9 F 181.

10 IBIS 9.

11 www.international-brigades.org.uk.

12 HTC 4–5.

13 TSCW (P) 159.

14 Edward VIII's "nanny boats" HMS *Grafton* and *Glowworm* were engaged in the blockade.

15 TSCW 934–44.

16 TT 392.

17 FF 99.

18 TT 393.

19 TSCW (P) 159.

20 TSCW (P) 160–1.

21 HTC 94–5.

22 In any event, Mola died on 3 June 1937 when his personal transport, an ancient wooden Airspeed Envoy, crashed into a hillside near Burgos.

23 TSCW 735.

24 F 226–7.

25 The variant of garrotting employed by the Nationalists involved tying the

victim to a wooden chair, placing a metal band (or collar) around his or her neck and tightening the band by a crank or a wheel until the victim was strangled to death or his neck broken.

26 IBIS 7.
27 And perhaps as many as 38% of the members of the largely-US Abraham Lincoln Brigade were of Jewish extraction; M Silberman, www.jewishvirtuallibrary.org.
28 TBFS 442.
29 NG 233.
30 HG 239.
31 Although it had some private viewings, the first public release in the US was in 1955, when the Museum of Modern Art, New York showed it shorn of three minutes they found offensive.
32 OA 312.
33 ALC 60.
34 NG 332.
35 *New York Times*, 15 November 2009.
36 *New York Times*, 27 December 1936.
37 NG 324.
38 *La Vanguardia Sports*, 8 October 2010.
39 *Nuremberg Trial Proceedings*, 81st Day, Morning Session.
40 TSH 493.
41 TSH 473.
42 TSCW (P) 301.
43 TSCW (P) 308–9.
44 TSCW (P) 317.
45 TBFS 464.
46 Wendell Phillips.
47 Charles Peguy.
48 John Wooden.
49 George Santayana.
50 George Santayana.

KEY TO SOURCES

AKS	Edward Windsor, *A King's Story* (Prion Books, 1999)
ALBA	*Abraham Lincoln Brigade Archives*, The Tamiment Library & Robert F. Wagner Labor Archives, New York University
ALC	Robert Forsyth, *Aces of the Legion Condor* (Osprey Publishing, 2011)
BG	Guy Walters, *Berlin Games* (Harper Perennial, 2007)
BTS	Evelyn de Lacy and Sally Foster, *Born to Swim* (Wakefield Press, 2014)
C	*CHIPS, The Diaries of Sir Henry Channon*, edited by Robert Rhodes James (Weidenfeld and Nicolson, 1967)
CB	Harry Otty, *Charley Burley and the Black Murderers' Row* (Tora Book Publishing, 2010)
DG	Larry Writer, *Dangerous Games* (Allen & Unwin, 2015)
Diary	Joseph Cooper, *Diary of the "Royal Cruise", 1 August–7 September 1936*, (National Maritime Museum Archives, Papers of Lady Yule)
F	Paul Preston, *Franco* (Fontana Press, 1995)
FDR	Dominic Tierney, *FRD and the Spanish Civil War* (Duke University Press, 2007)
FF	Peter Day, *Franco's Friends* (Biteback Publishing, 2012)
HG	Duff Hart-Davis, *Hitler's Games* (Harper & Row, 1986)
HO	Christopher Hilton, *Hitler's Games* (Sutton Publishing, 2006)
HTB	Colm Tóibín, *Homage to Barcelona* (Picador, 2002)
HTC	George Orwell, *Homage to Catalonia* (Penguin Classics, 2000)
IAS	David Boyd Haycock, *I am Spain* (Old Street Publishing, 2012)
IBIS	Ken Bradley, *International Brigades in Spain 1936–39* (Osprey Publishing, 2005)
KE8	Philip Ziegler, *King Edward VIII* (HarperPress, 2012)
LB	Joel Colton, *Léon Blum: Humanist in Politics* (Duke University Press, 1987)

Log	*Log Book of the Steam Turbine Yacht "Nahlin"* (National Maritime Museum Archives, Papers of Lady Yule)
NG	David Clay Large, *Nazi Games* (W.W. Norton, 2007)
OA	Terry Frei, *Olympic Affair* (Taylor Trade Publishing, 2012)
PPP	Frances Lannon, *Privilege, Persecution and Prophecy: The Catholic Church in Spain, 1875–1975* (Clarendon Press, 1987)
Report	*Official Report of the XIth Olympic Games, Berlin, 1936* (Wilhelm Limpert, 1937)
RFR	Agustín Guillamón translated by Paul Sharkey, *Ready for Revolution: The CNT Defense Committees in Barcelona, 1933-1938* (AK Press, 2014)
TBFS	Antony Beevor, *The Battle for Spain* (Phoenix, 2006)
TBITB	Daniel James Brown, *The Boys in the Boat* (Penguin Books, 2013)
TLCD	Diana Cooper, *The Light of the Common Day* (Penguin Books, 1959)
TLD	Denys Blakeway, *The Last Dance* (John Murray [Publishers], 2010)
TNO	Richard D Mandell, *The Nazi Olympics* (The Macmillan Company, 1971
TOOTABL	Peter Carroll, *The Odyssey of the Abraham Lincoln Brigade* (Stanford University Press, 1994)
TSCW	Hugh Thomas, *The Spanish Civil War* (Modern Library, 2001)
TSCW (P)	Paul Preston, *The Spanish Civil War* (Harper Perennial, 2006)
TSH	Paul Preston, *The Spanish Holocaust* (W.W. Norton, 2012)
TT	Juliet Gardiner, *The Thirties: An Intimate History* (Harper*Press*, 2011)
TW	Anne Sebba, *That Woman* (Phoenix, 2011)
TWS	J. Bryan III and Charles J.V. Murphy, *The Windsor Story* (Granada Publishing, 1979
17 Carnations	Andrew Morton, *17 Carnations* (Michael O'Mara Books, 2015)

INDEX

Abbà, Silvano 123, 142–3, 252
Aird, Jack 72, 175–6, 178, 213
Albritton, Dave 5, 125, 195, 217, 221
Alfonso XIII 77, 141, 215, 259
Allen, Jay 81–3, 242
Ansaldo, Juan Antonio 27, 242
Azaña, Manuel 13, 29–30, 241

Baillet-Latour, Henri de 96–8, 107–8, 110, 113–15, 127–8, 147, 227–8, 254
Baldwin, Stanley 106, 225, 230–2
Balmes, Amado 8–9
Balter, Sam 161
Bismarck, Otto von 149
Blomberg, Werner von 61, 70, 115, 147, 193
Blum, Léon 23, 45–6, 49–50, 54, 63–4, 66–8, 72, 112–13, 160, 172–3, 237, 259
Bolín, Luis Antonio 8, 15, 92
Boris III, King of Bulgaria 152
Bowers, Claude 13
Brundage, Avery 5, 11, 16, 48, 53, 56, 96–7, 180, 184, 203, 209, 222, 225–6, 249, 251, 254
Burley, Charley 3, 14, 28, 252–3
Butler, Gwendolyn "Poots" 176, 178, 213
Butler, Humphrey 176, 178, 213

Casals, Pablo 1–2, 7, 43–4, 260
Chakin, Alfred "Chick" 18, 22, 27, 252
Channon, Henry "Chips" 149, 151–2, 164, 186–7, 191–2, 201–2, 227
Chautemps, Camille 63, 66–7

Churchill, Winston 73, 231, 241
Ciano, Galeazzo 92–3, 257
Clark, Bob 154–7, 160–3
Companys, Lluís 2–3, 10, 12, 30–1, 257
Cooper, Diana 182, 213, 223
Cooper, Duff 182, 213, 225
Cot, Pierre 46, 54, 63–4, 67, 112
Coubertin, Pierre de 25, 95, 97, 103, 117, 120, 122, 254
Cunningham, Glenn 16, 149–51, 183, 195, 217

Daladier, Édouard 46, 67, 246
de Lacy, Evelyn 59–60, 127–8, 150, 153, 166, 169, 181, 200
de los Rios, Fernando 64–7
Delbos, Yvon 46, 63–4, 112
Diem, Carl 107, 115–16, 120–1, 134, 254
Dobriansky, Anatol 26
Draper, Foy 161–2, 169
Dudley Ward, Freda 38–9, 41, 190
Durruti, Buenaventura 58

Eden, Anthony 50, 106, 112, 142, 230, 241
Edstrom, Sigfrid 96
Edward, Duke of Windsor (Edward VIII) 35–6, 38–41, 71–4, 125–6, 174–8, 182–5, 189–91, 204–5, 224–5, 230–7
Eisenhower, Dwight 248
Elizabeth II 233, 236

281

Fanjul, Joaquin 20, 24
Ferris, Daniel 180, 221–2, 225–6
Fitzgerald, Helen 177–8, 213
Franco, Francisco 6, 8–10, 12, 15, 19, 26, 32, 46, 50, 53–4, 65–6, 68–70, 74, 76–83, 92–3, 98–100, 105, 109, 123–4, 141–2, 146, 153, 155–6, 160, 166–7, 188, 196–8, 212, 214–16, 237–8, 242–3, 247, 255, 257–60
François-Poncet, André 186–7, 202
Furness, Thelma 38–9, 190–1

Gallico, Paul 5, 47
George VI 233–4
Giral, José 13, 23, 45–6, 68, 133, 239
Glickman, Marty 161–2, 217
Göbbels, Joseph 101, 111, 115, 128, 149, 152, 164–5, 170–1, 186, 202, 218–20, 226, 255
Goded, Manuel 19–20, 75, 78, 188
Göring, Emmy 152, 201–3, 220
Göring, Hermann 70, 74, 111, 115, 152, 186–7, 201–4, 219–20, 251, 255–6
Gustaf Adolf, Crown Prince of Sweden 152

Handrick, Gotthard 123, 142–3, 148, 191, 251–2
Harper, Ernest 171–2
Hearst, William Randolph Jr 5, 97, 192
Hess, Rudolf 69, 138, 186
Hitler, Adolf 2–3, 22, 25, 49, 55, 57, 68–71, 74, 90, 95–6, 98–9, 103, 106–8, 111–19, 125, 127–8, 132, 138–9, 142, 148–9, 163–5, 167–8, 170, 172, 186, 191–5, 202, 206–7, 225, 227, 229, 234, 238, 241, 247, 249–50, 254–6, 258
Huber, Erwin 153–5, 157, 160, 162–3
Hull, Cordell 158, 179

Ibárruri, Delores "La Pasionara" 20–1
Ilundaín, Eustaquio 216

Jahncke, Ernest 96–7
Johnson, Cornelius 125, 127, 132–3, 217

Kantzow, Thomas von 203
Kiefer, Adolph 161
Kindelán, Alfredo 141–2, 259
Krauss, Käthe 137

Landon, Alf 247
Lascelles, Alan "Tommy" 178, 191
Lebrun, Albert 66, 73, 112
Léger, Alexis 49, 112
Leonard, Charles 55, 123, 142–3, 148, 252
Lewald, Theodor 56, 61, 107–8, 112, 114–15, 118, 120, 254
Long, Lutz 139–40, 155
Lorca, Frederico Garcia 222–3
Louis, Spiridon 117, 119
Lovelock, Jack 149–51, 217–18, 253
LuValle, James 195

MacArthur, Charles 5
Maisky, Ivan 240
Malraux, André 68, 104, 160, 242
March, Werner 103
Martin, Paul 90
Mastenbroek, Rie 198, 200
Maurras, Charles 49
Meadows, Earle 145, 217
Mercader, Caridad 51
Merryman, Bessie 40
Metcalfe, Ralph 131–2, 161–2, 169, 180, 195, 217, 248
Milch, Erhard 74, 91, 109, 147
Millán Astray, Jose 78, 216

Miller, Franz 136–7, 144, 150
Mitford, Diana 148–9
Mitford, Unity 148–9, 186
Mola, Emilio 6, 8–9, 12–13, 26–7, 32, 51, 58, 66, 78, 93, 99, 160, 188, 197, 215, 239, 247, 259
Molyneux, Hugh 177
Morris, Glenn 57, 62, 154, 155–7, 160, 162–3, 184, 191, 209, 249–51
Mussolini, Benito 49, 92–3, 96, 100, 167, 172, 238, 240, 257

Owens, Jesse 4, 16, 48, 55, 124, 128, 131–3, 139–40, 143–5, 161–2, 169, 179–80, 183–4, 191, 195, 198, 209, 217–18, 221, 223, 226, 247, 249, 257

Parker, Jack 154, 157, 160, 163
Phipps, Eric 164, 186–7
Poynton-Hill, Dorothy 198–9

Quiepo de Llano, Gonzalo 10, 51–2, 75, 78, 123–4, 155–6, 196, 215–16, 223, 259

Raffray, Mary "Buttercup" 37, 40–1, 230, 237
Ribbentrop, Joachim von 70, 109, 148–9, 164, 185–7, 202, 220
Riefenstahl, Leni 25–6, 84, 124–5, 128, 130, 132, 139, 145, 154, 156, 162–3, 199, 208–9, 249–51
Ritter von Halt, Karl 127–8
Robinson, Mack 144, 161
Roosevelt, Franklin Delano 57, 93–4, 105, 157, 179, 210
Rose, Billy 251

Sackett, Ada 23, 48

Samaranch, Juan Antonio 1, 42, 44, 254–5
Sanjurjo, José 26–7, 32, 78, 93, 242
Schilgen, Fritz 119
Sherrill, Charles 96–7
Simpson, Ernest 37–41, 230, 237
Simpson, Ernest Henry Child (Aharon Solomons) 237
Simpson, Wallis *see* Wallis, Duchess of Windsor
Snyder, Larry 195, 209, 221–3
Son, Kitei (Sohn Kee-chung) 168, 170–2, 253
Stephens, Helen 48, 131, 137–8, 170, 219, 248
Stoller, Sam 161–2

Tschammer und Osten, Hans von 106–7, 111, 132

Umberto, Crown Prince of Italy 152

Vansittart, Robert 164–5, 186–7, 192–4

Wallis, Duchess of Windsor (Mrs Ernest Simpson) 37–41, 72, 125–6, 174–8, 184–5, 189–91, 205, 213–14, 224–5, 230–1, 233–7
Walsh, Stella (Stanislawa Walasiewicz) 136–7, 248
Williams, Archie 170, 217
Williams, Joe 5, 47–8
Wykoff, Frank 131, 161–2, 169, 217

Yagüe, Juan 15, 78, 141, 167, 196–7, 211–12, 239, 246, 259

Zabala, Juan-Carlos 168, 170–2

ABOUT THE AUTHOR

Nicholas Whitlam majored in history at Harvard. *Four Weeks One Summer*, his third book, is the product of a long-held interest in the Spanish Civil War, the Olympic movement and the politics of the 1930s.

A career banker, he worked for major international banks in New York, London, Sydney and Hong Kong. On returning to Australia, he became CEO of a big Australian bank and then chairman of the country's largest insurance company. Nicholas Whitlam and his wife of more than forty years, the former Judy Frye, have three adult children and live in a coastal village south of Sydney.

www.whitlam.com.au

Lightning Source UK Ltd.
Milton Keynes UK
UKHW041052040319
338424UK00003B/690/P